9th IADIS International Conference Information Systems 2016

Vilamoura, Portugal
9 – 11 April 2016

Editors:

Miguel Baptista Nunes
Pedro Isaías
Philip Powell

ISBN: 978-1-5108-2369-3

Printed from e-media with permission by:

Curran Associates, Inc.
57 Morehouse Lane
Red Hook, NY 12571

proceedings.com

Some format issues inherent in the e-media version may also appear in this print version.

Printed by Curran Associates, Inc. (2016)

International Association for Development of the Information Society (IADIS)
Rua Sao Sebastiao Da Pedreira
No. 100, 30, 1050-209
Lisbon, Portugal

Phone: 351 21 3151373
Fax: 351 21 3151244

secretariat@iadis.org

Additional copies of this publication are available from:

Curran Associates, Inc.
57 Morehouse Lane
Red Hook, NY 12571 USA
Phone: 845-758-0400
Fax: 845-758-2633
Email: curran@proceedings.com
Web: www.proceedings.com

9th IADIS INTERNATIONAL CONFERENCE

INFORMATION SYSTEMS 2016

PROCEEDINGS OF THE
9th IADIS INTERNATIONAL CONFERENCE

INFORMATION SYSTEMS 2016

VILAMOURA, ALGARVE, PORTUGAL

9 - 11 APRIL, 2016

Organised by

iadis

international association for development of the information society

Official Carrier

TAP PORTUGAL

with arms wide open

A STAR ALLIANCE MEMBER

Edited by Miguel Baptista Nunes, Pedro Isaías and Philip Powell

Associate Editor: Luís Rodrigues

TABLE OF CONTENTS

FULL PAPERS

SHORT PAPERS

DOCTORAL CONSORTIUM

FOREWORD

These proceedings contain the papers of the 9th IADIS International Conference Information Systems 2016, which was organised by the International Association for Development of the Information Society in Vilamoura, Algarve, Portugal, 9 - 11 April 2016.

The IADIS Information Systems Conference 2016 aims to provide a forum for the discussion of IS taking a socio-technological perspective. It aims to address the issues related to design, development and use of IS in organisations from a socio-technological perspective, as well as to discuss IS professional practice, research and teaching. A set of key areas has been identified. However, these do not aim at being prescriptive, or set in stone, and any innovative contributions that do not fit into these areas have also been considered.

The following main tracks have been object of paper submissions:

- IS in Practice, Technology Infrastructures and Organisational Processes
- IS Design, Development and Management Issues and Methodologies
- IS Professional Issues
- IS Research
- IS Learning and Teaching

The IADIS Information Systems Conference 2016 had 85 submissions from 17 countries. Each submission has been anonymously reviewed by an average of 4 independent reviewers, to ensure the final high standard of the accepted submissions. Out of the papers submitted, 14 got blind referee ratings that published them as full papers, which means that the acceptance rate was 16%. Some other submissions were published as short papers and a doctoral consortium. Extended versions of the best papers will be selected to be published in a special issue of the Journal of Electronic Commerce in Organizations (JECO) journal (ISSN: 1539-2937) and also in the IADIS Journal on Computer Science and Information Systems (ISSN: 1646-3692) indexed by Emerging Sources Citation Index by Thomson Reuters.

The conference, besides the presentation of full papers, short papers and doctoral consortium also includes a keynote presentation and a tutorial from internationally distinguished researchers. We wish to thank Professor Kevin Grant, Kent Business School, University of Kent, UK, for accepting our invitation as keynote speaker and Professor Paul Nieuwenhuysen, Vrije Universiteit Brussel, Belgium, for his tutorial presentation.

The conference will also include a panel entitled "Challenges and Opportunities in Information Systems" with Profs. Philip Powell, Miguel Baptista Nunes, Pedro Isaías and Kevin Grant.

As we all know, a conference requires the effort of many individuals. We would like to thank all members of the Program Committee for their hard work in reviewing and selecting the papers that appear in the book of the proceedings.

Last but not the least, we hope that everybody will have a good time in Vilamoura, Algarve and we invite all participants for the next year edition of the IADIS International Conference of Information Systems 2017.

Professor Philip Powell, Executive Dean, University of London, UK
Conference Chair

Miguel Baptista Nunes, School of Information Management, Sun Yat-sen University, Guangzhou, China

Pedro Isaías, Universidade Aberta (Portuguese Open University), Portugal
Program Co-Chairs

Vilamoura, Algarve, Portugal
April 2016

PROGRAM COMMITTEE

CONFERENCE CHAIR

Professor Philip Powell, Executive Dean, University of London, UK

PROGRAM CO-CHAIRS

Miguel Baptista Nunes, School of Information Management, Sun Yat-sen University, Guangzhou, China
Pedro Isaías, Universidade Aberta (Portuguese Open University), Portugal

COMMITTEE MEMBERS

Abdelkrim Meziane, Cerist, Algeria
Adam Wojtowicz, Poznan University of Economics, Poland
Alexis Tejedor de Leon, Technological University of Panama, Panama
Amelia Badica, University of Craiova, Romania
Anastas Mishev, University of Ss. Cyril and Methodius, Macedonia
Anastasia Constantelou, University of the Aegean, Greece
Andreja Pucihar, University of Maribor, Slovenia
Annelie Ekelin, Linnaeus University, Sweden
Bulend Terzioglu, Australian Catholic University, Australia
Carmine Gravino, University of Salerno, Italy
Christos Kalloniatis, University of the Aegean, Greece
Crispin Coombs, Loughborough University, United Kingdom
David García Rosado, University of Castilla-la Mancha, Spain
Debasis Giri, Haldia Institute of Technology, India
Demetrios Sarantis, National Technical University of Athens, Greece
Dimitrios Vergados, University of Piraeus, Greece
Dimitris Kardaras, Athens University of Economics and Business, Greece
Eddie Soulier, Université de Technologie de Troyes, France
Edward Bernroider, Vienna University of Economics and Business, Austria
Efthimios Tambouris, University of Macedonia, Greece
Eleutherios Papathanassiou, IST College, Greece
Faiez Gargouri, Institut Superieur d'Informatique et de Multimedia, Tunisia
Fang Zhao, Edith Cowan University, Australia
Francisco Jose Silva Mata, Cenatav, Cuba
François Bergeron, TELUQ, Canada
George Vouros, University of Piraeus, Greece

KEYNOTE LECTURE

CHALLENGES OF TECHNOLOGICAL INNOVATION: IS A MORAL COMPASS NEEDED?

By Professor Kevin Grant,
Kent Business School, University of Kent, UK

Abstract

The discussion into technology and innovation continues to expand. Technology led innovation and organisational transformation refers to the process by which new products and processes are generated. When emergent technologies are deployed to bring about new ways of making existing products and services 'better', this is called process innovation. When they include entirely new products and services, the change is referred to as product/service innovation and, when something so disruptive changes how we work, rest and play, this is often termed paradigm shift based innovation.

A number of challenges and concerns still exist today with regards to our understanding and sense making of technology infused innovations. In this session, some thoughts and observations will be explored such as; hidden technological innovation, what is being measured and how, gender based technological innovation, how do we 'spot' emergent technologies, financial innovation, socially responsible innovation and new organisational forms and model of innovation to promote, enhance and deliver technology transfer. One developing concept is the notion that all IT led technology innovation is a good thing. We will explore/interrogate this further looking at the relationship between technology adoption and potential addiction factors of 'Generation Y' users as archetypical digital natives. We will also explore the possible need for us, as IT professionals, to incorporate a moral compass as technology led innovation continues to expand and permeate our everyday lives.

TUTORIAL

INFORMATION RETRIEVAL FROM THE INTERNET AND WWW, USING SEARCH BY IMAGE: A TUTORIAL

By Professor Paul Nieuwenhuysen,
Vrije Universiteit Brussel, Pleinlaan 2, 1050 Brussel, Belgium

Abstract

This tutorial workshop is based on a continuing investigation of the power, applicability, usefulness and limitations of search by image through the Internet. In this relatively new method for information retrieval, a query does not consist of text, but of an image file. The search results lead to images on the WWW and also to related texts. Other terms used for this method are:

- Search(ing) by example
- Reverse image search(ing)
- Reverse image lookup = RIL
- Backwards image search(ing)
- Inside search(ing)

- **Some of our findings:**
  1. Several online services are available free of charge to search by image.
  2. Differences among these services are substantial.
  3. The search service offered by Google performs relatively well.
  4. Google can reveal images present on the Internet, which are copies of the query/source image; however, the success is quite variable from case to case.
  5. This recall performance is strongly correlated with the performance of a more classical Google search by text to find copies of the query/source image file on the Internet.
  6. Even images that are modified versions of the query/source image can be revealed by Google; more specifically, such modified versions can differ from the source image in size and in colours; even fragments of the source image that are present on the internet can be revealed.

7. Our tests have demonstrated that since 2014 search by image can not only find images that are visually similar to the query/source image, but can even retrieve images that are semantically similar/related to the query/source image, even when visual similarity is not obvious. The search results may also include a description of the subject on the image, and this can of course be interesting if the user has not yet much knowledge about the subject, so that using a specific text query becomes possible. Furthermore, other information related to the image and relevant links may also be included in the search results.
8. The performance of search by image to find images that are semantically similar to the query/source image is improving.

- **Various applications can be shown:**
  - Starting from your own image, you may find copies or even modified versions on the WWW.
  - Starting from some interesting image, that you have not created, but that you consider as interesting, and that is perhaps not the original version, you may find other and better versions.
  - Starting from some interesting source image, you may find images with a subject that is related to the subject of that source image.

Keywords
Reverse image search, Google, information discovery, information retrieval, semantic gap

Full Papers

WORLDS APART – IT SUPPORT STRATEGIES FOR EVIDENCE BASED MEDICINE MEET REALITY

Hanife Rexhepi and Anne Persson
University of Skövde, Informatics Research Centre
P.O. Box 408, SE-541 28, Skövde, Sweden

ABSTRACT

When practitioners make decisions as well as treat and care for patients they interpret patient specific information according to evidence based medical knowledge. This process is complex as evidence is infrequently available in a form that can be acted upon at the time decisions must be made. The aim of this paper is to (1) explore how primary, secondary and municipality care in Sweden work with the process of managing knowledge, (2) explore how healthcare practitioners' experience, availability of medical knowledge when and where they need it and (3) conditions for developing a coherent IT-based knowledge portal for different areas of knowledge bases in healthcare. The results show significant deficiencies in the knowledge management process of the participating organizations. The knowledge management processes are not embedded in business processes, activities and relationships, which cause major difficulties for practitioners to keep up with the latest medical evidence.

KEYWORDS

Knowledge management, evidence based medicine, healthcare knowledge management.

1. INTRODUCTION

Delivering good quality care is a complex endeavor that is highly dependent on patient information and medical knowledge. When decisions about the care of a patient are made they must as far as possible be based on research-derived evidence rather than on clinical skills and experience alone. Evidence based medicine (EBM) is the conscientious, explicit and judicious use of current best evidence in making decisions about the care of individual patients (Sacketta, 1997). It aims to improve quality and safety of care by eliminating decision-making based on more traditional methods in favor of using (a) current best evidence in conjunction with (b) patient values and preferences, and (c) individual clinical expertise (Houser & Oman, 2011, p. 3) (see figure 1). Following the principles of EBM practitioners are required to formulate questions based on patients' medical history, current clinical problems, values and preferences, search the literature for answers, evaluate the evidence for its validity and usefulness, and finally apply the information to patients (Lenz & Reichert, 2007).

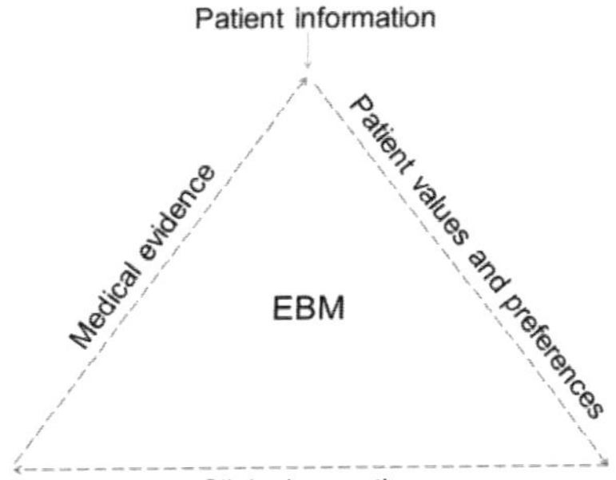

Figure 1. Evidence based medicine

Practicing EBM is challenging. One reason is inability to access patient's past and current medical history due to interpretability issues. It is also complicated, as practitioners usually do not have time to search for medical knowledge while the patient is in the office. Therefore, literature search usually takes place offline (Lenz & Reichert, 2007). Practitioners who search for knowledge all too often find that existing knowledge is not accessible in real time and may not necessarily map to the issue at hand (Clancy & Cronin, 2005). Some practitioners may even choose not to actively look for the needed knowledge as textbooks may be out of date, information in journals is too difficult, if not impossible, to translate into daily work practice and current information systems (IS) such as IT-based knowledge repositories are not widely used as they are not developed to meet practitioners' knowledge needs (Krasniqi & Persson, 2012). To alleviate this untenable situation, systematic reviews and medical guidelines are continuously developed in healthcare systems. It is, however, still challenging to ensure that healthcare practitioners actually apply the latest medical knowledge, as there is no single point of access to the needed knowledge. Medical guidelines and other important medical knowledge are contained in numerous autonomous IT-based knowledge repositories at different levels (local, regional, national). Each of these are developed based on the need to disseminate knowledge about a particular medical specialty to particular target groups with particular needs of knowledge (Krasniqi & Persson, 2012). Considering that a practitioner, such as a nurse within municipality care, needs to access knowledge about several specialties, the situation is sub-optimal, as the individual is forced to access several repositories in order to find the needed knowledge (Krasniqi & Persson, 2012).

The Swedish Ministry of health and social affairs have in their IT-strategy for Swedish healthcare (2006) emphasized the need to develop decision support systems and other knowledge-based support systems that provide timely and easy access to relevant medical knowledge. This is important since studies have supported the conclusion that patient outcomes are substantially improved when healthcare is based on evidence versus tradition or clinical expertise alone (Houser & Oman, 2011). The perceived benefits are faster dissemination of new knowledge, e.g., new treatment methods, and continuous competence development of healthcare practitioners. However, bringing evidence to the point of care requires more than investments in IT support. To realize the full potential of information technology that helps practitioners to access, use and share medical knowledge, knowledge management processes (KM) must be embedded in business processes, activities and relationships. The question that this paper addresses is how well the reality of current Swedish healthcare practice can live up to the national strategy.

The paper is based on a research project carried out in Swedish healthcare. The goal of the project was to investigate the possibilities to develop an IT-based knowledge repository that was intended to function as a single point of access to knowledge for healthcare practitioners in primary, secondary and municipality care. The target groups of this "knowledge portal" were nurses and nursing assistants. Physicians were excluded due to the results from a previous study (Krasniqi & Persson, 2012), which showed that the majority of the IT-supported knowledge repositories in Sweden had physicians as the main target group, while nurses and particularly assistant nurses were to a large extent neglected. As part of the project, the current knowledge management processes in the healthcare organizations of a region of Sweden comprising 15 municipalities, 4 hospitals and a large number of primary care units were studied. The aim of investigating these processes was to evaluate the healthcare organization's readiness to adopt an IT-based knowledge repository as a tool in daily healthcare practice. The results are reported in this paper. Extensive international research has been conducted regarding access to medical knowledge within the healthcare sector. However, little is known about how nurses and assistant nurses experience the availability of medical knowledge. In particular, no study has, to the best of our knowledge, addressed the problems experienced with availability of medical knowledge by practitioners within the three levels of healthcare at the same time; primary care, secondary care and municipality care. Therefore, the aim of this paper is to explore (1) how the three levels of healthcare worked with the process of managing knowledge, and (2) how practitioners experience access to medical knowledge (such as theoretical knowledge, systematic reviews, medical guidelines, scientific papers, and clinical expertise etc.), where and when they needed it. Attitudes towards using IT-based sources to access knowledge were also important to capture, since the goal of the project was to develop an IT-based knowledge repository.

The remainder of this paper is organized as follows. In section 2 the theoretical background to the work is presented. Section 3 describes the research approach while section 4 presents the findings. The findings are discussed in section 5.

2. THEORETICAL BACKGROUND

To achieve the goal of the paper, the theory of knowledge management (KM) and its relation to EBM has been used. Knowledge Management is a conscious strategy of getting the right knowledge to the right people at the right time and helping people to share and put knowledge into action in ways that strive to improve organizational performance. It involves processes for capturing, storing, sharing and applying knowledge. Within healthcare, KM is about managing the knowledge that is critical to providing high quality care to patients. Knowledge in this context includes both the experiences and understanding of practitioners (tacit knowledge) and the information available inside and outside the organization such as, medical guidelines (explicit knowledge). KM in the context of EBM creates a learning environment and ensures that "best practice" is systematically captured and disseminated. It is clear that healthcare organizations can profit from many advantages that KM provide, such as; improved patient care, safety and satisfaction, team-building across organizational boundaries and more informed decision-making by learning from others and building on individual experiences etc. (De Brún, 2007). The Swedish healthcare system, similar to other countries, faces significant challenges of delivering high-quality care, at lower costs. At the same time, there is growing recognition that healthcare organizations are knowledge-intensive and are suffering from information overload (Chen, Liu & Hwang, 2011). Healthcare organizations thus need to embrace KM strategies, processes, tools and techniques as it can support them to create greater value by delivering higher care quality more cost effectively (Wickramasinghe, Gupta & Sharma, 2005). Hence, a general model of KM has been used as a framework to study how the organizations involved in this study work with managing knowledge and how practitioners perceive availability of medical knowledge when and where it is needed. The model of the KM cycle presented by Persson & Stirna (2007) as described in Figure 2. will be used. It covers the whole lifecycle of knowledge in an organization and is adapted from O´Dell, Grayson & Essaides (1998).

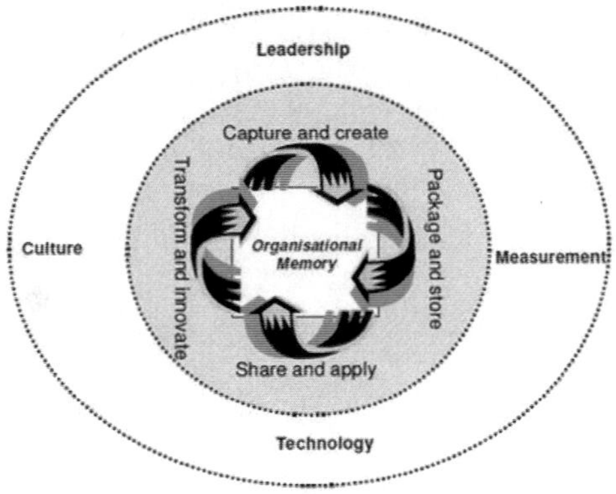

Figure 2. The knowledge cycle in organizations

Apart from the knowledge cycle at the center of the model, there are four factors that enable the successful implementation of KM. Successful KM is dependent on strong and determined leadership. The existence of a knowledge sharing culture also helps to implement KM practices. In order to assess whether or not new knowledge and practices are actually applied, different types of measurement procedures needs to be developed and implemented. Finally, information technology plays an important role in modern KM practices.

3. RESEARCH APPROACH

The research was conducted in three steps:

1. A preliminary review of literature describing related research was conducted, targeting literature from different research domains related to EBM and KM.
2. A qualitative study with interviews as the main data collection technique was carried out. 62 semi-structured interviews were conducted in primary care, specialist care and municipality care. The

interviews were taped and transcribed, and lasted approximately one to two hours each. The interview guide with associated questions was developed based on the KM cycle (Figure 2), which means that the following aspects were addressed:

- Processes for capturing and creating knowledge and
- Processes for packaging, storing, sharing, applying knowledge, and measurement of innovation and transformation.

The interview guide also included questions about the potential lack of medical knowledge in specific clinical situations and how the situation is managed. The interviewees represented two perspectives in the KM process:

- The management perspective (unit managers), assuming that they have the overall responsibility for ensuring that their unit apply the best available knowledge.
- The employee perspective (nurses and assistant nurses), assuming that they are responsible to access and apply the best available knowledge.

3. The recordings were transcribed into written documents. Analysis of the documents was inspired by grounded theory (Strauss & Corbin, 1990), and has been conducted in two steps:
    - Open coding started by reading through the interviews several times to create a deeper understanding of the respondents' statements and to relate them to identified categories and concepts.
    - Axial coding involved further exploration of the categories and concepts that were developed in the process of open coding. Axial coding was the process of identifying the relationship between and within categories. Axial coding did provide depth for the description of the identified concept, which evolved into a deep understanding of e.g., how practitioners capture new knowledge. Categories that emerged from open coding were reviewed in detail. When a deeper understanding of the categories occurred, a description of each category was made. These categories were then mapped into the KM process cycle (Figure 2).

We argue that the extensive empirical material together with the rigorous analysis method makes a strong case for the reliability of the results presented in this paper.

4. FINDINGS

The findings from the interview study are presented according to the knowledge cycle (Figure 2).

4.1 Capture and Create

Knowledge creation involves developing new knowledge or replacing existing explicit and tacit knowledge within the organization (Alavi & Leidner, 2001). Practitioners within primary, secondary and municipality care exchanged tacit knowledge through informal and formal networks, involving day-to-day interaction between people e.g., in a clinical situation, during breaks, and during joint activities such as meetings. They shared tacit knowledge by, e.g., assisting each other in terms of providing practical insights into "what solution will work in a particular situation, why it will work, and how to make it work". Through interaction practitioners obtained new insights that resulted in the creation of new knowledge. In other cases tacit knowledge was transferred from one member to another through discussions. Usually, important tacit knowledge that was transferred from one practitioner to another was not captured despite that the knowledge could be captured and were of importance to the organization as a whole. However, if practitioners converged to solve a complex clinical situation requiring an immediate solution, this knowledge was usually documented. The organizations had thus failed to establish a common space for creating and capturing tacit knowledge. There were, for example, no dialogue meetings or collaborative settings in place where individuals could share experiences, which later on could be captured. Another significant problem is lack of collaborative relationships with practitioners from other units within and outside the organization where practitioners could share experiences, gain new insights, create new tacit knowledge and capture explicit knowledge. The problem was particularly evident in municipality care and secondary care. A majority of the nurses, assistant nurses and managers asked for cross-communication and collaborative settings. There was a clear need to share experiences about "how others solve a specific clinical situation". Collaborative settings were especially important for nurses in municipality care as they usually work alone in their function that comprises treatment, counselling, supervision, and caring, with limited opportunities of daily contact with physicians.

The situation is somewhat different in secondary and primary care where the clinical situation requires close collaboration between nurses and physician. Furthermore, several of the nurses within the three levels of healthcare expressed a concern regarding the lack of a culture among nurses and assistant nurses to share knowledge and collaborate between departments within and outside the organization. They also expressed a feeling of injustice since they believe that the organizations prioritize physicians to connect and share tacit and explicit knowledge. Even managers argue that there is a tradition among physicians, that is not found among nurses and assistant nurses, "to connect people", to develop and cherish collaborative relationships with other practitioners by e.g., holding lectures, educating and sharing new research findings among each other. It is also common that physicians have internal training 1h/week where experiences are shared through face-to-face interactions and where tacit knowledge is converted to explicit knowledge and shared among other practitioners, an approach that is missing among nurses and assistant nurses. Additionally, managers emphasize that the effect of joint activities, especially seminars and conferences is not ideal, due to delays in knowledge creation, capture and knowledge transfer. They further argue that physicians and nurses are good at sharing tacit knowledge during joint activities, but less efficient at knowledge sharing in the day-to-day practice, and if knowledge sharing occurs, it is usually among colleagues within the department, and not entirely surprising knowledge is often shared between individuals within the same professional category. However, during this study, some nurses in secondary care gave examples of physicians who saw the importance of sharing their experience with nurses and assistant nurses, but these examples were few.

Capture of explicit knowledge within and outside the organization, especially within municipality care was seen as challenging. Not knowing what knowledge that flows through the organization and what knowledge is critical was considered problematic. Additional problems concerned, capturing of explicit knowledge from outside the organization. Not knowing where to find relevant knowledge and what type of knowledge that was relevant for the organization were evident. Capturing of explicit knowledge in the three levels of healthcare was mainly done through (1) individual responsibility of managers and practitioners and through (2) the "medical nurse in charge" (MNC). Individual responsibility means that each individual is responsible for capturing relevant knowledge in their subject area from inside and outside the organization and disseminate it among the organizational members. Nurses in municipality care and secondary care experienced capturing of new knowledge as challenging and time-consuming as the knowledge is dispersed and stored in various autonomous IT-repositories. Moreover, as these repositories are not comprehensive nurses expressed concerns that important knowledge may be overlooked. To simplify access and ensure application of knowledge that guides practitioners in delivering high quality care, practitioner expressed an urgent need to integrate knowledge such as medical guidelines with EHRs and to develop one comprehensive IT-supported knowledge repository, which also is integrated with the EHR. Some also requested integration of reminders within current information systems. Nurses and nursing assistant within municipality care and specialist care also emphasized the need for IT that supports sharing of tacit knowledge between practitioners within and outside the organization. Furthermore, nurses, particularly in municipality care, experience stress and worry about not being able to capture and access relevant knowledge at the right time, at the right place and in the right format as only one of ten municipalities paid for access to scientific databases. This was more pronounced among nurses within municipal care than for nurses in secondary care and primary care, due to the fact that the latter groups work closely with physicians and hence have better access to scientific medical knowledge. A nurse explains:

> *"Working evidence-based requires that we have access to scientific research, and scientific databases. To only use Google to find such knowledge is impossible [...]. Then I ask myself the question how can I educate and inform our assistant nurses on the ward when I cannot keep myself updated"*

Nurses in primary care have a national web-based knowledge portal that they use to acquire explicit knowledge. Therefore, the individual responsibility for capturing explicit knowledge was not perceived as problematic. Also, capturing of explicit knowledge, based on an individual responsibility within secondary, primary and municipality care occurs sporadically because of lack of enablers such as IT and culture, lack of time (to capture and document lessons learned), effort, interest and skills needed to find relevant knowledge.

Assistant nurses also have an individual responsibility for capturing knowledge. Unfortunately, 89 % of those interviewed felt that their individual responsibility for capturing knowledge, particularly evidence based research, is not relevant to their profession. Instead, they rely on nurses and managers to provide them with relevant knowledge. An assistant nurse explains:

> *"As an assistant nurse I do not think that it is important to search for the research. I've been working for 20 years, so I have a lot of experience [...] It is rare that I feel I need knowledge, and usually we have nurses who print out papers on things and put it in folders, which we then read, or the manager emails links with information, for example about dementia"*

An additional obstacle to nursing assistants' individual responsibility is (1) lack of knowledge and experience in searching for scientific medical knowledge and (2) lack of knowledge of what characterizes a scientific source. The nursing assistant who felt that the acquisition of knowledge is just as important for a nursing assistant as for a nurse or physician believes that the organization has failed to create an environment that supports capturing and sharing of knowledge.

The "Medical nurse in charge" is a nurse who has the primary medical responsibility of the department. She is also responsible for capturing, storing and disseminating explicit and tacit knowledge that may be relevant to other nurses and nursing assistants. The created and captured knowledge is often packaged in a document, stored on the intranet and/or printed and saved in a binder. Managers also have an important role in capturing, storing and disseminating knowledge. Knowledge outside the organization was captured, e.g., by following central directives and through organization-wide collaborations. It is evident that there is a tendency among both managers and practitioners to focus on the capturing of explicit knowledge from outside the organization. The tacit and explicit knowledge inside the organization does not seem to get as much attention. Perhaps the knowledge inside the organization is taken for granted? There was only one department at secondary care who consciously worked with the capture and creation of knowledge from inside the department.

4.2 Package and Store

While organizations capture, create new knowledge and learn they also forget acquired knowledge. Therefore, the storage and retrieval of organizational knowledge constitute an important aspect of KM (Alavi & Leidner, 2001). The key element in this process is to make the specific knowledge useful and easily accessible (Persson & Stirna, 2007). The interview results have demonstrated difficulties with the packaging, storing and access of knowledge. Knowledge is usually packaged in documents and then published on the intranet. This knowledge is difficult to absorb since the documents often are not adapted to the target groups. The use of multi-media such as film, animation and sound is hardly ever seen, even though this is often a feasible way to package tacit knowledge. A further complicating factor is that information is stored in variable form and in various places, e.g. on the computer, on the intranet, in different knowledge repositories and in paper folders. Hence, medical knowledge is inaccessible when needed. Some practitioners even choose to not actively look for the knowledge as existing tools are not adequate for answering the questions that arise and those who search for knowledge find that the provided knowledge usually do not map to the issue at hand. A nurse explains:

> *"Finding the right knowledge is difficult because you don't know if it is it stored on the intranet, on the computer, in the summaries of medical guidelines, in folders, news archives, on different web pages and so on"*

4.3 Share and Apply

An important part of KM is the sharing and use of knowledge. This process is not always simple as organizations often do not know what they know and/or they have weak systems for locating and retrieving knowledge that resides in them (Alavi & Leidner, 2001). Knowledge can be shared through different channels, such as meetings. However, informal channels such as unscheduled meeting and informal seminars aimed for sharing knowledge are rare among nurses and assistant nurses. Training is a common way of disseminating knowledge, but practitioners claim that it must be supplemented by other systematic efforts to ensure sustainable uptake of knowledge. The most common method used is that one practitioner is trained in a specific subject and is then expected to train their colleagues. This practice has proven to be problematic as knowledge gained from training often remains within the person who was first trained and tends not to reach other individuals in the organization. Experiences and insight from the training are usually presented orally and rarely documented. Additionally, it is difficult for managers to determine how much of the tacit knowledge gained from training is shared among individuals. Hence it is difficult to see the effect of such training.

IT is used within the three levels of healthcare as a "push-pull" approach. The push approach is characterized by a desire to capture knowledge in central repositories and then push it out to the organization, in this case by email, intranet and in conjunction with meetings. If a manager captured knowledge, e.g., from an external repository a web link was sent to employees by email and/or published on the intranet. Additionally, sharing is also dependent on the "pull" approach. This approach expects people to seek the knowledge they need, when they need it. As discussed previously the practitioners' lack of interest, time, skills and lack of adequate IT-support prevents a successful "push-pull" approach. This is worrying, as a successful and effective knowledge sharing and application is critical for transformation and innovation of knowledge - improvement of existing knowledge and creation of new knowledge (Persson & Janis, 2007). Moreover, managers in secondary care and to some extent in primary care express difficulties to assess whether employees have applied the disseminated knowledge. A manager even mentioned that explicit knowledge that has been captured from the outside organization is comparable to rain:

> *"Explicit knowledge is like a temporary and sudden rain of knowledge that washes through the organization without anyone knowing if someone has embraced it".*

Another argues:

> *"There we have a huge problem because we measure very badly how knowledge is assimilated or if the implemented knowledge, such as guidelines has contributed to any advantages to the patients. We have no feedback loop for how knowledge grows and is assimilated. Hence we don't know if it exists."*

Also, managers in municipality care perceive that monitoring the compliance to new knowledge is difficult. The majority of the municipalities have no specific processes developed for this. Sporadic follow-ups are common, and are conducted through verbal feedback from the nursing staff regarding her/his experience of how other medical staff follows new medical guidelines.

5. DISCUSSION AND CONCLUSION

A crucial role in the practice of evidence-based medicine is healthcare practitioners' possibility to access evidence based medical knowledge at the time when they need it. This study has confirmed that practitioners lack access to medical knowledge when preparing and conducting patient visits, as well as when making decisions about the care of the patient. One of the main reasons is that the participating organizations have failed to embed the KM process in everyday processes. It is evident that the processes and information flows are not understood and documented. For example, insights regarding what and how knowledge flows through the organization, what information is critical for which process, and how it is used as well as who uses it, is missing. Moreover, the findings have confirmed that the main barrier hindering the adoption of KM is related to people and organizational culture. There seem to be difficulties regarding getting people to share, participate and understand the roles and responsibilities that support KM and its importance and contribution to the organization. In addition, practitioners lack access to adequate IT-support for accessing and sharing knowledge. To simplify access and ensure application of knowledge that guides practitioners in delivering high quality care, practitioners expressed an urgent need to integrate medical guidelines and relevant knowledge sources with Electronic Health Records. There is also an urgent need for IT that supports sharing of tacit knowledge between practitioners within and outside the organization.

In conclusion, current Swedish healthcare practice, at least in the studied region, is far away from being able to live up the national IT-strategy as concerns IT-based knowledge support. We have no reason to believe that the situation is any different in other Swedish regions. The results of this study have made the leaders of the participating organizations aware of the problematic situation. They now realize that the KM processes needed for the successful implementation of an IT-based knowledge repository is simply not there.

It is evident that just implementing an IT-based knowledge repository will most probably not improve on the situation, as the main KM problems were related to people and to the organizational culture. As a result of this study, the 15 municipalities have decided to develop basic support for managers to start assessing their own units and start to systematize their KM processes. The support is based on the knowledge cycle (Figure 2) and includes simple tools and ways of working in each step. This will be a first step towards the vision of having an IT-based knowledge repository as a single point of access to relevant medical knowledge.

The study has been carried out in Swedish healthcare and the more general applicability of the results could therefore be questioned. The second author has been involved in several international studies of KM in various types of organizations and seen similar gloomy patterns there. We would, therefore, not be surprised if healthcare organizations in other countries experience the same problems. This needs to be further studied as we have not been able to find any studies to compare with.

REFERENCES

Abidi, S. S. R. (2007) Healthcare Knowledge Sharing: Purpose, Practices and Prospects In: Bali, R.K., Dwivedi, A. (eds.) *Healthcare Knowledge Management: Issues, Advances and Successes*, pp. 67–86. Springer, New York.

Alavi, M. & Leidner, D.E. (2001), "Review: knowledge management and knowledge management systems: conceptual foundations and research issues", *MIS Quarterly*. 25 (1), 107-36.

Bemmel, J.H. & Musen, M.A. (1997). *Handbook of Medical Informatics*. Bohn Stafleu Van Loghum, Houten, Netherlands.

Chen, Y-H., Liu, C-F & Hwang, H-G. (2011) Key factors affecting healthcare professionals to adopt knowledge management: The case of infection control departments of Taiwanese hospitals. *Expert Systems with Applications*. 38, 450–457.

Clancy, C.M. & Cronin, K. (2005) Evidence-Based Decision Making: Global Evidence, Local Decisions. *Health Affairs*. 24 (1), 151-162.

De Brún, C. (2007) Knowledge Management and the National Health Service in England In: Bali, R.K., Dwivedi, A. (eds.) *Healthcare Knowledge Management: Issues, Advances and Successes*, pp. 67–86. Springer, New York.

Glasziou, P. & Haynes, B. (2005) The paths from research to improved health outcomes. Evidence-Based Medicine. 10, 4-7.

Houser, J. & Oman, K.S. (2011) *Evidence-Based Practice: An Implementation Guide for Healthcare Organizations*. Jones & Bartlett Learning.

Krasniqi, H. & Persson, A. (2012), Web-based Knowledge Portals in Swedish Healthcare – Overview & Challenges, in Karlsson, D. et al,. (eds.), *Scandinavian Conference on Health Informatics* 2012, *Linköping* Electronic Conference Proceeding, no 70, Linköping University Electronic Press, Linköping, Sweden, IISBN: 978-91-7519.

Lenz, R. & Reichert, M. (2007) IT support for healthcare processes – premises, challenges, perspectives. *Data & Knowledge Engineering*. 61 (1), 39–58.

Ministry of health and social affairs (2006) *National Strategy for eHEALTH Sweden*. URL: http://www.sweden.gov.se/sb/d/1474 (visited on 09/12/2014).

O'Dell, C., Grayson, J.C & Essaides, N. (1998) *If Only We Knew What We Know: The Transfer of Internal Knowledge and Best Practice*. Simon & Schuster.

Persson, A & Stirna, J. (2007) *Making IT Happen and Making IT Stick - A Successful Case of Implementing a Knowledge Management System in a Healthcare Organization. Proceedings of the Fifteenth European Conference on Information Systems*, ECIS 2007, St. Gallen, Switzerland, 2007.

Rezazadeh, E., Hachesu, R.R., Rezapoor, A & Aliereza, K. (2014) Evidence-based medicine: going beyond improving care provider viewpoints, using and challenges upcoming. *Journal of Evidence-Based Medicine*. 7 (1), 26-31.

Sackett, D.L. (1997) Evidence-based medicine. *Fatal and Neonatal Hematology for the 21st Century*. 21 (1), 3–5.

Sackett, D., Straus, S.E., Richardson, W.S., Rosenberg, W & Haynes, R.B. (2000) *Evidence-based Medicine: How to Practice and Teach EBM*. Churchill Livingstone.

Strauss A, Corbin J. (1990) *Basics of qualitative research-Grounded Theory, procedures and techniques*. Newbury Park.

Wickramasinghe, N., Gupta, J.N.D. & Sharma, S.K. (2005) *Creating knowledge-based healthcare organizations*. IGI Publishing.

CONTENT CLUTTER AND ENTERPRISE SOCIAL MEDIA: A CASE STUDY

Jason Weir and David W. Wilson
Department of Computer Science and Information Systems, Birkbeck, University of London
Malet Street, London, WC1E 7HX, UK

ABSTRACT

A single case study of the UK subsidiary of a multinational corporation (Colpal) that currently utilizes enterprise social media technology to share organisational knowledge has revealed an emergent theme. The relational and cognitive dimensions of social capital and organisational leadership were found to play important influencing roles for knowledge sharing within the organisation's virtual communities. However, a new theme emerged from the case suggesting that the affordance of persistence offered by social media technology can actually hinder knowledge sharing once content reaches a certain level. Labelled as content clutter, it concerns the phenomenon whereby the amount of knowledge content becomes sufficient to discourage future knowledge sharing. As an organisation's use of enterprise social media starts to mature, these findings serve as a starting point for future research concerned with how to effectively manage knowledge content in virtual communities in a way that encourages effective knowledge sharing.

KEYWORDS

Content Clutter, Knowledge Sharing, Virtual Communities, Social Capital, Enterprise Social Media

1. INTRODUCTION

In current organisations, the ability to handle knowledge effectively is often considered a source of competitive advantage (Argote & Ingram, 2000) and a critical success factor to organisational development, leading to better internal strategic alignment and enhanced decision making (Kearns & Lederer, 2003). The emergence of virtual communities is offering ways for employees to exchange knowledge within the firm. Social networking is a critical organisational routine that enables knowledge sharing and knowledge creation (Sun, 2010), and has helped redefine our perception of "community", lowering geographical and physical boundaries. This study concerns knowledge sharing within organisational virtual communities.

We take knowledge sharing to be the process of two or more individuals transferring and acquiring knowledge through communication (Ku & Fan, 2009) Shared knowledge can be explicit knowledge, which can be easily articulated, codified and transferred , allowing the knowledge receiver to understand the know-what and know-why of 'something' (Hsu, Ju, Yen, & Chang, 2007). The other form of knowledge is tacit which develops in the knowledge receiver innate know-how and including know how to interact with known-whom around 'something'. Unlike explicit knowledge, tacit knowledge isn't easily articulated and codified, making it much harder to be transferred (Nonaka & Takeuchi, 1995). Often the key to acquiring tacit knowledge has been through a shared experience of two or more participants (Lam, 2000). Since it is much harder to imitate or copy tacit knowledge, facilitating tacit knowledge transfer gives the organisation a sustainable competitive advantage in the longer term (Liedtka, 1999). In organisational virtual communities an individual sharing a document with many people in exemplifies explicit knowledge sharing. Posting suggestions of how to approach a meeting where figures need to be explained exemplifies tacit knowledge sharing.

This study delineates the term virtual community as an "aggregation of individuals or business partners who interact around a shared interest, where the interaction is at least partially supported and/or mediated by technology mediation" (Porter, 2004, p1). Virtual communities are an informal platform to provide knowledge, support and friendship (Huang & Kuo, 2003). They allow participants to maintain existing social ties and seek new social ties as well. (Dabbish, Kraut, Fussell, & Kiesler, 2005).

Newly emerged social media technologies e.g. wikis, blogs and fora offer employees more simultaneous affordances compared with earlier tools, like email and instant messenger (Treem & Leonardi, 2012). Following the success of personal social media platforms many technology departments of larger organisations have implemented social media technologies for organisational use among their employees. Previous scholarship has examined factors that influence a person's ability and/or desire to share information and knowledge within an organisational virtual community. Contextual variables, such as the social media technology, organisational support and championship, right through to individual variables like incentive systems, extrinsic and intrinsic motivation, social capital, identity & personal cognition have all been theorised to play a role in the level of knowledge sharing within an organisation (Lin, Hung, & Chen, 2009; Shen, Yu, & Khalifa, 2010). The evolving role of technology, social aspects, and organisational support on knowledge sharing have been the most researched.

The specific question of why employees are motivated to share organisational or shy away from sharing knowledge in their organisational virtual communities is the overarching question of this study. It attempts to provide an in-depth analysis of the key themes that influence knowledge sharing. Furthermore, it seeks to contribute by clarifying the relationship between the technology and social and organisational aspects of knowledge sharing within organisational virtual teams.

Approaching this question, we employ a case study in, a UK subsidiary of a multinational consumer products company, henceforth named as 'Colpal' who, through their enterprise social networks, currently utilise virtual communities to share knowledge within the organisation.

2. LITERATURE REVIEW

We chose to focus on enterprise social media usage within a knowledge sharing context. Literature was collected to find major themes emerged. Social capital and organisational context were the main themes emerging. Social capital is important to knowledge sharing within virtual teams, evidenced by the research theorising social capital as an antecedent to knowledge sharing (Chai &Kim 2010); as a mediator to knowledge sharing (Ip & Wagner, 2008) and finally as a moderator to knowledge sharing (Fischer and Reuber 2011). Nahapiet & Ghoshal (1998) offered two characteristics of social capital. Firstly, it can't be owned by any one individual or be easily traded among groups. Secondly, it facilitates the most efficient actions of individuals operating within a social structure. Nahapiet & Ghoshal (1998) distinguished three different dimensions of social capital.

In the first structural dimension, this is taken to mean the intensity of relationships that exists in a network and the configuration structure of the network itself. In the context of virtual communities, it is the familiarity that members in the community, traditional or virtual, feel towards one another (Yu, Lu, & Liu, 2010). Key to understanding this dimension is the level of 'social ties' that occur between individuals within a group. Frequency of interaction, is important for two reasons. Firstly, it means that both strong and weak ties can exist in the virtual world and be developed over time, just like offline relationships. Secondly, it opens up the idea of virtual communities acting as a more effective information 'bridge' between strongly tied and weakly tied virtual communities, allowing for information and knowledge to diffuse faster than ever before. Overall, this structural dimension is reinforced by the relational and cognitive elements.

Trust and its effect on knowledge sharing has been deeply researched in the literature. Hsu et al. (2007), found that trust is a multi-dimensional concept that develops in stages, from the basic level of information-based trust, right through to identification-based trust whereby both parties have fully internalised the other's preferences, emerging from a history of interactions with one another (Rousseau, Sitkin, Burt, & Camerer, 1998). Being able to identify with other individuals breeds a mutual trust that is the key driver of knowledge sharing within virtual communities (Hsu et al., 2007; Grabner-Krauter, 2009). Additionally, while elements of relational capital drive the frequency of knowledge sharing within virtual communities, it has also been shown to increase the quality of the knowledge exchange (Chiu et al., 2006).

The third cognitive dimension refers to shared visions, shared, and shared interpretations that occur between individuals and groups (Lesser & Storck, 2001). Nahapiet & Ghoshal (1998) explain that shared language is a sort of social lubricant that enhances the capability of different parties to merge knowledge during social exchange. In the context of virtual communities, it provides an avenue in which participants can understand each other and work together to continually build up their common vocabulary and communicate in the most efficient and effective manner within their own domains (Chiu et al., 2006). Expanding on the notion of shared vision, Tsai & Ghoshal (1998) explain it to be "a bonding mechanism that helps different parts of the organisation to integrate or combine resources" (p467). Additionally, shared language and vision have been shown to act as an initial substitute for trust, allowing for early interactions that lead onto more enhanced levels of trust (Grabner-Krauter, 2009)

Huy and Shipilov (2012) defined emotional capital as the "aggregate feelings of goodwill toward a company and the way it operates" (p74). The key pillars supporting emotional capital are alignment expectation between the organisation and individual, employee recognition of achievement, community attachment between employees and senior management based on shared values, interests, and fun. In their study, they found that those companies that exhibited higher levels of emotional capital, engaged more frequently in knowledge sharing on their enterprise social media platform than companies with low emotional capital. However, Nahapiet & Ghoshal (1998) suggested that the existence of social capital is not always a beneficial resource. Janis (1982) posited that strong ties can produce 'collective blindness' that might have damaging consequences.

Overall, having a high presence of social capital has been empirically demonstrated to facilitate better knowledge sharing in physical communities (Yli-Renko, Autio, & Sapienza, 2001) and later on within virtual ones (Chao-Min et al., 2006; Yao, Tsai, & Fang, 2015). However, they are highly interdependent. In isolation, while each of the dimensions on their own doesn't always result in greater knowledge sharing, there is broad agreement that their combined affect does promote impacts on knowledge sharing within organisational virtual communities. It appears that social media technologies may act as a cognitive, structural and relational lubricant that help reinforce social capital.

The study of the organization's role in the context of knowledge sharing has largely been shown in previous research to be both an antecedent and moderator to knowledge sharing within offline and virtual communities (Tong, Tak, & Wong, 2015). The organisational environment that surrounds virtual communities can be broken down to mean the economic environment, the management style, the political context and the culture of the organisation itself (Barrett, Cappleman, Shoib, and Walsham (2004). Status and power distance are also considered as key influencers to knowledge sharing within virtual teams (Bhagat, Kedia, Harveston, & Triandis, 2002). To address the intertwining elements of management style and political context, an attempt has been made to categorise these under the following headings of organisational support, leadership, network formality, and structure.

This study characterises organizational support as the level of endorsement or formality an organisation gives to its virtual communities. Wenger, McDermott, and Snyder (2002) place this degree of formality on a continuum between the level of formality that makes the virtual community essentially 'unrecognisable' to the organisation and the level of endorsement on a virtual community being so great that is represents a fully institutionalised virtual community. In this scenario, the level of endorsement is also positively linked to the company resources dedicated to the virtual community. Romanelli and Tushman (1994) suggest that this level of resource must be sustained over time to ensure that the virtual community remains formal, characterising this as the level of 'organisational slack' a company has towards keeping a virtual community successful.

Another important organisational resource that drives knowledge sharing is the extent of leadership 'embeddedness' associated with such virtual communities (Majewski & Usoro, 2011). This was taken to mean the extent to which a person or a group of people motivate and inspire virtual members to engage in knowledge sharing (ibid.) At one end of the spectrum, usually where there is a high degree of formality, leadership roles are generally assigned by management (Gongla & Rizzuto, 2001; Lesser & Storck, 2001). At the other end of the spectrum where there is extremely low formality, leadership roles within the group are in a constant state of flux, emerging through the state of expertise of a given person or group (Lesser and Storck, 2001). While placed at either end of the spectrum isn't necessarily an advantage or disadvantage, when a virtual community grows in member size and importance. Linking back to the cognitive and relational dimensions of social capital, communities that operate good knowledge management in terms of keeping a common and consistent language (Tsai & Ghoshal, 1998), as well as ensuring that the information is kept up to date and relevant to people's jobs (M.-Hsu et al 2007), breeds more cognitive alignment and information based trust among participants, helping to contribute to higher rates of knowledge sharing.

Another organisational dynamic concerns the delicate balance of formal and informal mechanisms that support knowledge sharing within an organisational virtual community. Virtual communities that have organically evolved sometimes lack the formal mechanisms to manage the knowledge quality and may start to become unruly (McDermott and O'Dell, 2001). On the other hand, virtual communities that were created by the company's senior management team based on topics they deemed important may lack the informal mechanisms to sustain knowledge sharing in the first place (ibid.). Wherever the balance of formal and informal mechanisms may lie, having the capability in the organisation that allows leaders to strike such a balance to both motivate and manage knowledge sharing within virtual teams appears to be the key in driving knowledge sharing.

Finally, organisational structures have also been shown to have an impact on knowledge sharing within virtual communities. Nonaka and Takeuchi (1995) argue that flat, open, flexible, and decentralised structures best support the sharing of knowledge. Looking at the opposite end of organisational structure, those with a more centralised organisational structure inadvertently tend to create a non-participatory environment that discourages knowledge sharing. (Sivadas & Dwyer, 2000). Building on the notion of hierarchies, Tsai (2001 and 2002) sees these hierarchical structures create knowledge silos that have the potential to hamper knowledge sharing.

In an assessment of the key themes identified review that concern knowledge sharing within virtual communities, it is evident that the key influencers of knowledge sharing embody a dynamic interplay between more recent and continually evolving technological aspects and evolving social and organisational aspects.

Despite broad consensus in the literature that social media technology facilitates more socialisation and offers affordances that supersede more traditional CMC technologies, it can't generate and sustain knowledge sharing within virtual communities on its own. Similarly, while elements underpinning social capital like trust and shared language have been shown to drive more knowledge exchange in communities, both physical and virtual, outside the obvious need for a social media platform to exist within a virtual community, social media technologies have been shown to enhance the level of social capital, helping to have both a direct and indirect effect on knowledge sharing in such communities.

Whilst much recent scholarship has sought to test theories on social, organisational and technological aspects in relation to knowledge sharing in organisational virtual communities, the continuous and rapid evolution of technology, combined with its apparent mediating effect on the world in which it operates, calls for a fresh in-depth look to identify what themes are relevant today in a complex real-life organisational setting. By understanding if these major themes are still key influencers to knowledge sharing in an organisational setting and second, to uncover any other new contextual themes that may be worthy of future study.

3. RESEARCH QUESTIONS AND METHODOLOGY

The overall research question that this research addressed concerned the influencers to knowledge sharing within an organisational virtual communities.

In order to identify the key influencers, respondents were asked to provide reasons as to why they were most active and least active within their current organisational virtual communities. We wanted to understand if themes from the literature resonate in the case and also sought to identify emergent themes from the case that could have implications for future research directions.

According to its 2014 Annual Report submitted to the Securities and Exchange Commission, Colpal is a $17.3 billion US-based consumer products company serving people in more than 200 countries. The company enjoys market leading shares through its strong global brands in its core businesses – Oral Care, Personal Care, Home Care and Pet Nutrition. According to its website, it has identified three key strategic pillars to help support sustainable growth in these core businesses: 'Innovation for Growth', 'Leading to Win' & 'Effectiveness and Efficiency'. The key pillar of 'Effectiveness and Efficiency' concerns the re-investment of savings generated through on-going efficiency programs. Reinvestment is focused on innovation and brand building, enabling technology and analytics, digital engagement and driving growth in emerging markets.

The company's virtual communities persist on platforms from a single provider. They have grown from the CMC provision and now include profiled, blogs, wikis, and fora. In order to answer the questions on why respondents were least active and most active, an e-mail survey was sent by the General Manager to all 103 UK employees of 'Colpal'. There was a final open ended question asking respondents to provide one or two suggestions on what Colpal could do to increase knowledge sharing within their social media platform. Each individual response was checked to ensure that all answers given by respondents were detailed enough to give an accurate picture of their views. The survey received a 97% response rate from employees with all questions eventually answered in a satisfactory manner.

Two weeks before the survey was issued, informal observation of employees within Colpal was recorded across six business meetings where it was anticipated that the internal social media platform would be used and/or discussed. Observation can be defined as "the systematic description of events, behaviours, and artefacts in the social setting chosen for study" (Marshall & Rossman, 1989), p79. During such meetings, observations from participants concerning the internal social media platform were jotted down on notes and categorised as potential issues or potential positives to knowledge sharing within Colpal. Other interesting observations that were considered important to answering the research question were also noted. The researcher was also a participant in these meetings. Before the commencement of each meeting, informed consent to collect notes was obtained from participants.

This additional data collection method was necessary for the following reasons. Firstly, it allowed the research to be conducted in the respondent's naturalistic settings, revealing both their positive and negative reactions to engaging in knowledge sharing within the enterprise social media platform. DeWalt and DeWalt (2010) suggested that participant observation be utilised as a way to increase the research validity. These observations were important as it revealed both verbal and non-verbal reactions to this social phenomena that might otherwise not have made it into participant's survey responses. To help reduce observer bias, a specific observer template was created to ensure consistent information capture across each meeting.

4. RESEARCH FINDINGS, ANALYSIS & DISCUSSION

The first aspect emerging from the data concerned the member expectation of knowledge sharing within the virtual communities. In virtual communities where employees were most active in knowledge sharing, there existed a high level of expectation that all members contribute knowledge in some way. Reasons for the high level of contribution expectation were varied, with some respondents saying that it was "just part of my job" or "it was part of a business process". In virtual communities where there was the least knowledge sharing, there existed relatively low levels of expectation to share. Reasons for low level expectation were also varied, with some respondents saying that "why should I contribute when no one else appears to be" or "it wasn't made clear that I needed to contribute anything". Observational field notes suggested in two meetings that social expectation played a role with one meeting showing a potential link between high expectation and high knowledge sharing and low expectation and low knowledge sharing

This notion of expectation alignment forms part of the relational dimension of social capital put forward by Nahapiet & Ghoshal (1998) which supported previous research (Chui et al, 2006 ;Tsai & Ghoshal, 1998) showing this to be one of the key ingredients to increased knowledge sharing.

The second social aspect emergent from the data is the concern of trust. Trust in this situation concerned the accuracy of content in each page and whether the information was relevant. In virtual communities where employees were most active in knowledge sharing, the trust in information content appeared high. In most instances, respondents gave the example of certain market share files that were only available through a particular virtual community page. They were known to be accurate and relevant to most people within the organisation.

Like expectations, the multifaceted nature of trust forms part of the relational dimension of social capital and its effects on knowledge sharing have been well documented (Chui et all, 2006; Tsai & Goshal, 1998; Rousseseau et al. 1998). However, it was proposed by M.-Hsu et al (2007) that information based trust is the first level of trust and members must graduate through all the levels of trust to drive the most effective knowledge sharing. In the example regarding the market share reports, other than certain employees uploading and downloading the files, there were very little posted comments concerning the data. It is possible that in order to generate more commentary around such pages, additional levels of trust, might need to be achieved.

Interestingly, while Chiu et al (2006) showed a significant positive relationship between social capital and knowledge sharing, the study also tested social capital's effect on knowledge quality and found that, contrary to their expectations, increased levels of social capital generally had no relationship to knowledge quality.

There doesn't appear to be any studies that test the direct relationship between knowledge quality and knowledge sharing. Findings from the Colpal case suggest that a useful future area of inquiry would be to understand what relationship, if any, exists between the level of knowledge quality and the level of knowledge sharing in a virtual community. Furthermore, it would be also useful to understand at what point the level of knowledge sharing within a virtual community starts to dilute knowledge quality.

The third social aspect emerging from the data concerned the domain's metadata structures. In virtual communities where employees were most active in knowledge sharing, the metadata appeared to be structured in such a way that made content posted within these communities easy to find or easy to share for members. This intuitiveness of metadata structure was generally not present in communities where members engaged in lower levels of knowledge sharing. Furthermore, in communities where knowledge sharing seemed high, field notes from observational data noted that, out of six observed meetings, three meetings observed occurrences where problematic metadata structures were inhibiting the efficiency or finding content that was relevant to a meeting. It could be argued that metadata is a type of shared language that forms part of a cognitive interplay among virtual team members, enabling more efficient knowledge transfer. This notion of shared language is called out by Nahapiet & Ghoshal (1998), forming a component of the cognitive dimension of social capital. Evidence of shared language, in addition to other elements of cognitive capital it must be noted, act as an enabler to knowledge sharing with virtual communities is also evident in previous research by Chui et al (2006).

4.1 Organisational Themes and the Emergence of Content Clutter

The study emerged findings consonant with the concepts in the literature concerning management support, strategic leadership and envisioning, awareness of and responsibility for communication via virtual communities. At the same time elements of structural capital as an influencer to knowledge sharing in virtual communities were made reference to in the survey data but not the observational data.

However, one theme emerging from this case that didn't appear as a major theme in the literature review concerned the influence of content clutter on knowledge sharing within virtual teams. In virtual communities where employees were least active in knowledge sharing, information clutter appeared to be a key influencing factor. Not to be confused with content quality, meaning the quality of each individual piece of content within a virtual community, content clutter concerns the frequency of content, large and small, that sits within the community. It is suggested from the data that the high frequency of content on some virtual communities made it harder to find information that was relevant for employees to do their job. However, in the communities where employees said they were most active, references were made to content quality but not necessarily to the frequency of content in each community. A possible explanation for this may be the employee's interpretation of 'quality' as it could have also been taken to mean the ideal level of content frequency. Another possible explanation was that some of these most active communities contain a smaller number of participants which may have resulted in naturally smaller levels of content to begin with.

Interestingly, a secondary review of the literature focusing on this notion of content clutter revealed a paper by Yardi, Golder, and Brzozowski (2009) who explained through their study of corporate blogging that the more information that was added to a virtual community, the harder it became to find any specific piece of information. Here, the specific affordance of persistence (Treem & Leonardi, 2012) offered by social media may start to become a hindrance to knowledge sharing once the frequency of content researches a certain point.

5. CONCLUSIONS

Whilst there is a question arising out of the suitability of social media tools over more traditional CMC tools, the biggest revelation emergent from the study is that the persistence of such technology, can actually hinder knowledge sharing. Described as content clutter and supported by previous research (Yardi et al., 2009), this emergent theme may have turned an initial strength of social media technology into a possible weakness, suggesting that as the frequency of information content of a virtual community reaches a saturation point, whereby the organisation and search for specific knowledge starts to become confusing and cumbersome.

This emergent theme from the case highlights a potentially new issue in knowledge sharing suggesting that too much knowledge sharing could start to diminish the sharing.

Moreover, the influencers of knowledge sharing in virtual communities found in this case have helped identify potential shortfalls in organisational strategy concerning virtual communities. With many organisations recognising organisational knowledge as a key intangible resource that holds a potential key to competitive advantage (Grant, 1996), this will help business leaders within the organisation refine their strategies in the hope of making organisational social media the main medium of tacit and explicit knowledge exchange.

The emergence of content clutter as a potential future research topic warrants further qualitative and quantitative inquiry, especially in the context of how it interacts with other possible variables that impact knowledge sharing in organisational virtual communities.

REFERENCES

Argote, L., & Ingram, P. (2000). Knowledge transfer: A basis for competitive advantage in firms. *Organizational behavior and human decision processes, 82*(1), 150-169.

Bhagat, R. S., Kedia, B. L., Harveston, P. D., & Triandis, H. C. (2002). Cultural variations in the cross-border transfer of organizational knowledge: An integrative framework. *Academy of management review, 27*(2), 204-221.

Barrett, M., Cappleman, S., Shoib, G., & Walsham, G. (2004). Learning in Knowledge Communities:: Managing Technology and Context. *European Management Journal, 22*(1), 1-11.

Chai, S., & Kim, M. (2010). What makes bloggers share knowledge? An investigation on the role of trust. *International Journal of Information Management, 30*(5), 408-415.

Chiu, C.-M., Hsu, M.-H., & Wang, E. T. G. (2006). Understanding knowledge sharing in virtual communities: An integration of social capital and social cognitive theories. *Decision Support Systems, 42*(3), 1872-1888.

Dabbish, L. A., Kraut, R. E., Fussell, S., & Kiesler, S. (2005). *Understanding email use: predicting action on a message.* Paper presented at the Proceedings of the SIGCHI conference on Human factors in computing systems.

Fischer, E., & Reuber, A. R. (2011). Social interaction via new social media: (How) can interactions on Twitter affect effectual thinking and behavior? *Journal of business venturing, 26*(1), 1-18.

Grant, R. M. (1996). Toward a knowledge-based theory of the firm. *Strategic management journal, 17*(S2), 109-122.

Hsu, M.-H., Ju, T. L., Yen, C.-H., & Chang, C.-M. (2007). Knowledge sharing behavior in virtual communities: The relationship between trust, self-efficacy, and outcome expectations. *International Journal of Human-Computer Studies, 65*(2), 153-169.

Gongla, P., & Rizzuto, C. R. (2001). Evolving communities of practice: IBM Global Services experience. *IBM systems journal, 40*(4), 842-862.

Gray, D. E. (2014). *Doing research in the real world*: SAGE Publications Limited.

Hsu, M.-H., Ju, T. L., Yen, C.-H., & Chang, C.-M. (2007). Knowledge sharing behavior in virtual communities: The relationship between trust, self-efficacy, and outcome expectations. *International Journal of Human-Computer Studies, 65*(2), 153-169

Huang, C.-C., & Kuo, C.-M. (2003). The transformation and search of semi-structured knowledge in organizations. *Journal of Knowledge Management, 7*(4), 106-123.

Huy, Q., & Shipilov, A. (2012). The Key to Social Media Success Within Organizations. *MIT Sloan Management Review, 54*(1), 73-81.

Kearns, G. S., & Lederer, A. L. (2003). A Resource-Based View of Strategic IT Alignment: How Knowledge Sharing Creates Competitive Advantage. *Decision Sciences, 34*(1), 1-29.

Ip, R. K. F., & Wagner, C. (2008). Weblogging: A study of social computing and its impact on organizations. *Decision Support Systems, 45*(2), 242-250.

Janis, I. L. (1982). Groupthink: Psychological studies of policy decisions and fiascoes: Houghton Mifflin Boston.

Ku, E. C., & Fan, Y. W. (2009). Knowledge sharing and customer relationship management in the travel service alliances. *Total Quality Management, 20*(12), 1407-1421.

Lam, A. (2000). Tacit knowledge, organizational learning and societal institutions: an integrated framework. *Organization studies, 21*(3), 487-513.

Lesser, E., & Storck, J. (2001). Communities of practice and organizational performance. *IBM systems journal, 40*(4), 831-841.Liedtka, J. (1999). Linking competitive advantage with communities of practice. *Journal of Management Inquiry, 8*(1), 5-16.

Lin, M.-J. J., Hung, S.-W., & Chen, C.-J. (2009). Fostering the determinants of knowledge sharing in professional virtual communities. *Computers in Human Behavior, 25*(4), 929-939.

Majewski, G., & Usoro, A. (2011). Barriers of and incentives to knowledge sharing in (virtual) communities of practice: A critical literature review. *BU Acad. Rev, 10*, 387-405.

Marshall, C., & Rossman, G. B. (1989). Design qualitative research. *Calfornia: Sage.*

McDermott, R., & O'dell, C. (2001). Overcoming cultural barriers to sharing knowledge. *Journal of Knowledge Management, 5*(1), 76-85.

Nahapiet, J., & Ghoshal, S. (1998). Social Capital, Intellectual Capital, and the Organizational Advantage. *The Academy of Management Review, 23*(2), 242-266. doi:10.2307/259373

Nonaka, I., & Takeuchi, H. (1995). The knowledge-creating company: How Japanese companies create the dynamics of innovation: Oxford university press.

Sivadas, E., & Dwyer, F. R. (2000). An examination of organizational factors influencing new product success in internal and alliance-based processes. *Journal of marketing, 64*(1), 31-49.

Tong, C., Tak, W. I. W., & Wong, A. (2015). The Impact of knowledge sharing on the relationship between organizational culture and Job satisfaction: The perception of information communication and technology (ICT) practitioners in Hong Kong. *International Journal of Human Resource Studies, 5*(1), 19-47

Treem, J., & Leonardi, P. M. (2012). Social Media Use in Organisations: An Affordance Approach: Exploring the Affordances of Visibility, Editability,Persistence, and Association. Paper presented at the Communication Yearbook.

Tsai, W., & Ghoshal, S. (1998). Social capital and value creation: The role of intrafirm networks. *Academy of Management Journal, 41*(4), 464-476.

Porter, C. E. (2004). A Typology of Virtual Communities: A Multi-Disciplinary Foundation for Future Research. *Journal of Computer-Mediated Communication, 10*(1), 00-00.

Rousseau, D. M., Sitkin, S. B., Burt, R. S., & Camerer, C. (1998). Not so different after all: A cross-discipline view of trust. *Academy of management review, 23*(3), 393-404.

Romanelli, E., & Tushman, M. L. (1994). Organizational transformation as punctuated equilibrium: An empirical test. *Academy of Management Journal, 37*(5), 1141-1166.

Shen, K. N., Yu, A. Y., & Khalifa, M. (2010). Knowledge contribution in virtual communities: accounting for multiple dimensions of social presence through social identity. *Behaviour & Information Technology, 29*(4), 337-348.

Sun, P. (2010). Five critical knowledge management organizational themes. *Journal of Knowledge Management, 14*(4), 507-523.

Wenger, E., McDermott, R. A., & Snyder, W. (2002). *Cultivating communities of practice: A guide to managing knowledge*: Harvard Business Press.

Yardi, S., Golder, S. A., & Brzozowski, M. J. (2009). *Blogging at work and the corporate attention economy.* Paper presented at the Proceedings of the SIGCHI conference on human factors in computing systems.

Yin, R. K. (2013). *Case study research: Design and methods*: Sage publications.

Yli-Renko, H., Autio, E., & Sapienza, H. J. (2001). Social capital, knowledge acquisition, and knowledge exploitation in young technology-based firms. *Strategic management journal, 22*(6-7), 587-613.

Yu, T.-K., Lu, L.-C., & Liu, T.-F. (2010). Exploring factors that influence knowledge sharing behavior via weblogs. *Computers in Human Behavior, 26*(1), 32-41.

THE IMPORTANCE OF COMMUNICATION IN THE TRANSFER OF KNOWLEDGE AND IN THE CREATION OF A SHARED VISION - A CASE STUDY

Maria Terezinha Angeloni[1], Rafael Zimmermann Homma[2], Luiz Afonso Pereira Athayde Filho[2] and Aldo Cosentino[1]

[1]*Instituto de Estudos e Gestão Energética - INERGE*

[2]*Celesc Distribuição – CELESC*

ABSTRACT

This article aims to present a Communication Plan, to support the transfer of knowledge and the creation of a shared vision among the members of the Research and Development Project (R&D) for the sponsor / client company – Celesc, electric utility company in the State of Santa Catarina, Brazil and executed by the Institute for Studies and Energy Management - INERGE. The project is part of the R & D program of the National Electric Energy Agency - ANEEL[1] in accordance with the law 12.212 – January 20, 2010. The theoretical framework is based on the areas of Project Management, Knowledge Management and Organizational Communication. Methodologically it is characterized as an interorganizational, interproject research of experimental development. The results are not yet effective because of the short implementation time of the project, however, based on the actions implemented up to present time it can be inferred that the communication is an important element in the transfer of knowledge and the creation of a shared vision between the team members – interproject, as well as between the organizations involved – interorganizations.

KEYWORDS

Knowledge Management; Project Management; Organizational Communication.

1. INTRODUCTION

Communication is an area that is increasingly being considered relevant to the success of businesses and is changing the relationship dynamics among involved participants, being them internal or external to the organizations.

With the transformation from an industrial society to an information and knowledge society, organizations managed in Taylorian molds - where communication was not a priority - deals today with a new reality. To account for the volume of data, information and knowledge generated both in internal and external environment; a well established communication system must be implemented.

The importance of communication in the management of organizations in general and in project management cannot be denied and should aim to build a systemic and shared view, generating the same perception of its members.

For a better understanding of the importance of organizational communication, it is necessary to analyze it in the context in which it is inserted. Organizations inserted in the industrial society had different communication needs from those inserted in the information and knowledge society.

Based on the above, it's justified the relevance of this study, considering the importance of proceeding on those studies that interrelate areas of Communication, Knowledge Management and Project Management; and this movement is defined as the research question: Can communication contribute to the transfer of knowledge and the creation of a shared vision among the members of a Research and Development Project?

---

[1] The National Agency of Electrical Energy (ANEEL) is a regulatory agency linked to the Ministry of Mines and Energy (Ministério de Minas e Energia), that regulates and supervises the production, transmission and commercialization of electricity, according to the policies and guidelines from the federal government.

This article is divided into five (5) sections, the first being this introduction. The second presents the theoretical framework of the study. The third covers the methodological procedures. The fourth describes the Communication Plan. In the fifth section we present the final considerations.

2. INTER-RELATIONSHIP BETWEEN THE AREAS OF COMMUNICATION AND KNOWLEDGE MANAGEMENT IN RESEARCH AND DEVELOPMENT PROJECTS

The management of projects has systematized their practices, becoming a subject in the 1980s, and having as the leader in the consolidation of the area, the Project Management Institute (PMI), which in 1996 produced a Project Management Knowledge Guide- GUIDE PMBOK ® (Pinheiro, Siani, Guilhermino, Henriques, Quental and Pizarro, 2006).

The PMBOK® Guide (PMI, 2013), the fifth and final version, presents a methodology built on 47 management processes, structured into five groups of basic processes: initiating, planning, executing, monitoring and controlling, and closing.

The definition of project, in that guide, has the following characteristics: it is a temporary endeavor, which does not mean of short length; it has a defined beginning and end; and it is usually undertaken to create a lasting result that can be tangible or intangible.

A project can be either executed within and for the same organization – intra-organizational, or from one organization to another or others – inter-organizational. It may also focus on a single project – intra-project, or it may be thought to build a portfolio of projects within an organization oriented for projects – inter-project (Shinoda, 2013), also denominated intramural and extramural projects in the Frascati Manual (2015).

Frascati Manual (2015), a reference document about R&D (Research and Development), organizes the projects of research and experimental development in basic research, applied research and experimental development. Its definitions are accepted worldwide and its principles are used as base in the Oslo Manual (2005) and in the law 11.196/05, also known as "the Law of Good", that adopts the aforementioned three kinds of research.

Following the same approach, for ANEEL every project of R&D must be included in its development proposed phase within the innovation chain, and it may be classified as basic guided research, applied research or experimental development, adding to the types of research present in Frascati Manual, Oslo Manual and the Law of Good, other types of research such as top seeded, pioneer batch or insertion in the market, and they can be simultaneously, nationalization of products, as long as that shows some improvement or new functionality, characterizing the object of the research and necessary development, respecting the legislation about intellectual property (ANEEL , 2012).

> ANEEL (2012, p. 53 and 54) conceptualizes the types of research:
> Basic Guided Research – theoretical or experimental phase that aims the search of knowledge about new phenomena for the development of products and innovation processes [...]. Applied Research – phase to apply the acquired knowledge, for the development or improvement of products and processes. It guides to the discovery of knowledge application acquired at the basic guided research or new methods, and ways to achieve a specific objective [...]. Experimental Development: systematic phase, outlined from pre-existing knowledge, aiming the validation or the demonstration of technical viability or functionality of new products, processes, systems and services, or yet, the improvement of what has already been produced or established [...]. Top seeded – phase which considers aspects related to the improvement of the prototype obtained in a former R&D [...]. Pioneer Batch – phase that considers aspects related to the production in "pilot scale" of Top Seeded developed in a former project [...]. Insertion in the Market – phase that ends the innovation chain and aims diffusing the results in the electric sector [...]

Whatever type of project it may be, there is consensus that they generate data and information (PMI, 2013) or information and knowledge (Jamil 2005; Shinoda, 2012), and that they need to pass through the organization (s) and among members from one or more projects, that is, intraorganization, interorganization, intraproject and interprojects (Shinoda, 2012), and intramural and extramural (Manual de Frascati, 2015).

According to the PMBOK (PMI, 2013, p. 58), [...] throughout the project's life cycle, a significant amount of data and information is collected, analyzed, processed and distributed in various formats to the members of the project team and other stakeholders. [...] The collected data is analyzed in context and aggregated and transformed becoming project information [...]. The information can then be verbally communicated or stored and distributed as reports in various formats.

The concepts of data, information and knowledge are closely related to its utility in decision making and connected to the concept of communication.

The communication process is a sequence of events in which data, information and knowledge are transmitted from a sender to a receiver.

Decision making in organizations will increasingly demand teamwork and greater involvement of people, as in project teams. Teamwork put into evidence the dialog procedures which are based on the idea that in an organization, the communication should be encouraged for the establishment of a common thought (Angeloni, 1992). The establishment of a common thought consists in consider the point of view of each member of the team, so that the decisions taken in the organizations have a higher quality level. The decision-making process then passes from the individual level to the staff level.

Based on the above, we can infer that there is a strong interrelationship between the variables, data, information and knowledge with communication and decision processes, supported by an information technology environment, as shown in Figure 1.

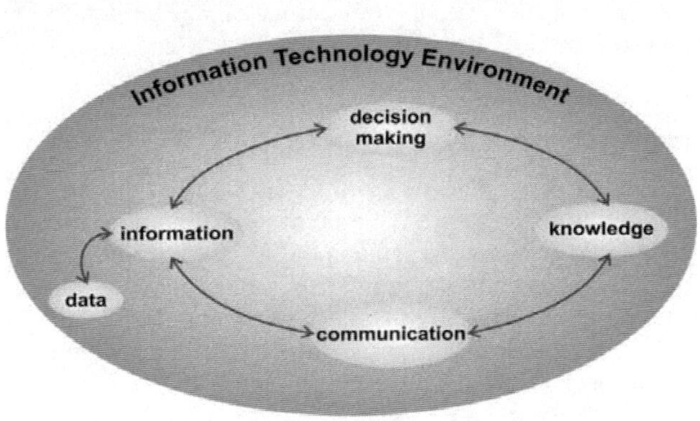

Figure 1. Elements involved in decision-making process. Source: Angeloni, 2010, p. 19

Information and knowledge must flow in the organization through an efficient communication system involving the installation of a suitable technological infrastructure. Only that way, the organization will have data, information and knowledge of high quality, in a timely manner to support the decision-making process.

The information technology options as a facilitator object for communication is especially due to the advent of telematics. Network connections, laser communication, optical fiber and large computer switching systems have grown significantly and spread across the business context an idea of connectivity.

Despite the major changes in the business environment and the prioritization of some variables over others, communication followed the path of management thought, increasing in importance and affirming its key role in the efficiency and effectiveness of business objectives. Imagining organizational success in the contemporary perspective, without working communication processes can be considered imprudent.

Krogh, Ichijo and Nonaka (2001), when dealing with knowledge organization, point out the importance of creating a sharing space, called enabling context or "ba", a word of Japanese origin, which is the roughly translated as a place in where a fact happens.

Thus, "ba" can be interpreted as the space or context where relationships take place. (Nonaka and KONNO, 1998). This context can be physical, such as an office or a meeting; virtual, such as e-mail, teleconferencing; mental, such as shared experiences, ideas or ideals; or any combination of these three elements. (OUTI and STRAUS, 2009).

The enabling conditions or "organizational space for knowledge" consists of the set of favorable conditions that must be afforded by the organization to facilitate or enable the emergence of ideas, innovations, sharing, collaborative problem solving and tolerance to honest mistakes, among others. Under this view, the understanding of the word management, upon their association with the word knowledge, should not be understood as synonymous with control. Management, in that context, means to promote activities that create and transfer knowledge, and it is embedded in the interpretative approach of knowledge management proposed by George, Iacono and Kling (1995); Schultze and Boland (2000); Stenmark (2001); Krogh, Ichijo and Nonaka (2001); Choo (1998), aiming tacit knowledge, being strictly related to the communication atmosphere. The other approach on knowledge management is functional (Dhaliwal and Benbasat, 1996; Gregor and Benbasat, 1999; Zhao, Kumar and Stohr, 2001) and benefits the explicit knowledge, treating it as a manageable object, that is, information and its consequent storage. It is important to emphasize that the transference of knowledge happens by either means of communication – tacit knowledge, or by its storage – explicit knowledge.

The present text is part of the interpretative approach, that according to Dazzi and Angeloni (2001), Dazzi and Pereira (2002), and Grotto and Angeloni (2004), who are experts in organizational communication, is responsible for the dissemination of information and knowledge through messages that run through the organization and the common meanings produced, that is a shared vision. Knowledge management expands an important facet of communication: the need to transfer knowledge generates the necessity to intensify communication processes in organizations. The communication is not only evidenced by the formal written channels, functional approach present in the other part of the plan known as information and knowledge management (Angeloni, Zimmermann, Cosentino and Athayde Filho, 2015), but mainly by the exchange of tacit knowledge, which depends largely on face-to-face communication, present in the current plan of communication.

Observing the nature, the flow, the direction of information, the written and oral media, we can define the degree of influence of this cultural element in the sharing of knowledge.

3. METHODOLOGY

The objective of this article is to present a Communication Plan, which aims to support the transfer of knowledge and the creation of a shared vision among the members of the Research and Development Project (R&D) for the sponsor / client company - Celesc Distribution, electric utilities company in Santa Catarina and executed by the Institute for Studies and Energy Management - INERGE.

The Research and Development Project, reason for the plan's definition, aims to develop an integrated system for autonomous inspection of overhead power lines, and it is part of ANEEL's R&D program, regulated by law 12.212 - January 20, 2010, which regulates the annual application of a percentage of net operating revenue in research projects and technological development of the electricity sector (ANEEL, 2012).

"R&D projects regulated by ANEEL are those aimed to the qualification and technological development of electrical companies, in order to generate new processes or products, or the improvement of their characteristics [...]. Every R&D project should be framed in its development proposed phase within the chain of innovation and classified as basic-driven research, applied research, experimental development, top seeded, pioneer batch or market insertion, and can be simultaneously additionally classified as nationalization of product, as long as that adds some improvement or new functionality, in order to characterize the research and development necessary content, respecting the intellectual property laws (ANEEL, 2012, p 14).

Supported by Frascati Manual (2015), which is an aid to the classification of the R&D activities regulated by ANEEL (2012), this project is considered an experimental development, according to ANEEL's innovation chain.

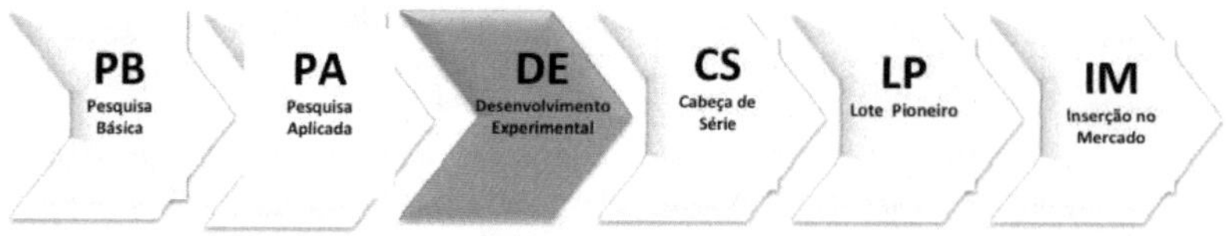

Figure 2. ANEEL's innovation chain. Source: Adapted from Pereira and Caciglieri Junior (2015)

"The Experimental Development is an outline survey from pre-existing knowledge in order to prove or demonstrate the technical and functional feasibility of new products, processes, systems and services, or even the improvement of what was already produced [.. .]. (ANEEL, 2012, p 53 and 54)."

The study is also characterized as intraproject and interorganizational (Shinoda, 2012) or extramural (Frascati Manual, 2013), because the plan was developed solely to this project and involved two companies, the sponsor / client company and the executing company.

The definition of the plan, considering the proposals of the research matter and the object of the project, is supported mainly by the interpretative approach of the knowledge management that prioritizes the tacit knowledge, but does not avoid actions from the functional approach when necessary.

To prepare the Communication Plan, 6 (six) people were consulted: manager and coordinator of the project, coordinators and sub coordinators from areas at Celesc and INERGE, who, knowing the communication actions of the Project Management Plan, gave their opinions about communication actions, responsibility, definition of the target audience, frequency/means used, documents, and definition of dates of occurrence.

To support the plan's implementation, Redmine was used as project management software.

4. PROPOSED PLAN COMMUNICATION

For the structuring of the communication management plan it was taken into account the theoretical aspects and plans and preparation of technical guidelines contained in the Project Management Plan, which define, regarding communication:

a) The manual for carrying out R&D for Celesc projects governs the relationship between Celesc and INERGE in the development of this project;
b) Celesc's project manager is the company's formal element of contact for any technical and administrative matters;
c) The Project Coordinator, by INERGE, is the formal element of contact with Celesc;
d) Without damage to the necessary integration among team members, any technical or administrative communication should be formalized through the nominated responsible person under b and c;
e) The manager and the project manager will have at least one monthly meeting to monitor and analyze the evolution of the project and related documents. This meeting may be open to other participants, at the request of either of them;
f) The project coordinator will hold at least a biweekly meeting with the technical areas leaders (Engineering, Avionics, Information Technology, Communication and Image, and Knowledge Management). These meetings may be individual or not, according to the project's needs. Conference call resources should be prioritized;
g) Internal follow-up meetings and as well as meetings with Celesc's staff should produce a Meeting Minutes, which must be reviewed and signed by all participants and subsequently filed in the project folder;
h) The project coordinator delegated the function of communication coordinator to the coordinator of the Knowledge Management area, who will be responsible for:
    - maintaining repository in electronic form of the documents produced by the project, as the folder structure defined;
    - maintaining repository of e-mails exchanged between the parties concerned with the project;
    - keeping a folder or file with the paper documents produced by the project and providing this information, according to their sensitivity and allocation to interested parties;
    - Creating environment for interaction among the members of the project, both the sponsor / client and the performing company.

The communication guidelines established above are summarized in the Communication Plan, presented in Table 1.

Table 1. Communication Plan. Source: Authors from the Project Management Plan

Type of Communication	Person in charge	Target Audience/Recipients	Goals	Frequency of Occurrence	Related Documents	Date (dd/mm/aaaa)
Contract Signature	Board of Directors Celesc-INERGE	Celesc and INERGE Staff	Formalize contract	Unique Event at the start of project	Signed Contract	14/10/2013
Starting Meeting	Manager (PM) and Coordinator (PC) and representative of DVEE	Celesc and INERGE	Start of the project: goals, planning. Interaction of teams	Unique event at the start of project	Minutes of Meeting	17/11/2013
First MeetingofProject Team	PM and PC	Celesc and INERGE Teams	Presentation of the project requirements and communication plan	Unique event at the start of project	Minutes of Meeting	03/12/2013
Project Plan Approval	PM and PC	Celesc and INERGE	Approval of the Project Plan	Unique event at the start of project	Minutes of Meeting and Project Plan Approved	-
Presentation of the Monitoring Matrix	PM and PC	Technical Teams	Present the Monitoring Matrix of the project, explaining activities, goals, and responbible members	Unique event at the start of project	Monitoring Matrix of the project	-
Monthly Meeting	PM and PC	PM, PC and guests	Analisys of the evolution os the project, its risks and discuss problems that could affect schedule or goals/results	Monthly (mensal) (Presential or by video conference	Minutes of meeting, technical or management reports	Every Monday and Thursday of the month (é como está no original)
Quarterly Workshop	PM and PC	CP, EP and guests	Presentation and Tracking of Results of the Period	Quarterly (Presential or by video conference	Minutes of meeting, technical or management reports	Jun, Sept and Dec 2015 - Mar, Jun, Sep and Dec 2016 - Mar, Jun and Sep 2017
Lessons Learned	PM and PC	PM and PC and R&D Celesc	Presentation and Discussion of Results of the Period	Quarterly	Specific Form	Monthly on Mondays and Wednesdays
Monthly Tracking Report	PC	PM and R&D Celesc	Presentation Tracking and Control of Results of the Period	Monthly	Monthly Report	Dead Line: the 18th day of the month

Eventual Technical Meetings	Called by PM and PC	PM, PC and guests	Analysis of technical problems	Eventual	Schedules and Reports	According to Necessities
Quarterly Tracking relatory	PC	PM and R&D Celesc	Tracking and Control of the Results in the Period	Quarterly	Reports	Delivered until the 18th day of Feb, Jun and Oct 2015 - Feb, Jun and Oct 2016 and Feb, Jun and Oct 2017
Technical Articles and participation in Meetings and events in Brazil or Abroad	PM and PC	External Technical Community	Presentation of Significative Results of the Project	Eventual	Article Presented or Published	4 submitted articles until Dec 2015, 4 submitted articles until Sept 2016 and 4 submitted articles until Jun 2017
Training Courses for Celesc's Staff	CP, EP e Celesc staff	Celesc Staff	Train Employees for the Transfer of Knowledge Acquired in the Project	3 courses	Didactic Material including Presentations	Still to define
Workshops with Celesc	PM, PC and Celesc R&D	PM, PC, Celesc and INERGE Staffs and Guests	Presentation of the Evolution of the Project, with eventual focus in Specific Areas or Subjects	Every 6 Months	Minutes of Workshop and Presentations	Apr and Oct 2015 - Apr and Oct 2016 - Apr 2017
Project Final Workshop	PM, PC and Celesc R&D	PM, PC, Celesc and INERGE Staffs and Guests	Presentation of Final Results and Closing of the Project	Unique event at the final of project	Minutes, Presentations of General Results, Summaries, Folders, Banners and Other Types of Material in Electronic or Printed Form	17/10/2017
Institutional broadcast	CP, EP, Celesc e Aneel	Celesc Board of Directors, all employees, ANEEL and General Public	Publish Relevant Information about Results of the Project	Unique event at the final of project	Information at Celesc's Site, Newspapers and ANEEL Seminars	17/10/2017
Final Report of the Project	PM and PC	Celesc Board of Directors and First Level of Staff and ANEEL	Presentation of Final Results and Closing of the Project	Unique event at the final of project	Final Report	17/10/2017

Presented the communication plan, it is important to point out that despite the continuous development of new media, traditional media are still being used, transforming the communication system increasingly rich into alternatives to convey the messages. That proves the importance to consider, in the development a communication plan, the mainstream media, whether it is traditional or supported in the information and communication technology - ICT.

5. FINAL CONSIDERATIONS

Finalizing the preparation of the communication plan one can note that there is a wide range of media from the most traditional ones to the most current ones supported in information and communication technologies. The most important feature when creating a communication plan is knowing how to choose the best way to meet the necessities of each specific situation.

Evidencing this evolution of the media, which takes place parallel to the evolution of information technology, Boff and Vargas (1996) believe that the evolution of technology is an important ally of the communication process, creating faster, more accurate and integrated media. However, the approach should not be focused exclusively on the technological aspects, but also on the people and the creation of an environment that allows the interaction of all the different components of the project.

It is noteworthy, however, that due to the fact that the project is on its one-third of its running time, it is still not possible to provide effective results and answers to the research question: Can communication contribute to the transfer of knowledge and the creation of a shared vision among the members of a Research and Development Project?

It can be considered, by the communication actions taken up to now, in the course of the project development, that communication is essential in the knowledge transfer and creation of a shared vision, mainly because it is an R&D project consisting of five teams with expertise in different areas coming from more than one company.

It is important to emphasize that the communication plan presented here can be an inspiration to other projects developed in different companies of different sectors and sizes.

As a recommendation for future work we suggest the definition of communication plans for project portfolios – interprojects and intraorganization, having as focus the organizational learning.

REFERENCES

ANEEL. Agência Nacional de Energia Elétrica (Brasil) (2012) - *Manual do Programa de Pesquisa e Desenvolvimento Tecnológico do Setor de Energia Elétrica.* Agência Nacional de Energia Elétrica. Brasília: ANEEL. Obtained on September 3, 2015 from: http://www.aneel.gov.br/aplicacoes/leitura_arquivo/default.cfm?idaplicacao=56.

Angeloni, M.T.; Zimmermann, R.H.; Cosentino, A.; Athayde Filho, L.A.P. (2015). Gestão da informação e do conhecimento em projetos de pesquisa e desenvolvimento – um estudo de caso. In *Simpósio Internacional de Gestão de Projetos, Inovação e Sustentabilidade*, São Paulo - SP.

Angeloni, M. T. (1992). Technologies de transmissión de l´information et consequences sur le processus des decisions des organizations. *Mémoire de DEA*. École Superieure des Affaires, Grenoble : France.

_______________. 2010. *Comunicação nas organizações da era do conhecimento*. São Paulo. Atlas.

Boff, L. H; Vargas, L. (1996). Cenários atuais da comunicação eletrônica: um exemplo do uso de bases de dados e métodos de tratamento da informação. in: Encontro Anual da Associação Nacional dos Programas de Pós-Graduação em Administração. 1996, Angra dos Reis. Anais... Rio de Janeiro: ANPAD, 1995. vol. 1. p. 309-325

BRASIL. Lei 11.196/05 – *Lei do Bem, de 21 de novembro de 2005*. Trata da concessão de incentivos fiscais às pessoas jurídicas. Obtained on November 17, 2014 from: <http://www.planalto.gov.br/ccivil_03/_ato2004-2006/2005/lei/l11196.htm.

Choo, C. W. (1998). *The Knowing Organization : How Organizations Use Information for Construct Meaning, Create Knowledge and Make Decisions*. New York : Oxford Press.

Dazzi, M.C.S.; Angeloni, M.T. (2001). Compreendendo o significado de gestão do conhecimento e a importância da comunicação em seu compartilhamento. In *International Symposium knowledge management/Document management*-ISKM/DM, 2001, Curitiba-PR. Anais do knowledge management/Document management-ISKM/. Curitiba : Editora Universitária Champagnat, 2001. v. 1. pp. 469-488.

Dazzi, M.C.S.; Pereira, T.M. (2002). A importância da comunicação no desenvolvimento de sistemas. In *International Symposium knowledge management/Document management*-ISKM/DM, 2002, Curitiba-PR. Anais do knowledge management/Document management-ISKM/. Curitiba : Editora Universitária Champagnat, 2002. v. 1. pp. 430-447.

DhaliwaL, J.; Benbasat, I. (1996). The use and effects of knowledge-based system explanations: theoretical foundations and a framework for empirical evaluation. *Information Systems Research*, 7, pp. 243-361.

George, J. F.; Iacono, S.; Kling, R. (1995). Learning in context: extensively computerized work groups as communities of practice. *Accounting, Management and Information Techgnologies*, 5, pp.185-202.

Grotto, D.; Angeloni, M.T. (2004). A influência da cultura organizacional no compartilhamento do conhecimento: um estudo de caso. *Encontro Nacional de Estudos Organizacionais*, 2004, Anais Atibaia. Encontro Nacional de Estudos Organizacionais.

Jamil, G. L. (2005). Gestão de informação e do conhecimento em empresas brasileiras: estudo de múltiplos casos. *Tese de Doutorado*. Programa de Pós-Graduação em Ciência da Informação. Universidade Federal de Minas Gerais.

Krogh, G.; Ichijo, K.; Nonaka, I. (2001). *Facilitando a criação de conhecimento*: reinventando a empresa com o poder da inovação contínua. Rio de Janeiro: Editora Campus.

Nonaka, I.; Konno, N. (1998). The concept of "Ba": building a foundation for knowledge creation. *California Management Review*, v. 40, n. 3, p. 40-41.

OECD/Eurostat (2005), *Oslo Manual: Guidelines for Collecting and Interpreting Innovation Data, 3rd Edition*, The Measurement of Scientific and Technological Activities, OECD Publishing, Paris. Obtained on September 14, 2015 from: http://ec.europa.eu/eurostat/documents/3859598/5889925/OSLO-EN.PDF

OECD (2015), *Frascati Manual 2015: Guidelines for Collecting and Reporting Data on Research and Experimental Development*, The Measurement of Scientific, Technological and Innovation Activities, OECD Publishing, Paris. Obtained on September 14, 2015 from: http://dx.doi.org/10.1787/9789264239012-en

Outi, N.S.; Strauhs, F.R. (2008). Aplicação nacional do processo de criação do conhecimento japonês – caso Denso do Brasil In Angeloni, M.T. *Gestão do conhecimento no Brasil* – casos, experiências e práticas. Rio de Janeiro. Qualitymark.

Pereira, A. P.; Caciglieri Junior, O. (2015). MOP&D: Modelo de desenvolvimento integrado de produto orientado aos projetos de P&D do setor elétrico brasileiro. *Espaço Energia.* Out. Obtained on December 29, 2015 from: http://www.espacoenergia.com.br/edicoes/23/EE023-09-12.pdf.

Plano de Gerenciamento do Projeto (2014). *Projeto desenvolvimento de metodologia e sistema para tratamento de imagem e reconhecimento de padrões para inspeção autônoma de linhas aéreas de transmissão e de distribuição. ANEEL / INERGE.*

PRJ. (2014) Arquivo referente ao formulário de Projeto desenvolvimento de metodologia e sistema para tratamento de imagem e reconhecimento de padrões para inspeção autônoma de linhas aéreas de transmissão e de distribuição. *ANEEL / INERGE.*

Project Management Institute (2013). *A Guide to the Project Management Body of Knowledge (PMBOK® Guide)*—Fifth Edition Newtown Square, Pennsylvania, USA, PMI.

Shinoda, A. C. M. (2012). Gestão do conhecimento em projetos: um estudo sobre conhecimentos relevantes, fatores influenciadores e práticas em organizações projetizadas. *Dissertação de Mestrado.* Universidade de São Paulo, São Paulo.

Zhao, J. L.; Kumar, A.; Stohr, E. A. (2001). Workflow-centric information distribution through e-mail. *Journal of Management Information Systems*, 17, pp. 45-72.

RANKING-TYPE DELPHI STUDIES IN IS RESEARCH: STEP-BY-STEP GUIDE AND ANALYTICAL EXTENSION

Jörn Kobus[1] and Markus Westner[2]
[1]*TU Dresden, Germany*
[2]*OTH Regensburg, Germany*

ABSTRACT

Ranking-type Delphi is a frequently used method in IS research. However, besides several studies investigating a rigorous application of ranking-type Delphi as a research method, a comprehensive and precise step-by-step guide on how to conduct a rigorous ranking-type Delphi study in IS research is currently missing. In addition, a common critic of Delphi studies in general is that it is unclear if there is indeed authentic consensus of the panelists, or if panelists only agree because of other reasons (e.g. acquiescence bias or tiredness to disagreement after several rounds). This also applies to ranking-type Delphi studies. Therefore, this study aims to (1) Provide a rigorous step-by-step guide to conduct ranking-type Delphi studies through synthesizing results of existing research and (2) Offer an analytical extension to the ranking-type Delphi method by introducing Best/Worst Scaling, which originated in Marketing and Consumer Behavior research. A guiding example is introduced to increase comprehensibility of the proposals. Future research needs to validate the step-by-step guide in an empirical setting as well as test the suitability of Best/Worst Scaling within described research contexts.

KEYWORDS

Delphi, Best/Worst Scaling, MaxDiff, Maximum-Difference-Scaling

1. INTRODUCTION

In Information System (IS) research the Delphi method has been used for almost three decades and enjoys increasing popularity (Paré et al., 2013, p. 207). Research using Delphi covers a wide range of IS topics. Recent publications include, e.g., complexity in IS programs (Piccinini et al., 2014), critical skills for managing IT projects (Keil et al., 2013), or investigations of key issues in IS security management (Polónia and Sá-Soares, 2013). In addition, the adaption and evolution of the Delphi method is of research interest, e.g., in order to explore the application of Delphi as forecasting tool in IS research (Gallego and Bueno, 2014), assess rigor (Paré et al., 2013), or identify possibilities to build theory (Päivärinta et al., 2011).

While different types of Delphi studies exist (explained later in this paper), ranking-type Delphi can be considered as the most relevant for IS research. It focusses on classical IS research topics, e.g., identification and ranking of Critical Success Factors (CSF), identification of components of research frameworks, or prioritization of selection criteria. In addition its use is indicated "*[i]n business to guide future management action [...]*" (Paré et al., 2013, p. 208).

Thus, this paper contributes to IS research by: (1) Providing a rigorous step-by-step guide for conducting ranking-type Delphi studies through synthesizing results of existing research; and (2) Offering an analytical extension in order to increase the likelihood for authentic panelist consensus through introducing Best/Worst Scaling. Best/Worst Scaling is a method originating from Marketing and Consumer Behavior research but is relatively new to IS research.

Regarding (1), the paper synthesizes existing research regarding rigorous application of ranking-type Delphi (Okoli and Pawlowski, 2004; Paré et al., 2013; Schmidt, 1997). Although these papers deal with several main criticisms of ranking-type Delphi studies, e.g., regarding (a) The selection of appropriate experts (Okoli and Pawlowski, 2004, p. 16); (b) The inappropriate use of statistics (Schmidt, 1997, pp. 764–768); or (c) The missing report of response and retention rates (Paré et al., 2013, p. 207), none of them provides comprehensive and precise instructions by themselves. Therefore, we consolidate the main contributions of these papers and suggest a step-by-step guide with increased density and a higher level of completeness of information as a result.

Regarding (2), the paper proposes an analytical extension of the ranking-type Delphi method to decrease a general problem of (ranking-type) Delphi studies: Response style biases (Paulhus, 1991, p. 17). An example for response style biases is the pressure to conform with group ratings (Witkin and Altschuld, 1995, p. 188). This could happen for example if participants agree to a consensus only because they are tired of arguing and not because they got convinced.

The paper is structured as follows. Section 2 explains and defines relevant terms. Section 3 proposes a step-by-step guide for ranking-type Delphi studies which consolidates existing research. Section 4 extends this guide by adding Best/Worst Scaling to it. The final chapter concludes the paper and briefly discusses the proposals.

2. CONCEPTS AND DEFINITIONS

2.1 Delphi Method

The objective of the Delphi method is to achieve the most reliable consensus in a group of experts. This is done by questioning individual experts during several rounds. In between rounds, feedback on the other experts' opinions is provided. Direct confrontation of the experts is avoided. (Dalkey and Helmer, 1963, p. 458)

Originally, Delphi was used for forecasting. However, it continuously evolved during the last decades and is used today in a variety of research types. Paré et al. (2013, p. 208) – based on Okoli and Pawlowski (2004), Schmidt (1997), and Rauch (1979) – distinguish four types of Delphi studies: (1) Classical Delphi focusing on facts to create a consensus; (2) Decision Delphi focusing on preparation and decision for future directions; (3) Policy Delphi focusing on ideas to define and differentiate views; and (4) Ranking-type Delphi focusing on identification and ranking of key factors, items, or other types of issues.

In the paper at hand we will focus especially on type (4): Ranking-type Delphi as (a) It is widely used – Paré et al. (2013, p. 209) found that 93% of investigated Delphi papers from 1984-2010 used this type – and (b) it fulfills the requirements of IS research best (see above).

2.2 Best/Worst Scaling

Best/Worst Scaling (also referred to as Maximum Difference Scaling or MaxDiff) is based upon random utility theory (Louviere et al., 2013, pp. 293–300). It is defined as *"[...] a choice-based measurement approach that reconciles the need for question parsimony with the advantage of choice tasks that force individuals to make choices (as in real life)"* (ibid, p. 292). Best/Worst Scaling can be seen as a way to overcome some major shortcomings of common rating approaches (e.g. ties among items, response style bias, and standardization difficulties (Cohen and Orme, 2004, p. 32)).

Best/Worst Scaling builds on a body of items. A set consists of a number of items from the body. A respondent gets presented a series of sets and is asked to choose one best item and one worst item in each set. (Lee et al. 2008)

Compared to the Paired Comparison method, which also can overcome the above-mentioned shortcomings, Best/Worst Scaling is more efficient (Cohen and Orme, 2004, p. 34) as more statistical relevant information are provided by respondents in each comparison round. To ensure the validity of the Best/Worst Scaling approach, a careful design is necessary to decide which items are shown in which sets. This includes especially (1) Frequency balance, meaning that each item appears an equal number of times during all sets; (2) Orthogonality, meaning that each item is paired with each other item an equal number of times during all sets; (3) Connectivity, meaning that the sets are designed in a way that it is possible to infer the relative order of preference for all items; and (4) Positional balance, meaning that each item appears an equal number of times on the left and right side. (Sawtooth, 2013, p.7).

Because of the previously mentioned benefits regarding preference mapping, Best/Worst Scaling is a frequently used method in Marketing and Consumer Behavior research (e.g. Louviere et al., 2013, Cohen, 2009, Cohen and Orme, 2004). However, it seems not to be commonly used in IS research and hence provides an interesting and original method which can contribute to the methodological development of the research field. Applied to the given research context, Best/Worst Scaling is proposed as a ranking mechanism to enrich the data analysis phase of a ranking-type Delphi study in a IS research setting as described later.

2.3 Guiding Example

In order to make it easier to follow our proposal, we use a consecutive example of a ranking-type Delphi study to illustrate each phase. The guiding example takes a strategic IS perspective and investigates the identification and ranking of Critical Success Factors (CSFs) for the implementation of a process improvement method in an IT organization. The example was inspired by own research, however was simplified and complemented with fictional data where appropriate.

3. STEP-BY-STEP GUIDE FOR RANKING TYPE DELPHI STUDIES

An overview on our proposed guideline to conduct rigorous ranking-type Delphi studies can be found in Figure 1. Phase 1 is based on Okoli and Pawlowski (2004, pp. 20–23), who themselves built on Delbecq et al. (1975). Phase 2 to 4 is based on Paré et al. (2013, p. 210) and Schmidt (1997, pp. 768–771). Especially Schmidt (1997) states that ranking-type Delphi got very popular in IS research and introduced a consistent approach for data collection (phase 2), analysis (phase 3), and presentation (phase 4).

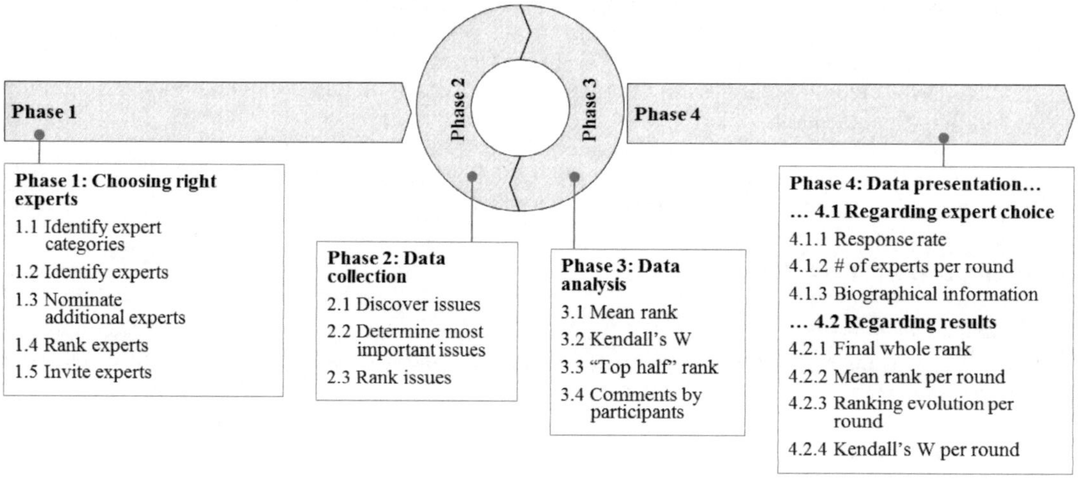

Figure 1. Proposed guideline for ranking-type Delphi study based on (Okoli and Pawlowski, 2004; Paré et al., 2013; Schmidt, 1997).

Figure 2 provides a detailed overview which elements of the ranking-type Delphi guideline are described by which authors. We decided to build around these papers as they recently provided an overview on rigor in IS ranking-type Delphi studies (Paré et al., 2013), are highly cited[1] (Okoli and Pawlowski, 2004), or are the first that introduced a structured approach to ranking-type Delphi studies (Schmidt, 1997).

[1] As of September 2015, citations in (1) Web of Science: 366 and (2) Google Scholar: 1238.

	(1) Chosing right experts					(2) Data collection			(3) Data analysis				(4) Data presentation						
													(a) Expert choice			(b) Results			
	1.1	1.2	1.3	1.4	1.5	2.1	2.2	2.3	3.1	3.2	3.3	3.4	4.1.1	4.1.2	4.1.3	4.2.1	4.2.2	4.2.3	4.2.4
Paré et al. 2013	✓	✓	(✓)	(✓)	(✓)	✓	✓	✓	✓	✓	✓	✓	✓	✓	✓				
Okoli and Pawlowski 2004	✓	✓	✓	✓	✓	✓	✓	✓	✓	✓	✓	✓							
Schmidt 1997						✓	✓	✓	✓	✓	✓	✓	✓	✓	✓	✓	✓	✓	✓

✓ Mentioned in guideline (✓) Referenced in discussion

1.1 Identify expert categories; 1.2 Identify experts; 1.3 Nominate additional experts; 1.4 Rank experts; 1.5 Invite experts.
2.1 Discover issues; 2.2 Determine most important issues; 2.3 Rank issues.
3.1 Mean rank; 3.2 Kendall's W; 3.3 "Top half" rank; 3.4 Comments by participants
4.1.1 Response rate; 4.1.2 # of experts per round; 4.1.3 Biographical information
4.2.1 Final whole rank; 4.2.2 Mean rank per round; 4.2.3 Ranking evolution per round; 4.2.4 Kendall's W per round

Figure 2. Sources for elements of ranking-type Delphi guideline.

3.1 Phase 1 – Choosing Right Experts

The choice of the right experts for Delphi studies is described as *"[...] perhaps the most important yet most neglected aspect*" (Okoli and Pawlowski, 2004, p. 16). Since Delphi study results depend mainly on the answers of chosen experts, it is necessary to define a thorough process for their appropriate selection. Adapting Okoli and Pawlowski (2004, pp. 20–23), we propose a five steps approach to choose appropriate experts as initial phase of the study: (1.1) Identify expert categories; (1.2) Identify expert names; (1.3) Nominate additional experts; (1.4) Rank experts; and (1.5) Invite experts.

Step (1.1) aims at developing selection criteria for experts, e.g., regarding disciplines or skills, organizations or literature (academic or practitioner authors). Step (1.2) then identifies experts meeting those selection criteria. A personal list of experts can serve as an initial starting point. Step (1.3) sends a brief description of the Delphi study to the already identified experts and asks them to nominate further experts in the field. Additionally, as much biographical information as possible about all (already identified and nominated) experts' demographics and profiles are documented. Step (1.4) then ranks the experts in priority for invitation to the Delphi study based on their qualification. Step (1.5) invites the experts to the study in descending order of the ranking. The subject, required procedures, and the type and extent of experts' commitments are explained. This step is repeated, until an appropriate number of experts agreed on their participation. Anonymity of expert participants has to be ensured at all times.

Guiding example: (1.1) A success factor study typically aims to incorporate the perspective of experts with considerable experience on the topic of interest. In our case – CSFs for the implementation of a process improvement method in an IT-organization – emerging expert categories could be (line) managers and consultants with relevant expertise and experience. We decided for consultants.

(1.2) Since researchers' personal networks can be a source to recruit experts (Paré et al., 2013, p. 210), we use our network to contact a renowned global IT-consulting company. We set the threshold for consultants to be able to participate to having supported at least seven implementations of the process improvement method. Together with the main contact of the consulting firm, a list of 10 potential panelists is created.

(1.3) By reference of four members from the established list, seven additional possible panelists are identified. Therefore, in total 17 possible panelists are identified.

(1.4) We rank the panelists in descending order by the number of implementations they have supported.

(1.5) While there seems no agreement on an optimal number of panelists for a ranking-type Delphi study, the number of participating experts "*[...] should not be too large (in order to facilitate consensus)*" (Paré et al., 2013, p. 208). We therefore decide to invite the 12 highest ranked experts. If one of these experts is unable to take part, we invite the highest ranked of the remaining list instead until we achieve the number of 12 committed participants.

3.2 Phase 2 – Data Collection & Phase 3 – Data Analysis

In the Delphi method data is repetitively collected, analyzed, and reconciled with experts. Therefore, we describe data collection (phase 2) and data analysis (phase 3) together as they cannot be separated distinctively.

Before the iterative data collection (phase 2) can start, an initial instrument pre-test (i.e., instruction and questionnaire) is conducted to ensure that all experts understand tasks and objectives (Paré et al., 2013, p. 210). The following data collection phase itself consists of three steps (Schmidt, 1997, pp. 768–771): (2.1) Discover issues; (2.2) Determine most important issues; and (2.3) Rank issues.

An issue hereby could be for example an item or a factor. (2.1) To discover the most important issues, first and foremost as many issues as possible have to be identified. Clear instructions are provided to experts and there is no restriction on the number of answers experts can give. After the initial data collection, the researchers consolidate and group familiar answers through content analysis (Mayring, 2000, pp. 4–5). The consolidated results then need to be verified by the experts again to ensure the correct understanding of the intended meaning and appropriateness of grouping.

(2.2) To not overwhelm the experts by the amount of issues they should rank in step (2.3), a further focus on the most important issues might be necessary (as a rule of thumb the list should comprise approximately 20 issues or less (Schmidt, 1997, p. 769)). For this, the consolidated and validated list of issues is randomly ordered, and sent together with clear selection instructions to the experts. The researchers then delete all issues that were not selected. In case there are still too many issues left, step (2.2) can be repeated.

In step (2.3) the experts are asked to rank the issues in descending order, from most important to least important. As the Delphi method is an iterative approach, step (2.3) is repeated until an appropriate trade-off between level of consensus and feasibility (defined as indulgence of respondents and researcher's resources and additional time requirements) is reached. Within each new ranking round, respondents can revise their ranking decision supported by a controlled feedback based on (3.1) Mean rank; (3.2) Kendall's W – a coefficient of concordance (Kendall and Gibbons, 1990); (3.3) Top half rank (percentage of experts who ranked respective item in their top half); and (3.4) Relevant comments/justifications by respondents.

Stopping criteria for the Delphi data collection are either a strong consensus or a clear indication that no more differences in answers can be expected. Kendall's W, assuming values between 0 and 1 can serve as a quantitative measure for this purpose. Values around .1 indicate very weak agreement; values around .5 moderate agreement, and values around .9 very strong agreement (Schmidt, 1997, p. 767).

Guiding example: Before data collection starts, the instrument is pre-tested with two consultants whose experience (five projects) is not sufficient to be included into the final participation list.

(2.1) In order to discover as many implementation success factors as possible, it seems necessary to provide an efficient and convenient way for experts to take part in the Delphi study. For this, we offer the panelists to either e-mail their input, conduct a call, or use a web-survey with personalized hyperlinks. In case of ambiguity, the respective panelist is asked to clarify its input. There is no limit to the number of success factors an expert can mention. In total 47 success factors are mentioned. Once the initial gathering is finished, these 47 success are qualitatively investigated (Mayring, 2000, pp. 4–5) to check for duplicates and grouping possibilities (e.g. 'Leadership needs to role model the change' and 'Active leadership' could possibly be merged to one group of success factors named 'Leadership involvement'). Further researchers review the results independently to ensure consistency. A description for each category is created. After this, every expert verifies if their mentioned success factors are correctly reflected in the grouping logic.

(2.2) After consolidation and grouping, 12 CSF remain. This means that there is no need to reduce the number of success factors for the upcoming ranking round further.

(2.3) In the next round the panelists are asked to rank the list of 12 CSF. They start with the one they believe is most important as first ranked, down to the one which they believe is least important as twelfth ranked. In addition, the experts can justify their decision. After a ranking round, the experts are provided with (3.1) Mean rank; (3.2) Kendall's W; (3.3) Top-half rank and (3.4) Relevant comments/justifications.

We conduct two rounds of ranking. After the first round, the level of consensus is perceived as moderate ($W_1 = 0.51$). Therefore, we provide the experts with results (3.1-3.4) of the first round and conduct another ranking round. It results in a strong consensus ($W_2 = 0.73$). As for round 2 already several reminders were necessary to keep the experts motivated and impatience was expressed by some experts we decide to not do a third round as the results are deemed a satisfactory compromise between consensus and indulgence of respondents.

3.3 Phase 4 – Data Presentation

In the data presentation phase the final study results are presented. Regarding the choice of experts, this includes (4.1.1) The response rate for the initial call for participation (as indication if experts consider the exercise as relevant/important); (4.1.2) The number of participants for each Delphi round (as indication of flagging interest and for replicable calculations); and (4.1.3) The documentations of profiles of participating experts.

Regarding results, sub-results, and calculations, it is necessary to provide sufficient raw data to support the accountability of statistics. At least the (4.2.1) Final whole rank; (4.2.2) Mean ranks for each round; (4.2.3) Evolution of ranks of an item in each round; and (4.2.4) Kendall's W for each round should be reported. Additionally, the total number of issues generated in the first phase of data collection (2.1), and transparency on consensus level of the pared list at the end of the second phase (2.2) need to be reported.

Guiding example: (4.1.1) The response rate for the initial participation call was around 83% (from the first 12 experts asked, 10 took part. The two experts who have not taken part are replaced by two experts from the remaining list). (4.1.2) In total, two ranking-type Delphi rounds were necessary. All 12 experts have taken part in the two Delphi rounds. (4.1.3) Table 1 illustrates how the profiles of experts could be depicted for this example.

Table 1. Template to illustrate expert profiles of Delphi panel.

Describtion/ expert ID	Role/Position	Main country of involvement	Eperience (# of projects)
Expert 1	Partner	Germany	11
Expert 2	Partner	Sweden	10
Expert 3	Senior expert	UK	20+
Expert 4	Senior expert	Germany	30+
Expert 5	Partner	Spain	12
Expert 6	Partner	Norway	10
Expert 7	Partner	Czech Republic	30+
Expert 8	Partner	Germany	9
Expert 9	Partner	France	10
Expert 10	Partner	Sweden	20+
Expert 11	Partner	UK	8
Expert 12	Partner	Denmark	7

(4.2.1-4.2.4) The number of CSF generated in the first phase of data collection (step 2.1) is 47. After consolidation and grouping (step 2.2), all 47 CSF can be assigned to 12 groups. This means there was full consensus on the list shown in Table 2. The remaining study results can be obtained from Table 3. As the order of the mean ranks (4.2.2) did not change in between the two rounds, we omit the information on evolution in ranks (4.2.3).

Table 2. Remaining CSF after consolidation (step 2.2).

Success factor/ expert ID	Expert 1	Expert 2	Expert 3	Expert 4	Expert 5	Expert 6	Expert 7	Expert 8	Expert 9	Expert 10	Expert 11	Expert 12	Σ	%
CSF 1	x	x	x		x	x	x	x	x	x	x		**10**	**83%**
CSF 4		x		x	x	x	x	x	x	x	x	x	**10**	**83%**
CSF 6			x		x		x	x	x	x	x	x	**8**	**67%**
CSF 2	x		x		x		x	x	x	x			**7**	**58%**
CSF 9			x		x	x	x	x		x	x		**7**	**58%**
CSF 12	x	x	x	x	x					x			**6**	**50%**
CSF 8	x		x		x	x		x				x	**6**	**50%**
CSF 3			x	x			x		x		x	x	**6**	**50%**
CSF 10	x		x	x		x				x			**5**	**42%**
CSF 11		x			x			x		x		x	**5**	**42%**
CSF 5	x		x			x		x				x	**5**	**42%**
CSF 7		x				x	x			x			**4**	**33%**
Total	**6**	**5**	**9**	**4**	**8**	**7**	**7**	**8**	**5**	**9**	**5**	**6**		

Table 3. Results of ranking (step 2.3) rounds 1 and 2 of the Delphi study.

Success factor	Mean rank (round 1)	Mean rank (round 2)	Final rank
CSF 6	4,38	2,45	**1**
CSF 9	5,87	3,81	**2**
CSF 1	6,74	4,56	**3**
CSF 2	6,98	5,03	**4**
CSF 4	7,23	5,56	**5**
CSF 12	7,56	6,32	**6**
CSF 8	8,12	6,89	**7**
CSF 11	8,89	7,66	**8**
CSF 10	9,10	9,33	**9**
CSF 3	9,23	10,11	**10**
CSF 7	10,11	10,89	**11**
CSF 5	10,21	11,01	**12**
Kendall's W	**0,51**	**0,73**	

Based on these results the discussion of the findings would take place. However, as this is highly content- and less process-related, this is out of scope for the paper at hand.

4. ANALYTICAL EXTENSION FOR RANKING TYPE DELPHI STUDIES USING BEST/WORST SCALING

IS ranking-type Delphi studies use several ranking mechanisms. These include direct ranking of items (Kasi et al., 2008); ranking based on ratings on a predefined scale – for example on a Likert scale (Liu et al., 2010; Nakatsu and Iacovou, 2009); or ranking based on expert allocation of points from a predefined pool (Nevo and Chan, 2007). However, all these mechanisms do have several well-known and documented disadvantages related to response style biases. Paulhus (1991, p. 17) enumerates the three most prominent response style biases as (1) Social desirability bias (tendency to lie or fake); (2) Acquiescence bias (tendency to agree); and (3) Extreme response bias (tendency to use extreme ratings). A way to overcome these biases in ranking-type Delphi studies is the introduction of Best/Worst scaling as a ranking mechanism (Lee et al., 2008, p. 335). Since a subjective preference order can be calculated based on numerous smaller decisions, it gets much harder for the panelist to predict/deliberately influence the final ranking list. In order to apply Best/Worst Scaling to the introduced step-by-step guide, an extension of it is proposed as shown in Figure 3.

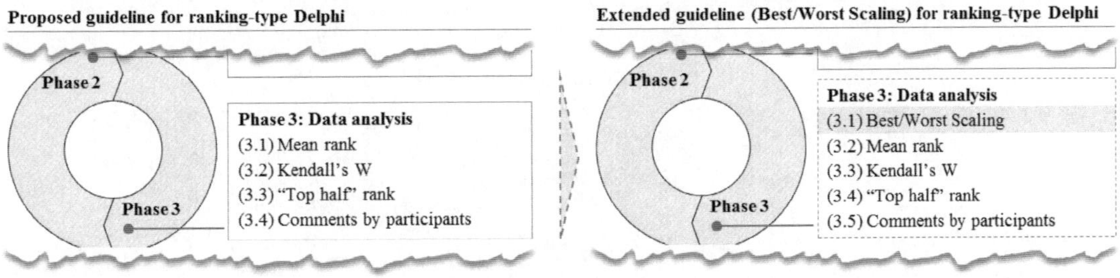

Figure 3. Extended guideline for ranking-type Delphi study featuring Best/Worst Scaling for Data analysis.

Extended Phase 3 – Data analysis: (3.1 – new) In order to use Best/Worst Scaling as ranking mechanism in ranking-type Delphi studies, proper (a) Design, (b) Execution, and (c) Analysis need to be defined.

(a) Regarding design, the list of all remaining issues (result of phase 2.2) serves as body of items. In addition, it needs to be decided on the number of sets (questions) experts get asked; the number of items per set; and the appearance of items in sets considering frequency, orthogonality, connectivity and positional balance (compare section 2.2).

(b) Regarding execution, it should be easy for the experts to take the questionnaire. While it would be possible to use paper and pen or regular e-mail communication for this, a web-based version of the questionnaire seems to be the most appropriate form for taking the survey.

(c) Regarding analysis, several possible options exist to transform the results of Best/Worst Scaling on individual level to a ranking. The simplest option is to calculate 'best minus worst' (# of times when issue was selected best - # of times when issue was selected worst). However, more sophisticated options include for example the application of linear probability models, conditional logit models, or rank-ordered logit models (Louviere et al., 2013, pp. 295–296).

(3.2-3.5) The steps of Mean rank, 'Top-half' rank and Kendall's W and comments by participants are identically to the previously introduced step-by-step guide.

Guiding Example: (3.1 – new) While it is possible to manually design and conduct Best/Worst Scaling, we follow Louviere et al. (2013, p. 295) and use more sophisticated statistical software in order to prepare for non-trivial analyses. We decided to use a web-based solution from Sawtooth Software (Sawtooth, 2015) to design and analyze our proposed ranking. We did so, as provided technical papers (Sawtooth, 2013) offered transparent and sufficient information on functionality and proficiency of the software.

(a) Design: As the body of items consists of 12 CSF, we decide to let the experts rank 12 sets (Sawtooth, 2013). In each set, four items are shown of which the experts select the best and the worst CSF. The appropriate appearance (frequency, orthogonality, connectivity and positional balance) of CSFs in the sets was ensured by the software. Figure 4 provides an example for a set.

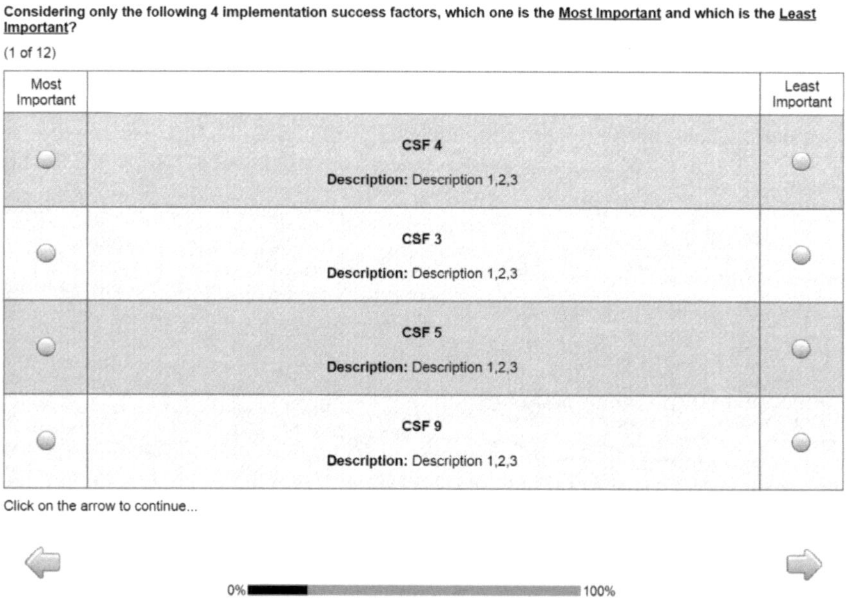

Figure 4. Example of set in web-survey.

(b) Execution: We decided for a web-survey as this provided the participants freedom to take the survey whenever and wherever they wanted. In addition, it turned out that a smartphone compatible version is important.

(c) Analysis: Using statistical software we calculated the results for each individual expert based on conditional logit models, which can be used to investigate choice behavior (McFadden, 1974, pp. 105–106). Table 4 provides a sample result for an expert. The row 'Value' provides the zero-centered interval scores derived by the conditional logit model. A higher value indicates more importance of the CSF. In our example Table 4 is calculated for each expert and used to obtain respective ranking of CSF.

Table 4. Result for expert ranking derived using Best/Worst Scaling.

Rank	**1**	**2**	**3**	**4**	**5**	**6**	**7**	**8**	**9**	**10**	**11**	**12**
CSF	3	1	8	11	10	9	6	4	2	5	7	12
Value	49,0	23,4	23,4	3,0	0,1	- 2,1	- 2,7	- 3,6	- 4,0	- 5,2	-30,3	-51,0

(3.2-3.5) After having obtained the ranking of each individual expert with the help of a conditional logit model, we can obtain mean rank, 'Top-half' rank and Kendall's W and comments by participants as described in above step-by-step guide.

5. CONCLUSION

The study at hand contributes to IS research twofold.

First, it introduces a rigorous step-by-step approach to conduct ranking-type Delphi studies, which are used widely in IS research. In addition, a guiding example is introduced which provides possible visualizations and helps IS scholars to think and act end-product oriented, while conducting a ranking-type Delphi study.

Second, it introduces an analytical extension for ranking-type Delphi studies which can further increase rigor. The level of consensus should neither be influenced by response style bias, nor by the researchers' persistency (i.e., by asking experts again and again until some of them give in to achieve consensus) but only by the real opinions of the experts. Through the introduction of Best/Worst Scaling as ranking mechanism the problem of illusionary consensus of Delphi panelists can be reduced. In Best/Worst Scaling the experts are forced to choose a CSF deliberately as most/least important compared to other CSFs. In this way a subjective preference order can be calculated and it gets much harder for the panelist to predict/deliberately influence its final ranking list. In addition, the guiding example introduces an easy-to-conduct, time efficient and cognitive low demanding way for panelists to conduct a ranking based on Best/Worst Scaling.

While the study was inspired by a real world research example, its main limitation is that it has not yet been applied in full to a real world research question. While we are confident that the described process would yield expected results, future research still needs to prove that.

In addition, future research needs to investigate in detail if Best/Worst Scaling could even replace more of phase 3 (Data analysis) as the only ranking mechanism. While Kendall's W is a well-established and used measure of consensus in ranking-type Delphi studies, future research should investigate what other measures would be suitable with the additional data on preferences gained by described ranking mechanism.

REFERENCES

Cohen, E. (2009) 'Applying best-worst scaling to wine marketing', *International Journal of Wine Business Research*, vol. 21, no. 1, pp. 8–23 [Online]. DOI: 10.1108/17511060910948008.

Cohen, S. and Orme, B. (2004) 'What's your preference? Asking survey respondents about their preferences creates new scaling decisions', *Marketing Research*, vol. 16, pp. 32–37.

Dalkey, N. and Helmer, O. (1963) 'An experimental application of the Delphi method to the use of experts', *Management Science*, vol. 9, no. 3, pp. 458–467.

Delbecq, A. L., Van de Ven, A. H. and Gustafson, D. H. (1975) *Group techniques for program planning: A guide to nominal group and Delphi processes*, Scott, Foresman Glenview, IL.

Gallego, D. and Bueno, S. (2014) 'Exploring the application of the Delphi method as a forecasting tool in Information Systems and Technologies research', *Technology Analysis & Strategic Management*, vol. 26, no. 9, pp. 987–999.

Kasi, V., Keil, M., Mathiassen, L. and Pedersen, K. (2008) 'The post mortem paradox: a Delphi study of IT specialist perceptions', *European Journal of Information Systems*, vol. 17, no.1, pp. 62–78 [Online]. Available at http://dx.doi.org/10.1057/palgrave.ejis.3000727.

Keil, M., Lee, H. K. and Deng, T. (2013) 'Understanding the most critical skills for managing IT projects: A Delphi study of it project managers', *Information & Management*, vol. 50, no. 7, pp. 398–414.

Kendall, M. G. and Gibbons, J. D. (1990) *Rank correlation methods*, 5th edn, London, New York, NY, E. Arnold; Oxford University Press.

Lee, J. A., Soutar, G. and Louviere, J. (2008) 'The best-worst scaling spproach: An alternative to Schwartz's values survey', *Journal of Personality Assessment*, vol. 90, no. 4, pp. 335–347.

Liu, S., Zhang, J., Keil, M. and Chen, T. (2010) 'Comparing senior executive and project manager perceptions of IT project risk: a Chinese Delphi study', *Information Systems Journal*, vol. 20, no. 4, pp. 319–355 [Online]. DOI: 10.1111/j.1365-2575.2009.00333.x.

Louviere, J., Lings, I., Islam, T., Gudergan, S. and Flynn, T. (2013) 'An introduction to the application of (case 1) best–worst scaling in marketing research', *International Journal of Research in Marketing*, vol. 30, no. 3, pp. 292–303.

Mayring, P. (2000) 'Qualitative Content Analysis', *Forum: Qualitative Social Research*, vol. 1, no. 2, pp. 1–10.

McFadden, D. (1974) 'Conditional logit analysis of qualitative choice behavior', in Zarembka, P. (ed) *Frontiers in econometrics,* New York, NY: Academic Press, pp. 105–142.

Nakatsu, R. T. and Iacovou, C. L. (2009) 'A comparative study of important risk factors involved in offshore and domestic outsourcing of software development projects: A two-panel Delphi study', *Information & Management*, vol. 46, no. 1, pp. 57–68 [Online]. DOI: 10.1016/j.im.2008.11.005.

Nevo, D. and Chan, Y. E. (2007) 'A Delphi study of knowledge management systems: Scope and requirements', *Information & Management*, vol. 44, no. 6, pp. 583–597 [Online]. DOI: 10.1016/j.im.2007.06.001.

Okoli, C. and Pawlowski, S. D. (2004) 'The Delphi method as a research tool: An example, design considerations and applications', *Information & Management*, vol. 42, no. 1, pp. 15–29 [Online]. DOI: 10.1016/j.im.2003.11.002.

Päivärinta, T., Pekkola, S. and Moe, C. E. (2011) 'Complexity in IS programs: A Delphi study. ICIS 2011 proceedings.'.

Paré, G., Cameron, A.-F., Poba-Nzaou, P. and Templier, M. (2013) 'A systematic assessment of rigor in information systems ranking-type delphi studies', *Information & Management*, vol. 50, no. 5, pp. 207–217.

Paulhus, D. L. (1991) 'Measurement and control of response bias', in Robinson, J. P., Shaver, P. R. and Wrightsman, L. S. (eds) *Measures of personality and social psychological attitudes,* New York: Academic, pp. 17–59.

Piccinini, E., Gregory, R. and Muntermann, J. (2014) 'Complexity in IS programs: A Delphi study. ECIS 2014 proceedings.'.

Polónia, F. and Sá-Soares, F. de (2013) 'Key issues in Information Systems security management. ICIS 2013 proceedings.'.

Rauch, W. (1979) 'The decision Delphi', *Technological Forecasting and Social Change*, vol. 15, no. 3, pp. 159–169 [Online]. DOI: 10.1016/0040-1625(79)90011-8.

Sawtooth (2013) *The maxdiff system technical paper. Access date: 25.08.2015* [Online]. Available at https://www.sawtoothsoftware.com/download/techpap/maxdifftech.pdf (Accessed 15 September 2015).

Sawtooth (2015) *SSI web: maxdiff. Access date: 15.08.2015.* [Online]. Available at https://www.sawtoothsoftware.com/products/maxdiff-software/maxdiff (Accessed 15 September 2015).

Schmidt, R. C. (1997) 'Managing delphi surveys using nonparametric statistical techniques', *Decision Sciences*, vol. 28, no. 3, pp. 763–774 [Online]. DOI: 10.1111/j.1540-5915.1997.tb01330.x.

Witkin, B. R. and Altschuld, J. W. (1995) *Planning and conducting needs assessments: A practical guide*, Thousand Oaks, CA, Sage Publications.

CULTURE AND E-COMMERCE ACCEPTANCE IN INDONESIA

Arief Rahman and Wahyu Wardhani Putri
Universitas Islam Indonesia

ABSTRACT

The purpose of this research was to examine the impacts of Indonesia national culture in the consumer e-commerce acceptance. Based on Hofstede's cultural dimensions, this research investigates the moderating effect of power distance, individualism, masculinity, uncertainty avoidance, and long-term orientation. The Partial Least Square (PLS) method was employed to analyze of the model. Involving 172 respondents through online and direct survey, this study found that all variables of national culture except masculinity and long-term orientation moderate e-commerce acceptance in Indonesia. The research contributes to the theory as well as to the practice. The discussion on the implications for theory and practice are included in the paper.

KEYWORDS

e-commerce, national culture, acceptance, Indonesia

1. INTRODUCTION

E-commerce refers to the business type, which enables a company or individual to conduct business through electronic network, especially Internet. E-commerce has allowed companies to establish a market presence, or to enhance its current market position, by providing a cheaper and more efficient distribution chain for their products or services. Nowadays, almost any product or service can be offered via e-commerce, from hotels, banks, and financial services to accessories, books, and songs. The phenomenon of e-commerce, hence, has been one of the fruitful topics for many researchers.

Despite the numbers of research in e-commerce, only few studies have focused on the effects of culture on e-commerce acceptance. Previous studies show that behaviour in e-commerce different from one country to another (Goethals, Carugati, and Leclercq 2008; Yoon 2009). Therefore the main objective of this research was to explore the impact of national culture in the e-commerce consumer acceptance. In doing so, current study examined e-commerce consumer acceptance by examining model of Gefen, Karahanna, and Straub (2003) in Indonesia and using Hofstede's cultural values as moderating variables in the model.

Tabel 1. E-Commerce Buyer Penetration Worldwide, by Region (% of internet users)

Region	2013	2014	2015	2016
North America	72.0%	73.6%	74.9%	76.3%
Western Europe	64.0%	65.2%	66.3%	76.3%
Asia-Pacific	42.1%	44.1%	46.8%	48.9%
Central & Eastern Europe	41.6%	43.4%	44.3%	44.4%
Middle East & Africa	31.3%	33.1%	34.0%	35.0%
Latin America	28.2%	29.9%	30.9%	31.8%
Worldwide	41.3%	42.7%	44.3%	45.4%

Source: (eMarketer 2014)

2. THEORETICAL FRAMEWORK

2.1 e-Commerce Customer Acceptance

Derived from the Theory of Reasoned Action (TRA) (Ajzen and Fishbein 1980), Technology Acceptance Model has been validated and modified many times and therefore is one of the robust model. The model posits that Perceived Ease of Use (PeoU) and Perceived Usefulness (PU) determine user intention and technology usage behaviour (Davis 1989).

However, this research modifies the model by incorporating Trust in the model. Trust is vital since the nature of e-commerce where the sellers and buyers do not really meet face to face. Anxiety about security, trust of the vendor and privacy influence the willingness of the customers to involve in e-commerce (Gefen 2000; McKnight and Chervany 2002; Doney and Cannon 1997; Pavlou 2003). Gefen, Karahanna, and Straub (2003) argue that intention to use online shopping were determined by the assessment of the system by the customers and trust in the online shopping. They found that PEoU and PU along with Trust were the antecedents of e-commerce acceptance. Hence, we employ the integrated model of trust as the foundation model of this research.

2.2 National Culture Dimensions

Study by Hofstede (1984) on cultural dimensions provides a theoretical foundation for exploring the impact of cultural dimensions on the acceptance of IT-based innovations such as e-commerce. Culture can be defined as the mind's collective programming that is then differentiating members of a group of society from those of another (Hofstede 1983). Hofstede describes five dimensions to identify national cultures; they are power distance (PDI), individualism (IDV), masculinity (MAS), uncertainty avoidance (UAI), and long-term orientation (LTO). Table 2 presents the dimensions along with a brief description of each.

Table 2. Hofstede's Cultural Dimensions

Dimensions	Abbrv.	Description
Power distance	PDI	Degree of inequality among members which the society considers normal
Individualism	IDV	Degree of preference for an independence social framework
Masculinity	MAS	Degree of preference for achievement, heroism and assertiveness
Uncertainty avoidance	UAI	Degree to which the individuals in the society feel comfortable with uncertainty
Long-term orientation	LTO	Degree of orientation towards future rewards

2.3 Impacts of Cultural Dimensions on e-Commerce Acceptance

Culture shapes customers' point of view toward him/herself and toward the other, and therefore influences attitude. Suh and Kwon (2002) argue that customers with different culture have different attitudes, preferences and values. The differences cause them reluctant to buy foreign products although we are in globalization era. Previous research in the impact of culture on IT acceptance provides useful insight. Yoon (2009) found that national values affect customers' acceptance in China, while Capece et al. (2013) also found similar results in Italia, and Wahlberg (2015) in Sweden. Furthermore, Straub, Keil, and Brenner (1997) concluded that different culture accept technology differently. A study by Goethals, Carugati, and Leclercq (2008) provides an evidence that e-commerce behavior is different even in two culturally similar countries.

3. RESEARCH MODEL AND HYPOTHESES

To fulfill the research objective, this study incorporates Hofstede's cultural dimensions of PDI, IDV, MAS, UAI, and LTO as moderators in a technology acceptance model. Figure 1 summarizes hypotheses in the current research.

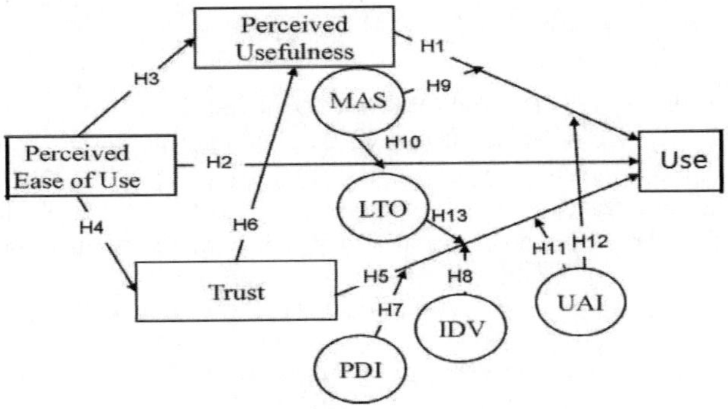

Figure 1. Research Model and Hypotheses

3.1 e-Commerce Acceptance Model

Based on Gefen, Karahanna, and Straub (2003), we propose these following hypotheses for e-commerce acceptance:

Hypothesis 1. *Perceived Usefulness (PU) has a positive impact on e-Commerce Use.*
Hypothesis 2. *Perceived Ease of Use (PEoU) has a positive impact on e-Commerce Use.*
Hypothesis 3. *Perceived Ease of Use (PEoU) has a positive impact on Perceived Usefulness (PU).*
Hypothesis 4. *Perceived Ease of Use (PEoU) has a positive impact on Trust.*
Hypothesis 5. *Trust has a positive impact on e-Commerce Use.*
Hypothesis 6. *Trust has a positive impact on Perceived Usefulness (PU).*

3.2 Power Distance

Power distance, refers to the acceptance by the individuals in the society toward power. Individuals in Large Power Distance societies accept a hierarchical order in which all of the society members has a place and further justification is not required. Contrary, individuals in Small Power Distance (low PDI) societies try to find power equalization and require justification for power inequalities. In a small power distance, customers believe that companies will be less likely to behave unethically than customers in Large Power Distance (high PDI) (Straub, Keil, and Brenner 1997). Hence, customers in high PDI society have less trust toward e-commerce than do customers from low PDI.

Hypothesis 7. *The higher the degree of Power Distance (PDI), the lower the effect of Trust on e-Commerce Use.*

3.3 Individualism

Individualism is a preference for an independent social framework, whereas Collectivism is a preference for a tightly knit social framework. Collectivistic society tend to emphasize on strong relationships and interdependence, therefore they are sensitive to boundaries (Triandis, Bontempo, and Villareal 1988). Trust is more important in a collectivistic society, and they are less likely to trust individuals from outside their group. In other words, an individualistic society may have more trust toward e-commerce than a collectivistic.

Hypothesis 8. *The higher degree of Individualism (IDV), the higher the effect of Trust on e-Commerce Use.*

3.4 Masculinity

Because Perceived Usefulness (PU) is strongly related to achievement of task goals (Srite and Karahanna 2006), thus the higher the degree of Masculinity (MAS), the higher the effect of PU on IT adoption. On the other hand, because high Perceived Ease of Use (PEoU) is related with less frustating work, while the Feminine values concern on quality of work life, hence the lower the degree of MAS, the higher the effect of PEoU on IT adoption. Based on those propositions, we propose the following hypotheses:

Hypothesis 9. *The higher degree of Masculinity (MAS), the higher the effect of Perceived Usefulness (PU) on e-Commerce Use.*

Hypothesis 10. *The higher degree of Masculinity (MAS), the lower the effect of Perceived Ease of Use (PEoU) on e-Commerce Use.*

3.5 Uncertainty Avoidance

Innovation, by its nature, is associated with greater risks and uncertainty (Kirton 1976). Technological innovations, such as e-commerce, will be accepted if the benefits earned by its users exceed the risks or costs (Ellen, Bearden, and Sharma 1991). However, members of societies with high uncertainty avoidance tend to feel threatened by ambiguity, risky and uncertain situations. Trust, hence, would be likely to have less effect on members of society on a high UAI values.

Hypothesis 11. *The higher the degree of Uncertainty Avoidance (UAI), the lower the effect of Trust on e-Commerce Use.*

UAI has been refered as a determinant of IT adoption (Straub, Keil, and Brenner 1997). Societies with low UAI are tolerant with innovation. They are willing to try out new technologies. Furthermore, Png, Tan, and Wee (2006) posit that the higher UAI culture, the less likely to adopt IT.

Hypothesis 12. *The higher the degree of Uncertainty Avoidance (UAI), the lower the effect of Perceived Usefulness on e-Commerce Use.*

3.6 Long-term Orientation

Along with Trust, which is closely related to risk of uncertainty, people with high Long-term Orientation (LTO) values believe in secure future rewards. Although future rewards are contingent assets which is not yet certain. People with high LTO values, hence have a strong beliefs that let them to take risk.

Hypothesis 13. *The higher degree of Long-term Orientation (LTO), the higher the effect of Trust on e-Commerce Use.*

4. RESEARCH METHOD

This research involved 172 valid questionnaires of e-commerce users in Indonesia. The respondents for this study are those who have experience in using online e-commerce transaction. The questionnaires are directly distributed as well as through online survey. Among respondents, 62 are males and 110 are females. In term of age, most of the respondents (91.3%) are below 20 years old, and 77.9% of the respondents are university students. More than 95% respondents have more than 3 years experience in using e-commerce transactions. More detail descriptive statistics of the respondents are presented in Table 3.

Measurements in the questionnaire for PU, PEoU, Trust and e-Commerce Use are based on the studies by Gefen (2000); Gefen, Karahanna, and Straub (2003); Pavlou (2003), while for the cultural dimensions of PDI, IDV, UAI, MAS, and LTO are based on research by Hofstede (1983, 2009); Srite and Karahanna (2006). Using a Likert score, the questionnaire is ranging from 1 (strongly disagree) to 6 (strongly agree). Smart PLS was applied to analyze the questionnaires.

Table 3. Descriptive Statistics of Respondents

Measure	Characteristics	Frequency	Percentage
Gender	Male	62	36%
	Female	110	64%
Age	Below 20	15	8.7%
	Over 20	157	91.3%
Occupation	University students	134	77.9%
	Highschool students	2	1.2%
	Civil servants	4	2.3%
	Entrepeneurs	10	5.8%
	Others	22	12.8%
e-Commerce experience	More than 3 years	8	4.7%
	Less than 3 years	164	95.3%

5. RESULTS

Two-step procedures were undertaken in the PLS analysis: measurement model assessment and structural model assessment. The following sections present the results of each assessment:

5.1 Measurement Model Assessment

The assessment was undertaken to ensure the reliability and validity of the measurements, by examining three indicators: (1) item reliability, (2) internal consistency, and (3) discriminant validity. The minimum value for the item loading was 0.6, as suggested by Gefen, Straub, and Boudreau (2000), while the threshold for average variance extracted (AVE) was 0.50 (Fornell and Larcker 1981; Hair, Ringle, and Sarstedt 2011). In terms of internal consistency, Bagozzi and Yi (1988) and Chin (1998) suggested that all variables should exceed 0.6. Based on those criteria, the results demonstrate that the measurement model was sufficient. Furthermore, results of Discriminant Validity and Cross-loading Analysis show that the items in the questionnaire are valid.

5.2 Structural Model Assessments

The assessment of structural model was divided into two categories, main effects and interaction model. The main effects examination was carried out to test the relationships among main variables (PU, PEoU, Trust and e-Commerce Use). While the assessment of interaction model was undertaken to test the moderation effect of cultural dimensions (PDI, IDV, MAS, UAI, and LTO) on the main variables. Table 7 presents the results of both assessments.

From the results of main effects assessment, we can come to a conclusion that all relationships are significant because *t-values* exceed *T-table* (significance level of 0.05), hence the hypotheses 1 until hypothesis 6 are statistically proven. Furthermore, in order to examine the moderation effects of cultural dimensions on the main variables, this research analyzed interaction effect as suggested by Chin, Malcolin, and Newsted (2003). By applying PLS, we follow a hierarchical process.

Table 4. Results of structural model assessment

Hipotesis	Path	Path Coefficient	t value	R^2
		Assessment of Main Effects		
H1	PU → Use	0.216	2.100*	0.593
H2	PEoU → Use	0.295	3.644*	
H3	PEoU → PU	0.431	4.432*	0.365
H4	PEoU → Trust	0.358	3.849*	0.128
H5	Trust→ Use	0.200	2.210*	
H6	Trust → PU	0.296	2.843*	
		Assessment of Interaction Model		
H7	Trust→ Use	0.382	3.216*	
	PDI → Use	0.587	5.592*	
	Trust*PDI→Use	-0.324	2.584*	0.366
H8	Trust → Use	0.297	1.709*	
	IDV → Use	-0.344	1.828*	
	Trust*IDV→Use	0.627	4.748*	0.306
H9	PU → Use	0.106	0.808	
	MAS → Use	0.293	2.696*	
	PU*MAS→ Use	0.450	2.745*	0.530
H10	PEoU→Use	0.287	1.424	
	MAS → Use	0.501	3.498*	
	PEoU*MAS→Use	0.029	0.111	0.453
H11	Trust→Use	0.580	6.598*	
	UAI→Use	-0.395	4.223*	
	Trust*UAI→Use	0.514	4.933*	0.445
H12	PU → Use	0.574	6.985*	
	UAI→Use	-0.333	4.009*	
	PU*UAI→Use	0.401	4.501*	0.474
H13	Trust→Use	0.168	0.840	
	LTO→Use	0.333	1.678*	
	Trust*LTO→Use	0.216	0.727	0.337

**significant at the 0.05 level*

Totally, 14 structural models from 7 hypotheses (H7-H13) were examined and the results are shown in Table 4. The moderation effects in the table are indicated by the last line of each calculation in each hypothesis. We found that H7, H8, H9, H11, and H12 have been proven statistically significant. Based on the results, we concluded that those relations are quasi moderating effects, since the direct effects of the cultural dimensions on e-commerce use are significant as well. None of the moderators is pure moderator in the interaction.

However, the interaction effects of PEoU x MAS and Trust x LTO have insignificant effects on e-Commerce Use. Thus, H10 and H13 are rejected. But the t-value and path coefficient in the main effects model indicated that MAS and LTO both have significant effects on e-Commerce Use directly at the level of 0.05. Hence, we suggest that MAS and LTO are not moderator variables but an antecedent of e-Commerce Use.

6. DISCUSSION, IMPLICATIONS AND CONTRIBUTIONS

Based on this research, which involved 172 e-commerce users in Indonesia, we found that dimension of Uncertainty Avoidance is the most influential cultural dimension impacting consumer e-commerce acceptance. The dimension moderates the relationships between Perceived Usefulness on e-Commerce Use as well as between Trust on e-Commerce Use. The moderating effect on Trust on e-Commerce Use is the strongest, though.

Value of uncertainty avoidance closely relates to the attitude toward innovations. As e-commerce is one of the innovations in the digital era, different individual may have different attitude toward it. The attitude is determined by personal values, including cultural values (Doney and Cannon 1997).

The findings indicate that in Indonesia where the people tend to avoid uncertainty, building trust is fundamental. Trust is an essential factor for innovations acceptance (Warkentin et al. 2002). Without trust, people reluctant to use new technologies. To build trust, companies and e-commerce developers as the service providers as well as government as the regulators have an important role. Companies and e-commerce developers should provide secure systems which guarantee to proper use and protection of personal data of the users. Government on the other hand, has a role to enact laws in protecting customers. Both parties can work together to educate people and make them knowledgeable about new technologies.

This research generates insight in the relationship between variables of Perceived Ease of Use and e-Commerce Use, which is proven to be the most significant. When companies are dealing with customers who have various background and knowledge about new technology, developing user-friendly system is substantial. The system should be easy to use and provide a clear steps of transaction, so that the customers can maintain their expectation.

Contrary to the propositions, Masculinity does not have a moderating effect of the relationship between Perceived Ease of Use and e-Commerce Use. The result and also the characteristics of respondents which is dominated by female customers are surprising facts. One possible explanation for the results is that because this research is about shopping, which is closely associated with women. The result that Long-term Orientation has no mediating role on the relationship between Trust and e-Commerce Use is also unexpected.

This study contributes to the research on technology acceptance in general, and especially in the developing countries. The results showed that national culture affects e-commerce customers' acceptance. The findings of this research also contribute to the practice: companies, e-commerce developers and government as discussed in the earlier section.

7. LIMITATIONS AND FUTURE RESEARCH DIRECTIONS

This research was conducted by involving respondents through direct distribution of questionnaire as well as through online survey. Direct survey mostly involved university students. This might have affected the external validity of the results. Therefore in the future research which involving respondents with more various background is needed. The determinant coefficient in the research was low, which indicates that the research model can be improved in the future by incorporating other variables. Future research might apply other relevant theories to improve the model.

REFERENCES

Ajzen, Icek, and Martin Fishbein. 1980. *Understanding Attitudes and Predicting Social Behavior*. Upper Saddle River, NJ.: Prentice-Hall, Inc.

Bagozzi, Richard P., and Youjae Yi. 1988. "On the Evaluation of Structural Equation Models." *Journal of the Academy of Marketing Science* 16 (1): 74-94.

Capece, Guendalina, Armando Calabrese, Fransesca Di Pillo, Roberta Costa, and Valentina Crisciotti. 2013. "The Impact of National Culture on E-Commerce Acceptance: The Italian Case." *Knowledge and Process Management* 20 (2): 102-112.

Chin, Wynne W. 1998. "The Partial Least Squares Approach to Structural Equation Modeling." In *Modern Methods for Business Research*, ed. George A. Marcoulides, 295-336. Mahwah, New Jersey: Lawrence Erlbaum Associates, Publisher.

Chin, Wynne W., Barbara L. Malcolin, and Peter R. Newsted. 2003. "A Partial Least Squares Latent Variable Modelling Approach for Measuring Interaction Effects: Results from a Monte Carlo Simulation Study and an Electronic-Mail Emotion/Adoption Study." *Information Systems Research* 14 (2): 189-217.

Davis, Fred D. 1989. "Perceived Usefulness, Perceived Ease of Use, and User Acceptance of Information Technology." *MIS Quarterly* 13 (3): 319-340.

Doney, Patricia M., and Joseph P. Cannon. 1997. "An Examination of the Nature of Trust in Buyer-Seller Relationships." *Journal of Marketing* 61 (2): 35-51.

Ellen, Pam Scholder, william O. Bearden, and Subhash Sharma. 1991. "Resistance to Technological Innovations: An Examination of the Role of Self-Efficacy and Performance Satisfaction." *Journal of the Academy of Marketing Science* 19 (4): 297-307.

eMarketer. 2014. Worldwide E-Commerce Sales to Increase Nearly 20% in 2014. http://www.emarketer.com/Article/Worldwide-Ecommerce-Sales-Increase-Nearly-20-2014/1011039.
Fornell, Claes, and David F. Larcker. 1981. "Evaluating Structural Equation Models with Unobservable Variables and Measurement Error." *Journal of Marketing Research* 18 (1): 39-50.
Gefen, David. 2000. "E-Commerce: The Role of Familiarity and Trust." *Omega* 28: 725-737.
Gefen, David, Elena Karahanna, and Detmar W. Straub. 2003. "Trust and Tam in Online Shopping: An Integrated Model." *MIS Quarterly* 27 (1): 51-90.
Gefen, David, Detmar W. Straub, and Marie-Claude Boudreau. 2000. "Structural Equation Modeling and Regression: Guidelines for Research Practice." *Communications of the Association for Information Systems* 4 (7): 1-77.
Goethals, Frank G., Andrea Carugati, and Aurelie Leclercq. 2008. "E-Commerce Behavior in Different Countries." France: IESEG School of Management.
Hair, Joe F., Christian M. Ringle, and Marko Sarstedt. 2011. "Pls-Sem: Indeed a Silver Bullet." *Journal of Marketing Theory and Practice* 19 (2): 139-151.
Hofstede, Geert. 1983. "Cultural Dimensions in Management and Planning." *Asia Pacific Journal of Management* 1 (2): 81-99.
———. 1984. "National Cultures Revisited." *Asia Pacific Journal of Management* 2 (1): 22-28.
———. 2009. Cultural Dimensions. ITIM International. Accessed August, 10th 2010, http://www.geert-hofstede.com/.
Kirton, Michael. 1976. "Adaptors and Innovators: A Description and Measure." *Journal of Applied Psychology* 61 (5): 622-629.
McKnight, D. Harrison, and Norman L. Chervany. 2002. "What Trust Means in E-Commerce Customer Relationships: An Interdisciplinary Conceptual Typology." *International Journal of Electronic Commerce* 6 (2): 35-59.
Pavlou, Paul A. 2003. "Consumer Acceptance of Electronic Commerce: Integrating Trust and Risk with the Technology Acceptance Model " *International Journal of Electronic Commerce* 7 (3): 101-134.
Png, IPL., BCY. Tan, and Khai-Ling Wee. 2006. "Dimensions of National Culture and Corporate Adoption of It Infrastructure." *IEEE Transactions on Engineering Management* 48 (1): 36-45.
Srite, Mark, and Elena Karahanna. 2006. "The Role of Espoused National Cultural Values in Technology Acceptance." *MIS Quarterly* 30 (3): 679-704.
Straub, Detmar, Mark Keil, and Walter Brenner. 1997. "Testing the Technology Acceptance Model across Cultures: A Three Country Study." *Information & Management* 33 (1): 1-11.
Suh, Taewon, and Ik-Whan G. Kwon. 2002. "Globalization and Reluctant Buyers." *International Marketing Review* 19 (6): 663-680.
Triandis, Harry C., Robert Bontempo, and Marcelo J. Villareal. 1988. "Individualism and Collectivism: Cross-Cultural Perspective on Self-Ingroup Relationships." *Journal of Personality and Social Psychology* 54 (2): 323-338.
Wahlberg, Arvid. 2015. "The Effects of National Culture Values on Consumer Acceptance of E-Commerce: The Swedish Case." Industrial Engineering and Management, KTH Royal Institute of Technology, Stockholm, Sweden.
Warkentin, Merril, David Gefen, Paul A. Pavlou, and Gregory M. Rose. 2002. "Encouraging Citizen Adoption of E-Government by Building Trust." *Electronic Markets* 12 (3): 157-162.
Yoon, Cheolho. 2009. "The Effects of National Culture Values on Consumer Acceptance of E-Commerce: Online Shoppers in China." *Information & Management* 46 (3): 294-301.

DEVELOPMENT OF A TEMPORAL ONTOLOGY: AN APPROACH TO REPRESENT FLIGHT OCCURRENCES

Deborah Mendes Ferreira and Flávio de Barros Vidal
Department of Computer Science, University of Brasilia, C.P. 4466, Brasilia - DF 70910-900, Brazil

ABSTRACT

The Semantic Web is becoming fundamental in the Web. The amount of data available in the Web is increasing in great proportions, it is very important to find ways to deal with this trend. The Semantic Web can help with this, by giving meaning to this data in a way that machines can understand what information it contains and automatically process it. In this paper we present an ontology to represent flight occurrences, such as incidents and accidents. To build this ontology we use the Temporal Web Ontology Language (tOWL), an extension to the Web Ontology Language (OWL), which allow us to build ontology that supports temporality.

KEYWORDS

semantic web, temporal ontology, flight occurrences, knowledge representation

1. INTRODUCTION

One of the biggest obstacles to provide better support for Web users is the fact that a large part of the Web content is not accessible by machines (Berners-Lee, Hendler and Lassila, 2001). There are tools capable of collecting texts, separating it in parts, verifying its orthography and counting words. However, regarding the interpretation of phrases and extracting useful information for the users, the current tools are very limited (Antoniou and Harmelen, 2004). To be able to understand information contained in the Web, machines and humans need to share some understanding of the real world, i.e, we need to be able to represent the world or parts of the world inside the machine.

When representing the world, we want this representation to be as close to reality as possible to avoid making false assumptions about the world. To be able to do this, we also need to be capable of representing time. Time is an important aspect of human life. Many environments requires temporal awareness, one known example is Air Traffic Control (ATC), that each aircraft needs to follow a strict schedule to avoid any incidents. Therefore, time should also be part of real world representations (Ter Meulen, 1997).

The Temporal Ontology Language (tOWL), proposed by (Milea, Frasincar and Kaymak, 2012), is a temporal language build as an extension for the first version of OWL. With tOWL we can represent complex aspects of time, such as points in time and intervals. This language adds Concrete Domains (CD) to OWL, making it possible to use Concrete Domains predicates and datatypes, but limiting the expressiveness of the language to avoid undecidability (Baader and Hanschke, 2011).

In this paper we present a temporal ontology approach to represent flight occurrences, such as accidents, incidents, crimes, kidnapping and others. It is important to be able to represent this information. Using an ontology to store this knowledge we can learn from previous occurrences and avoid it happening again. Serious accidents/incidents can generate great human losses and also economical losses for airlines and government (Williams, 2004), it is important to find ways to avoid that these accidents/incidents occur. We use tOWL language as a base framework for this ontology, therefore, we can represent temporality in our ontology. The flight phases are cyclic, that means we can represent it as a state machine and tOWL allows this kind of representation. In the current state of art, we did not find ontologies with similar function, specially capable of representing time.

This paper is divided as follows: Section 2 presents the tOWL language, used to implement the ontology for flight occurrences. Section 3 details the implementation and design of the ontology. Section 4 presents a brief analysis of the ontology. Section 5 presents the conclusions of this work.

2. TOWL LANGUAGE

The tOWL (Milea, Frasincar and Kaymak, 2012) (Temporal Web Ontology Language) is an OWL extension that allows the communication between machines in contexts including temporal information. The tOWL language allows inferences of implicit knowledge in contexts that need temporality when a temporal dimension is involved.

Language tOWL was developed as an extension of OWL DL (Patel-Schneider, Hayes and Horrocks, 2008), a profile from the first version of OWL, with addition of the time unit. The OWL DL fragment considered was SHIN(D), i.e., OWL without the use of nominals

The tOWL implements two aspects of time: temporal infrastructure and change. Temporal infrastructure refers to the representation of time as intervals or instants.

Using tOWL, changes can happen in values of concrete attributes, in relationship between entities and in transition of states.

The language was developed in three layers: (i) Layer of Concrete Domains, (ii) Layer of Temporal Reference and (iii) Layer of 4D Fluents.

2.1 Layer of Concrete Domains

In tOWL we can represent feature chains, $f_1 \cdots f_n$, composed with a concrete feature g, creating a concrete feature path (CFP), which is equivalent to the following composition:

$$\mathrm{f}_1 \circ f_2 \circ ... f_n \circ g, \qquad \text{(Equation 1)}$$

where $n \in N$. The CFP is added to tOWL as the construct `ConcreteFeatureChain`. One example of such composition would be the abstract feature `time` composed with the concrete feature `start`, in the following manner:

$$\text{time} \circ start. \qquad \text{(Equation 2)}$$

Table 1. Semantics for the Layer of Concrete Domains(Milea, Frasincar and Kaymak, 2012)

tOWL abstract syntax	Theoretical Model semantics
ConcreteFeatureChain(f_1 f_2 ... f_n g)	$\{(a_1, b) \in \Delta^{\mathcal{I}} \times \Delta_{\mathcal{D}} \mid \exists! a_2 \in \Delta^{\mathcal{I}}, ..., \exists! a_{n+1} \in$ $\in \Delta^{\mathcal{I}} \wedge \wedge\ \exists! b \in \Delta_{\mathcal{D}} : (a_1, a_2) \in f_1^{\mathcal{I}}, ...$ $(a_n, a_{n+1}) \in f_n^{\mathcal{I}} \wedge g^{\mathcal{I}}(a_{n+1}) = b\}.$
dataSomeValuesFrom(u_1 u_2 p_d)	$\{x \in \Delta^{\mathcal{I}} \mid \exists! q_1 \in \Delta_{\mathcal{D}}, \exists! q_2 \in \Delta_{\mathcal{D}} :$ $u_1^{\mathcal{I}}(x) = q_1 \wedge u_2^{\mathcal{I}}(x) = q_2 \wedge\ (q_1, q_2) \in p_d^{\mathcal{I}}\}.$
dataAllValuesFrom(u_1 u_2 p_d)	$\{x \in \Delta^{\mathcal{I}} \mid \forall q_1 \in \Delta_{\mathcal{D}}, \forall q_2 \in \Delta_{\mathcal{D}} :$ $u_1^{\mathcal{I}}(x) = q_1 \wedge u_2^{\mathcal{I}}(x) = q_2 \wedge\ (q_1, q_2) \in p_d^{\mathcal{I}})\}.$

The constructs added in these layers are:

1. `ConcreteFeatureChain`: Defines that the interpretation of such concept is formed by all the pairs of individuals from the abstract domain and the concrete domain, such that each one of the abstract individuals is in the interpretation of the abstract feature f_1 next with exactly one other abstract individual, a_2. In its turn, is in the interpretation of f_2, next with exactly one individual, a_3, and so on, until a_{n+1}. Finally, the interpretation of the concrete feature g in the individual a_{n+1} must be defined and take only a concrete value, in this case, named b.
2. `dataSomeValuesFrom`: Defines that the interpretation of such concept consists in all the individuals of the abstract domain when two concrete feature chain u_1 and u_2 are interpreted over these individuals. The result consists of the concrete values q_1 and q_2, that are in the interpretation of the concrete domain p_d.
3. `dataAllValuesFrom`: Similar to the previous construction, however, in this case the relation p_d must be true for all the values of q_1 and q_2.

2.2 Layer of Temporal Reference

This layer presents timepoints, relationships between timespoints and intervals. The intervals are defined using the predicate of concrete domain $<$ and two concrete features, `start` and `end`, to define that the beginning of an interval must be strictly smaller than the end of the interval, as described in Equation 3.

$$\text{ProperInterval} \equiv \exists(begin, end).< \qquad \text{(Equation 3)}$$

2.3 Layer of 4D Fluents

This layer presents a perdurantist view of individuals, allowing representation of complex temporal aspects, as state transitions in processes. Table 2 presents the axioms of TBox corresponding to the timeslices/fluents layer.

Table 2. tOWL axioms for the Layer of 4D Fluents (Milea, Frasincar and Kaymak, 2012).

Constructs tOWL 4dFluents	tOWL Axioms in OWL-DL$^-$
Class(TimeSlice)	$\exists$time.Interval $\sqcap$ (= 1 time) $\sqcap$ $\exists$timeSliceOf. $\neg$(TimeSlice $\sqcup$ Interval $\sqcup$ rdfs:Literal)$\sqcap$ (= 1 timeSliceOf)
Class(Interval)	$\exists$(start, end). $\leq$ $\sqcap\exists$start.dateTime$\sqcap$ $\sqcap\exists$end.dateTime $\sqcap$ (= 1 start) $\sqcap$ (= 1 end)
Class(FluentProperty)	FluentProperty $\sqsubset$ rdf:Property
Class(FluentObjectProperty)	FluentObjectProperty $\sqsubset$ FluentProperty
Class(FluentDatatypeProperty)	FluentDatatypeProperty $\sqsubset$ FluentProperty
Property(timeSliceOf)	$\geq$ 1 timeSliceOf $\sqsubseteq$ TimeSlice $\top \sqsubseteq \forall$timeSliceOf.$\neg$(TimeSlice $\sqcup$ Interval$\sqcup$ $\sqcup$rdfs:Literal)
Property(time)	$\geq$ 1 time $\sqsubseteq$ TimeSlice $\top \sqsubseteq \forall$time.Interval
Property(start)	$\geq$ 1 start $\sqsubseteq$ Interval $\top \sqsubseteq \forall$start.dateTime
Property(end)	$\geq$ 1 end $\sqsubseteq$ Interval $\top \sqsubseteq \forall$end.dateTime

`TimeSlice` is defined as all individuals to which the `time` property is defined and takes values of the type `Interval` and to which the property `timeSliceOf` is defined and takes a value that is not a `Interval`, a `TimeSlice`or a `Literal`.

`Interval` is defined as all individuals whose properties `start` and `end` are defined and take a value from XML Schema `dateTime`, such that the value associate with a start point must be smaller than the value of the end point.

`FluentProperty` is defined as a subclass of a the Resource Description Framework (RDF) property class, and it is a superclass of `FluentObjectProperty` and `FluentDataProperty`. The property `timeSliceOf` is defined as a property that can be applied to timeslices, intervals or literals. `Time` property is defined as a property that takes values of the type `Interval` and can be applied to individuals of the type `TimeSlice`. The properties `start` and `end` are defined as properties that are set for the intervals and take values from XML Schema `dateTime`.

3. BUILDING THE ONTOLOGY

In this section we present how the ontology was built, we show the implementation of the Tbox and the Abox, components of a knowledge representation system.

The data used in this work was collected from the Website *Aviation Safety Network* (http://aviation-safety.net/). This database contains more than 15 thousand occurrences, ranging from 1919 to 2015.

3.1 Ontology Modeling

Figure 1 shows the temporal ontology to represent flight occurrences. The attributes represented by complete rectangles are of Instance type and the ones represented by dotted rectangles have data types (String, Number, Boolean, Enumerated). There are three major classes: Occurrence, Flight and Aircraft. Occurrence is linked to the Flight class and the Flight class is linked to Aircraft class. Figure 1 also represents all the properties that connect classes to their predicates. This figure omitted details of minor classes such as Destination Airport, Departure Airport, Location.

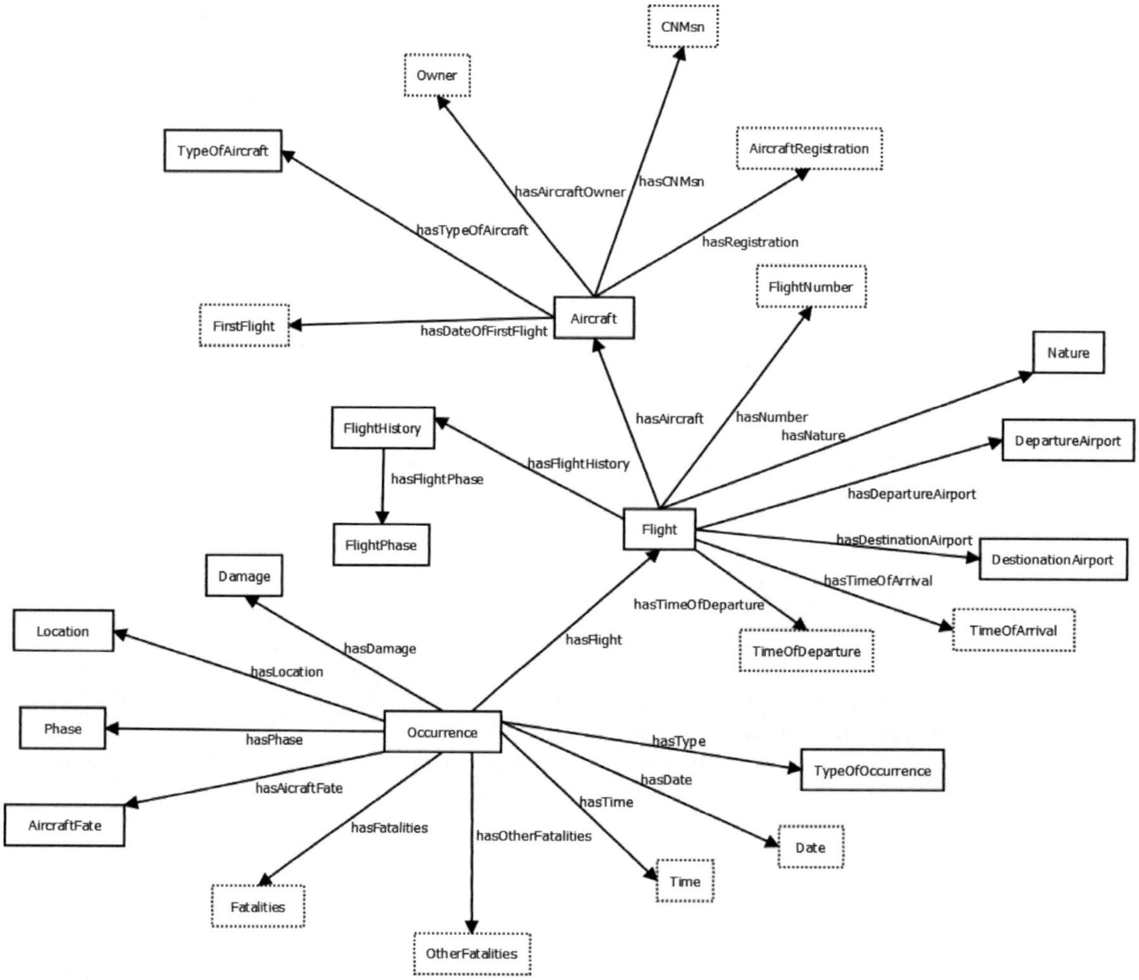

Figure 1. Ontology for flight ocurrences.

The temporal aspects of this ontology are: date of first flight of the aircraft, estimated time of arrival and departure, date and time of the occurrence and flight history. Flight history is divided into phases, as shown in Figure 2. Each stage has two possible outcomes: success or failure. Success occurs when the flight follows its normal stages. Failure occurs when the flight goes to an emergency situation. When an emergency fails, the flight changes to a stage named Abort, this stage means that the recovery from the emergency failed and an accident/incident may have occurred. Each stage of this diagram is represented in the ontology as a TimeSlice.

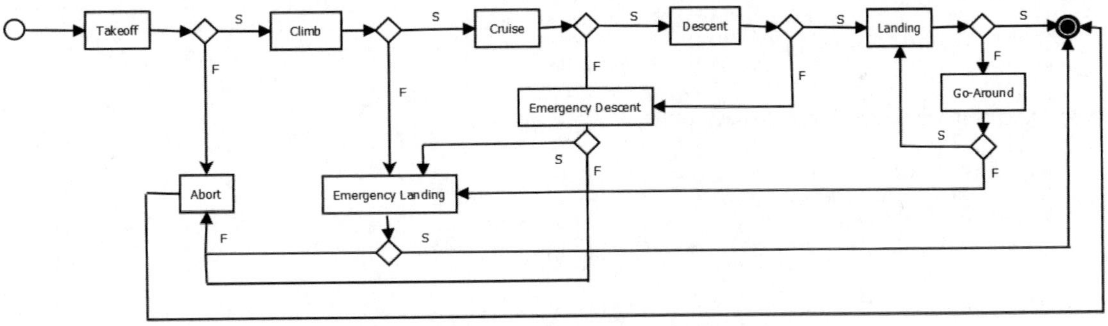

Figure 2. Sequence diagram for flight phases.

3.2 Implementing the TBox

TBox is the part of implementation that allows us to create the terminology for the ontology. In this work, the TBox is the conceptual information about flight occurrences. First we declare all ontology classes:

```
Class( :Occurrence )
Class( :Flight )
Class( :Aircraft )
Class( :TypeofOccurence )
Class( :AircraftFate )
Class( :Phase )
Class( :Location )
      ...
```

Then we define the fields and scopes of the properties that connect classes to instances:

```
ObjectPropertyDomain( :hasDamage :Occurrence )
ObjectPropertyRange( :hasDamage :Damage )
ObjectPropertyDomain( :hasLocation :Occurrence )
ObjectPropertyRange( :hasLocation :Location )
ObjectPropertyDomain( :hasPhase :Occurrence )
ObjectPropertyRange( :hasPhase :FlightPhase )
ObjectPropertyDomain( :hasAircraftFate :Occurrence )
ObjectPropertyRange( :hasAircraftFate :AircraftFate )
      ...
```

We also define fields and scopes for the properties that are connected to data type classes:

```
DataPropertyDomain( :hasTime :Occurence )
DataPropertyRange( :hasTime xsd:time )
DataPropertyDomain( :hasDate :Occurence )
DataPropertyRange( :hasDate xsd:date )
      ...
```

We add the following construct to indicate that fatalities can be passengers, crew or others (those at the ground, for example):

```
SubClassOf ( :Passenger :Fatalities )
SubClassOf ( :Crew :Fatalities )
SubClassOf ( :OtherFatalities :Fatalities )
```

Each flight phase is represented as a subclass of class FlightPhase:

```
Class( :TakeOff partial :FlightPhase )
Class( :Climb partial :FlightPhase )
Class( :Cruise partial :FlightPhase )
Class( :Descent partial :FlightPhase )
Class( :Landing partial :FlightPhase )
Class( :Abort partial :FlightPhase )
```

```
Class( :Go-Around partial :FlightPhase )
Class( :EmergencyLanding partial :FlightPhase )
Class( :EmergencyDescent partial :FlightPhase )
```

And all phases are disjoint to each other:

```
DisjointClasses( :TakeOff, :Climb, :Cruise, :Descent, :Lading, :Abort,
       :Go-Around, :EmergencyDescent, :EmergencyLanding )
```

Class of Flight History timeslice is defined as follows:

```
Class(FlighHistory_TS complete
       restriction(timeSliceOf(someValuesFrom FlightHistory)))
```

Each flight phase also has its own timeslice, defined as follows:

```
Class(TakeOff_TS complete restriction(timeSliceOf(someValuesFrom TakeOff)))
Class(Climb_TS complete restriction(timeSliceOf(someValuesFrom Climb)))
Class(Cruise_TS complete restriction(timeSliceOf(someValuesFrom Cruise)))
Class(Descent_TS complete restriction(timeSliceOf(someValuesFrom Descent)))
Class(Landing_TS complete restriction(timeSliceOf(someValuesFrom Landing)))
Class(Abort_TS complete restriction(timeSliceOf(someValuesFrom Abort)))
Class(Go-Around_TS complete restriction(timeSliceOf(someValuesFrom Go-Around)))
Class(EmergencyLanding_TS complete
       restriction(timeSliceOf(someValuesFrom EmergencyLanding)))
Class(EmergencyDescent_TS complete
       restriction(timeSliceOf(someValuesFrom EmergencyDescent)))
```

For each stage, we define a functional property to connect each Flight History timeslice to the stage belonging to this history:

```
ObjectProperty(:takeOff domain(:FlighHistory_TS) range(:TakeOff_TS))
FunctionalObjectProperty(takeOff)
 ObjectProperty(:climb domain(:FlighHistory_TS) range(:Climb_TS))
FunctionalObjectProperty(climb)
 ObjectProperty(:cruise domain(:FlighHistory_TS) range(:Cruise_TS))
FunctionalObjectProperty(cruise)
 ObjectProperty(:descent domain(:FlighHistory_TS) range(:Descent_TS))
FunctionalObjectProperty(descent)
       ...
```

Then we define the InPhase fluent, which points each timeslice of a flight to the stage where he is.

```
FluentObjectProperty(inPhase domain(
restriction (timeSliceOf(someValuesFrom Flight))) range(
restriction (timeSliceOf (someValuesFrom FlightPhase))))
```

The Flight History timeslices are defined by the sequence of phases that a flight can follow. This depends on the use of a composition chain roles (Equation 1) . The following construction defines that the initial phase of the flight should always be the phase of take off.

```
Class(FlightHistory_TS partial restriction(
       DataSomeValuesFrom(DataPropertyChain(takeOff time), time, starts))))
```

3.3 Implementing the ABox

In the Abox, we represent information about a specific flight, for this example we choose the Flight 9525 from Germanwings. First we create the instance of the 4U9525 flight:

```
Individual (:iFlight4U9525 type(:Flight))
```

Then we create all phases that the flight has followed using timeslices format, this flight had an accident at the cruise phase (En Route), we believe that he went through Emergency Descent before crashing.

```
Individual (:iFlightHistory_TS1 type (:FlightHistory_TS)
                    value (:timeSliceOf :iFlightHistory_TS1)
                    value (:takeOff :iTakeOff1_TS1)
                    value (:climb :iClimb1_TS1)
                    value (:cruise :iCruise1_TS1)
                    value (:descent :iDescent1_TS1)
                    value (:abort :iAbort1_TS1)
                    value (:goAround :iGoAround1_TS1)
                    value (:emergencyDescent :iEmergencyDescent1_TS1))
```

We created the timeslice associated with the first phase of flight, take-off, as shown in Figure 3:

```
Individual(:t1 type(:Interval))
Individual(:iTakeOff1
      type(:TakeOff_TS))
Individual(:iTakeOff1_TS1
      type(:TimeSlice)
      value(:timeSliceOf :iTakeOff1)
      value(:time :t1))
Individual(:iFlight4U9525_TS1
      type(:TimeSlice)
      value(:timeSliceOf :iFlight4U9525)
      value(:time :t1)
      value(:inPhase :iTakeOff1_TS1))
```

In the same way, we implemented timeslices for all other phases of this flight.

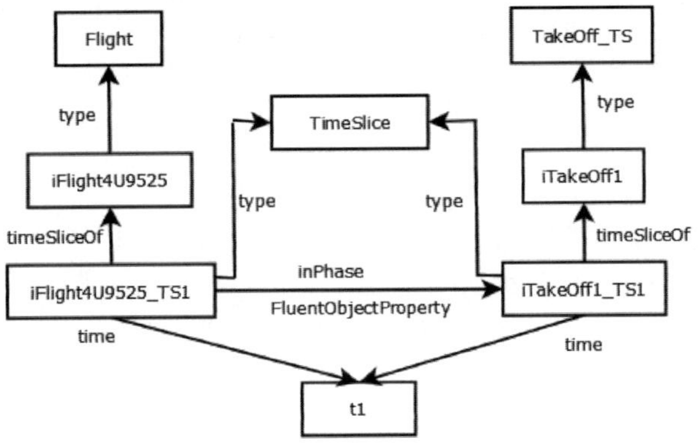

Figure 3. Flight 4U9525 association to the takeoff phase.

4. ANALYSIS OF THE ONTOLOGY

To analyze if the ontology is appropriate, we define some competency questions and verify if the ontology is capable of answering them, as described by (Grüninger and Fox, 1995).

Question 1: What accidents occurred simultaneously in the same period?

The ontology represents the time in which an accident occurred, it is possible to isolate periods of months and years, analyzing accidents which occur in the same period. Answering this question, we can verify if there is any relation between two different accidents.

Question 2: Where has the biggest number of occurrences happened in a certain period?

The ontology has a property to represent the location where were incidents and accidents happened, we can analyze location and time of occurrence. With this information, we can verify if there are times and places where/when an accident is more likely to happen.

Question 3: What type of aircraft was involved in the largest number of occurrences?

The ontology stores the type of aircraft involved in the accident using class Aircraft, we can find the types of aircraft that were involved in a greater number of occurrences. If we have this information, we can verify if there is any problem with the aircraft, that could be provoking a higher number of accidents.

Question 4: In which flight phase occur more occurrences?

This ontology stores phases of the flight and in which phase of the flight the incident or accident occurred, so we can answer that question. If we know in which phase there are more occurrences, we can work on improving the problems on that phase.

Question 5: Can we find some kind of pattern between time and number of air accidents?

In this ontology we know which accidents occurred in a given period, so we can see if there is a relationship between the analyzed period and the number of air accidents. With this information we can check what time of the year there are more accidents and then analyze what aspects of that part of the year could collaborate for the occurrence of accidents.

All these questions can be answered with queries using SPARQL. SPARQL is the W3C candidate recommendation query language for RDF (Pérez, Arenas and Gutierrez, 2006).

5. CONCLUSION

In this work we present a temporal ontology to represent flight occurrences, such as incidents and accidents.

This ontology can be used to represent knowledge about flight occurrences and connect different sources of information related to Air Traffic Control, in general, and can be extend to other situations/applications in air traffic management. Also, this ontology is built using the tOWL Language, which allows us to represent time and reason with it. We can find implicit knowledge about flight occurrences, reasoning with the ontology presented in this paper.

As future work, we plan to improve this ontology, connecting it to other sources of information and verifying its consistency, building more complex applications as a reasoner capable of dealing with the time aspects presented by the tOWL language.

REFERENCES

Annex, I. C. A. O. (1994). 13: aircraft accident and incident investigation.

Antoniou, G. and Van Harmelen, F. (2004). *A semantic web primer*. MIT press.

Baader, F. and Hanschke, P. (2011). A scheme for integrating concrete domains into concept languages.

Berners-Lee, T., Hendler, J. and Lassila, O. (2001). The semantic web. *Scientific american*, *284*(5), 28-37.

Davis, R., Shrobe, H. and Szolovits, P. (1993). What is a knowledge representation?. *AI magazine*, *14*(1), 17.

Milea, V., Frasincar, F. and Kaymak, U. (2012). tOWL: A Temporal Web Ontology Language. *IEEE Trans. Syst., Man, Cybern. B*, 42(1), pp.268-281.

Patel-Schneider, P. F., Hayes, P. P. and Horrocks, I. (2008). OWL 2 web ontology language: Profiles: Owl-r. W3C Working Draft.

Williams, K. W. (2004). *A summary of unmanned aircraft accident/incident data: Human factors implications* (No. DOT/FAA/AM-04/24). FEDERAL AVIATION ADMINISTRATION OKLAHOMA CITY OK CIVIL AEROMEDICAL INST.

BYOD VS. CYOD – WHAT IS THE DIFFERENCE?

Martin Brodin
University of Skövde
Box 408, S-541 28 Skövde

ABSTRACT

During the last years mobile devices have become very popular to use both for work and pleasure. Different strategies have evolved to increase productivity and to satisfy the employees. In this paper, we look at the two most popular strategies and look at the strengths and weaknesses of those. This is done by a systematic literature review and semi-structured interviews with CIO's or equivalent roles. We conclude that BYOD and CYOD comes with similar strengths, but CYOD brings a little fewer security risks.

KEYWORDS

BYOD, CYOD, Information Management, Mobile Devices, Mobile strategy, Smartphone, Bring Your Own Device.

1. INTRODUCTION

During the last years Bring Your Own Device (BYOD) has gained in popularity and opportunities, and threats have been discussed widely in both scientific and business articles (Brodin et al. 2015). But lately its popularity in the USA has decreased and in Europe, it has never really taken hold. Choose Your Own Device (CYOD) is a more popular approach in Europe and is gaining in popularity in the US (Kane et al. 2014).

The objective of this article is to investigate the difference between BYOD and CYOD issues using literature study techniques and interviews with CIOs. The following research questions will be addressed:

- RQ1: Which managerial issues are connected to both BYOD and CYOD?
- RQ2: What is the difference between BYOD and CYOD from a managerial perspective?

The paper is structured as follows. In section 2 the research method and analysis model are explained. Section 3 presents an introduction to BYOD, section 4 presents an introduction to CYOD and section 5 presents a comparison and discussion. Finally, section 6 gives the conclusions of the analysis, and offers directions for future research.

1.1 Ways to Manage Devices

Traditionally, when it comes to ISIT-devices, the employer received their working tools with the words; use what you are told (UWYT). IT then got a pre-determined list of approved devices which they control and has configure for work purpose. A variation is a list of allowed devices that depends on the role of the employee, where some roles can get much freer choice than others. The role based list approach is a mix of UWYT and CYOD. When moving from UWYT to CYOD the IT-department leave the choice of device completely to the user, but still buy and control the device. In this category, there are some variations between level of private use and control. When the organisation lets go even more of the control they let the employee buy the device by themselves, but with money from the organisation, if it will be a private or proprietary device may vary. The final step in device freedom is when the organisation is completely left outside the devices and the employee use their own private device even at work. This gives us three ways to see manage these devices, figure 1. In this article, the strategies that fall under BYOD or CYOD are of interest.

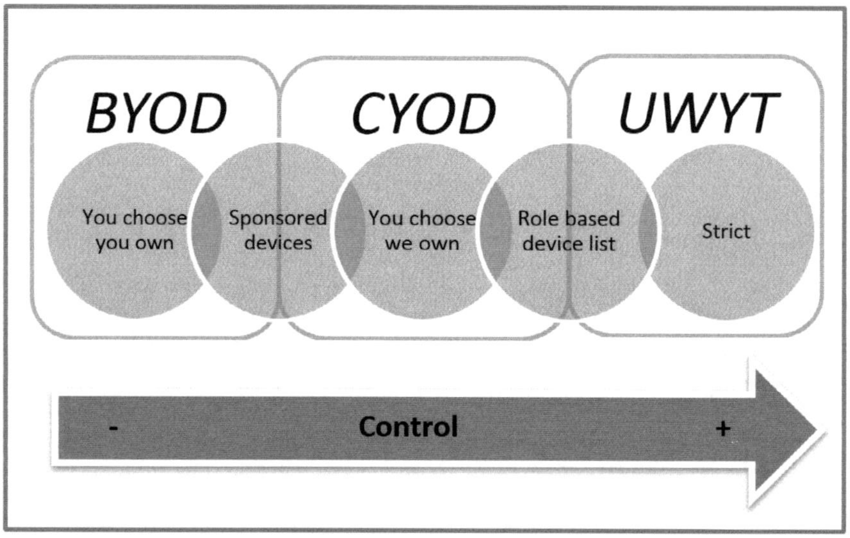

Figure 1. Strategies for mobile devices and the amount of control from the organisation

2. METHOD

This study uses a qualitative research methodology. First, a literature review was conducted with an approach from Webster and Watson (2002). The steps used in the literature review were:

1. An extensive literature search using the WorldCat search engine with different search terms connected to BYOD.
2. Manual screening for relevance (where relevance requires that the article both falls within the mobile/dual-use definition and focuses on policy, management or strategic issues, rather than technical issues).
3. Backward chaining by reviewing the citations in the articles identified as relevant in step 2.
4. Complementary forward chaining search in Web of Knowledge, Academic Search Elite, ScienceDirect, ACM, Emerald, Springer, IEEE and Wiley.

After a literature review, 12 semi-structured interviews were conducted with CIO, CSO, CFO, CSIO or head of IT in food industry, manufacturing industry, defence industry, health care, municipality and different types of consulting firms. The size of their organisations goes from 50 to 15 000 employees. The objective is 'to gather data on attitudes, opinions, impressions and beliefs of human subjects' (Jenkins 1985).

Data analysis was conducted using content analysis (Silverman 2001; Berelson 1952; Krippendorff 2004). As a technique, content analysis yields 'a relatively systematic and comprehensive summary or overview of the dataset as a whole' (Wilkinson, 1997;170). It operates by observing repeating themes and categorizing them using a coding system. Categories can be elicited in a grounded way or can (as in our case) originate from an external source such as a theoretical model (Wilkinson 1997). The coding scheme was developed from the framework presented in the next section.

2.1 Analysis Framework

Webster and Watson (2002) also require that a literature review be concept-centric, where the concepts determine the 'organizing framework' of the review. Concepts may derived from the analysis, but a common practice is to adopt a suitable conceptual framework from the literature. Brodin (2015) created a framework for BYOD adoption which later was used by Brodin et al. (2015) to identify management issues for BYOD. The chosen framework for this paper derived from the seven BYOD management issues, figure 2, that Brodin et al. (2015) identified before moving on to designing a strategy.

Framework category		BYOD management issues
Analysis	expectations	1. *personal productivity*
		2. *time/space flexibility*
		3. *user satisfaction*
	environment	4. *information control*
		5. *device protection*
	resources and capability	6. *awareness*
		7. *support*

Figure 2. The framework used in this analysis, adapted from Brodin et al. (2015)

3. BYOD

In literature about BYOD there are three main benefits that usually are highlighted; increased personal productivity, increased flexibility of time and place and increased user satisfaction (Brodin et al. 2015). Studies show that users which are allowed to use the same device for both private and work purpose works a lot more than others and saves hundreds of hours each year for their company (Miller & Varga 2011; iPass 2011; Barbier et al. 2012). This is due to the flexibility to work whenever and wherever the employee wants. This flexibility may not only be a benefit, not to the private life at least. In a study the respondents talks about how their partners are planning holidays where there is no mobile coverage or caught them in the middle of the night reading e-mails (Orlikowski 2007). Another study concluded that this flexibility is proven to increase work overload (Yun et al. 2012). While the increased use of mobile devices may harm the family life, a life without mobile devices could be painful for the user. In a study by iPass, 52 percent gave a negative emotional response to a week without their mobile device and almost 50 percent said that their mobile work environment contributed positively to their overall health (iPass 2011).

The mobile work climate will lead to a work and private life overlap and if the user does not have to switch between a personal and a work device the satisfaction will increase. A side effect will be that personal and work data may be mixed and questions about privacy may be raised. (Anderson 2013) Users tend to resist functions like encryption and remote wipe, when they are forced to them by their organisation, they consider that it encroaches on their privacy (Pettey & Van Der Meulen 2012). This makes it more difficult for the organisation to make sure that all devices that contain organisational data are secured to a minimum level. With devices all around the world with questionable security level the control over the information gets harder to keep. What will happen to the data when the device that it is stored on is lost or stolen, or if the employee leaves the organisation?

The security awareness is a problem in a lot of organisations. In a survey, 40 % said that they do not update their software and 25 % did not understand why you should update at all (Skype et al. 2012). Another study showed that even if the device is updated the security level is low; only 10 % of all tablets and 25 % of all smartphones got auto-locking and for laptops the share is 33 % (Camp 2012). Walker-Brown (2013) observes that "users only think about security when they either lose their data, or are blocked from accessing it", which seems to be true according to the surveys above. Another awareness problem comes with the policies, there are a lot of studies that shows that users do not obey and in many cases not even aware of BYOD and security policies (Cisco 2013; Oliver 2012)

Support for BYOD is a tricky question, the users expect the same level of support as they had with their company owned standard devices (Brooks 2013). At the same time causes the new flora of devices, with different operating system, problem for IT managers and their existing IT infrastructures (Intel 2012). This gives an increasing cost for support and administration, which reduces productivity in other areas for the IT professionals (Walters 2013). In the end, the saved money from devices were eaten up by increased cost of managing the IT environment (Harris et al. 2012).

Table 1. Management issues for BYOD

Management issues	BYOD
1. ***personal productivity***	Increase since the employees can work from any place at any time and go a device that they are familiar with.
2. ***time/space flexibility***	Very high
3. ***user satisfaction***	High, since they use a device they know and like. Although lower if they used to CYOD.
4. ***information control***	Unsure, organisational data may remain on private devices.
5. ***device protection***	Up to the user.
6. ***awareness***	More important since private, uncontrolled devices are used.
7. ***support***	Problem mainly for the network. Complex with a lot of different devices with no control software.

4. CYOD

When the users are allowed to choose their own devices without having to pay for them, a lot of the benefits from BYOD occur and a bit more control remains in the organisation. A key here is that the employer own the device and got the right to some control in exchange, the employee is allowed to, to some extent, also use the device for private purpose. The respondents, which uses CYOD, had a problem to see any argument for changing to BYOD. As one of the respondents said: "Yes, we would have saved some hundred dollars every year if we had asked staff to bring their own devices, get the installations and the images they need to do their job. But then we lose a competitive advantage that we have over our competitors. Then the staff would say; okay, I'll now have to pay €1500 every two years out of my own pockets, just to get the right tools to do my job. And then they start at our competitors instead."

So, what are the benefits with CYOD? Compared to a non-mobile or strictly on workplace strategy we got, just like BYOD, flexibility of time and place. That comes, of course, with every strategy that allows the user to bring their device outside the organisation wall. Almost all respondents said that one of the most important benefits with go-mobile is that their users can work whenever and where ever they like. Although not everyone sees this as a pure benefit, four of the respondents highlighted this as a problem, if the employees start to work more or less 24 hours a day and gets available even after regular working hours. In one of these organisations they just implemented a system where the employees got two phone numbers, one which the colleagues and clients gets and that is turned off after work hours and one for friends and relatives. The other three had had discussions about turning off mail-sync on evenings and weekends or instructing managers to think about the time they send email to their employees.

Personal productivity is raised both as a benefit and a threat. Most of the respondents can see an increased productivity connected to the new flexible way to work, although one respondent could see a risk that the users started to pay more attention to private social media and games during work hours and thus reduces productivity. Two of the respondents thought that the benefit of employees working on private time is eaten up by the time they spend on private internet browsing and mailing during work hours.

When it comes to user satisfaction, it is more about convenience than who owns the device. If the user is allowed to use the device for private purposes as well and do not need to carry, for instance, two smartphones the satisfaction level will increase. On the other hand, the satisfaction rate depends on what the user got before. Almost all respondents say that their employees do not want to go from CYOD to BYOD. One respondent replied to the question about BYOD with; "Yes, though it's not interesting in Sweden. It adds nothing. There is not potential for it. There is no way for it financially and no incentive to do that so it's not a fact as I see it."

Although CYOD brings a lot of positive things there are some concern. The concerns are based on the mobility and the increased exposure of information and devices. Or as one respondent expressed it: "The most dangerous thing we have, we'd rather not use mobile devices. But we have to, because otherwise we need to sit at the customer at all times. Sometimes we have to take some risks but we try to avoid mobile media as far as possible."

A major concern is control of information and the fact that information gets more exposed when it get outside the organisations walls. The biggest concern in this context is crosstalk and shoulder surfing while working on trains and other public places. The concern goes also to the private time: "You do not carry around on a computer when you are at the pub, but a phone, you can actually take with you to the pub." One of the respondent said that their work with a mobile device strategy was motivated by taking back control. "We had said no to tablets and saw that we had 5-600 linked to our network, though we said no. It was just a paper policy, nothing else that ruled… This one had just grown freely. So the focus of making mobility was that we felt that we must take control over our mobile devices and ensure that the data stays at the company."

Related to the concern about control is the one about device protection -how to keep information safe even if a device is lost or stolen. Some of the respondents felt safe with their MDM-tool and PIN-lock while others did not fully trust the safety functions on the phone in the same manner as the ones on the laptops. Although very few had experienced this threat in reality in any significant way.

Almost all respondents believed more in training than policies. "Since we think that the human is the weak link, we push hard on education." It was a common sense that users do not fully understand and know the content of long policies. A lot of the respondent tries to keep their policies on one page and focus to work with education and the culture, at least in the SME. One example is to integrate the security in other context, like when introducing something new or at an internal annual sales conference. "We try and get it as an integral part, and not just a bunch of requirements and horrible policies, read 20 pages and sign you will get your... It should rather hang together and be natural in my opinion. And then we try to introduce it in a selling mode as well."

One respondent thought that the employees are good at policies that concern them. "But it's just like, I do not know all the regulations surrounding shapes and colours that you can use, I have been reprimanded for that. ... Nah, I don't think it is possible, we have our field and must be clear in our communications and show good examples and be able to follow up. We have a mission to ensure information rivers, computers and data." In one of the companies they try to avoid policies and believed in another form of communication. "From the company, we have said that we do not want to throw us into and become structurally organized in every detail, but we want the be a company that keeps our flexibility and employee's ability to think and make their own decisions, but if we notice that there is a problem, many make a mistake or in a way that is not good or many begin to come to me with questions, many are asking questions about the same thing. Then we see that there is a need to structure the information and make a policy to clarify things."

The introduction of mobile devices has not increased the workload for the support team. Even though the total number of different devices in the organisation has increased, most of the respondents still got the same amount of employees in their service desk. This is due to smother synchronization tools and easy to use operating systems on the devices. And since all devices are owned by the organisation they can make sure that all accounts work, synchronization is in place and the device is connected to the right network before it is handed out to the user.

Table 2. Management issues for CYOD

Management issues	CYOD
1. personal productivity	Increase since the employees can work from any place at any time and go a device that they are familiar with.
2. time/space flexibility	Very high
3. user satisfaction	High, since they choose device by them self and do not have to pay for it.
4. information control	Information may be stored outside the organisation.
5. device protection	Organisation control the device.
6. awareness	Important
7. support	Organisation configure and control the device. Same pressure on service desk as before mobile devices.

5. COMPARISON AND DISCUSSION

In many ways, BYOD and CYOD are quite similar. The perceived benefits are the same, both solutions provide increased productivity, flexibility, and user satisfaction. In the interviews the respondent felt that a user that can choose any device they like but do not have to pay for it do not want to start pay for the same device. A company owned device, which the user is allowed to use for private purpose as well gave a higher value than if the user ha to bring their own device. Although using only a private device are better than a strictly work device.

The main difference is found in what the literature describes as concerns, in this case the control and protection of information and devices. The control part is largely the same, when the information leaves the organisation's safe embrace creates a concern. Where is the information? Regardless of whether the unit is private or not, there is a high risk that the organisation's data is mixed with private data, and in the end, it will be difficult to distinguish on who owns what. For BYOD there is an extra factor which creates even more concern; what will happen to the data when the employee leaves the organisation? The person will still keep the device where the data is stored.

When a device is private, the responsibility for the protection of it are handed over to the user. The move from organisational control of the device to private raises a lot of security concerns and increases the demand on the user for security awareness. This concern still exists for CYOD, but since the device, in a broader sense, are controlled by the organisation the concern is more related to the trust on the technology.

Security awareness has always been important and with the new mobile climate it is even more important, no matter who owns and control the device. Since the organisation can force the user to adjust to a minimum level of security on the device the organisation control the awareness is even more important for users of private devices. They have to understand why the security is needed and what can happen if the device not meet the requirement.

The impact on the support has been discussed in literature about BYOD and it goes from very little to major impact. The problem is not the devices by them self, most of the users know their device and how to handle them. The problem is more about making them work in the organisational infrastructure and connect to the right resources. For CYOD, this become less of a problem since the IT department configure the device and make sure it works in the environment before handing it over to the end user. With BYOD there may be a lot of devices in the network, since a single user may bring a lot of private devices, for CYOD the organisation know exactly how many devices each employee got and how much pressure the network has to handle.

Table 3. Comparison of management issues for BYOD and CYOD

Management issues	BYOD	CYOD
1. personal productivity	Increase since the employees can work from any place at any time and go a device that they are familiar with.	Increase since the employees can work from any place at any time and go a device that they are familiar with.
2. time/space flexibility	Very high	Very high
3. user satisfaction	High, since they use a device they know and like. Although lower if they used to CYOD.	High, since they choose device by them self and do not have to pay for it.
4. information control	Unsure, organisational data may remain on private devices.	Information may be stored outside the organisation.
5. device protection	Up to the user.	Organisation control the device.
6. awareness	More important since private, uncontrolled devices are used.	Important
7. support	Problem mainly for the network. Complex with a lot of different devices with no control software.	Organisation configure and control the device. Same pressure on service desk as before mobile devices.

6. CONCLUSIONS

In this article we investigated the difference between BYOD and CYOD from a management perspective. We have conducted a structured literature review and interviewed 12 CIO's in different organisations, both private and public. Our findings is that most of the benefits that come with BYOD also come with CYOD, but the concerns may not give the same impacts.

- RQ1: Which managerial issues are connected to both BYOD and CYOD?

Our findings are that it is mostly the benefits that are connected to both approaches. The personal productivity does apply to both, although for inexperienced users it may be a greater profit with BYOD. This since they will use something they already know, on the other hand, with CYOD, they will probably select the kind of device that they already are familiar with. If a CYOD device is allowed to be used even for private purposes the increased flexibility of time and space will be the exact same for both BYOD and CYOD. These two benefits will, in both cases, lead to an increased user satisfaction.

- RQ2: What is the difference between BYOD and CYOD from a managerial perspective?

Most of the differences appear around the security aspects, how to protect information on mobile devices. When a device is owned by the organisation they have more control of the device and can apply policies to it. On a privately owned device, it is up to the user to secure the device and its information. When an employee leaves the organisation a CYOD device can be completely erased, but for a BYOD device, it is up to the user to remove all data that belongs to their former employer. If the user allows the employer to use an MDM-tool on their device, the control gap between CYOD and BYOD decreases. Another issue that separates CYOD from BYOD is the possibility of deeper investigation in cases of suspected policy violation. If the device is CYOD the employer can take the device and commit a forensic investigation, if it is BYOD the employer has no right to apprehend the device and cannot carry out the investigation. Furthermore, the workload for the IT-department increases when handling BYOD. With BYOD the user can have more than one device on the network, which requires more network capacity and secondly, more devices require more help from the IT-Support.

Our conclusion is that, even if the cost of the devices themselves are higher with CYOD, the increased level of security and information control outweigh the economical disadvantages.

REFERENCES

Anderson, N., 2013. Cisco Bring Your Own Device - Device Freedom Without, San Jose: Cisco Systems, Inc.

Barbier, J. et al., 2012. Cisco IBSG Horizons Study. , p.5.

Berelson, B., 1952. Content analysis in communicative research, New York: Free Press.

Brodin, M., 2015. Combining ISMS with Strategic Management: The case of BYOD. IADIS International Conference Information Systems, pp.161–168.

Brodin, M., Rose, J. & Åhlfeldt, R.-M., 2015. Management issues for Bring Your Own Device. , 2015, pp.1–12.

Brooks, T., 2013. Classic enterprise IT: the castle approach. Network Security, 2013(6), pp.14–16. Available at: http://linkinghub.elsevier.com/retrieve/pii/S1353485813700709 [Accessed November 22, 2013].

Camp, C., 2012. The BYOD security challenge - How scary is the iPad, tablet, smartphone surge. Available at: http://blog.eset.com/2012/02/28/sizing-up-the-byod-security-challenge [Accessed July 15, 2013].

Cisco, 2013. Cisco Security Intelligence - Annual Security Report & Cisco Connected World Technology Report,

Harris, J., Ives, B. & Junglas, I., 2012. IT Consumerization: When Gadgets Turn Into Enterprise IT Tools. MIS Quarterly, 2012(September), pp.99–112.

Intel, 2012. Insights on the current state of BYOD in the Enterprise – Intel's IT Manager Survey,

iPass, I., 2011. iPass Global Mobile Workforce Report 2011Q3. Workforce, pp.1–27.

Jenkins, A.M., 1985. Research Methodologies and MIS Research. In E. Mumford, ed. Research Methods in Information Systems. Amsterdam, Holland: Elsevier Science Publishers B.V.

Kane, C. et al., 2014. Building The Business Case For A Bring-Your-Own-Device (BYOD) Program,

Krippendorff, K.H., 2004. Content Analysis: An Introduction to Its Methodology, Thousand Oaks, CA: Sage Publications Ltd.

Miller, R.E. & Varga, J., 2011. Benefits of Enabling Personal Handheld Devices in the Enterprise - Intel, IT@Intel White Paper.

Oliver, R., 2012. Why the BYOD boom is changing how we think about business it. Engineering and technology, 7(10), p.28.

Orlikowski, W.J., 2007. Sociomaterial Practices: Exploring Technology at Work. Organization Studies, 28(9), pp.1435–1448. Available at: http://oss.sagepub.com/cgi/doi/10.1177/0170840607081138.

Pettey, C. & Van Der Meulen, R., 2012. Gartner identifies three security hurdles to overcome when shifting from enterprise-owned devices to BYOD. Gartner Inc. Available at: http://www.gartner.com/newsroom/id/2263115 [Accessed July 20, 2013].

Silverman, D., 2001. Interpreting qualitative data, London: SAGE Publications Ltd.

Skype, Norton & TomTom, 2012. Survey finds nearly half of consumers fail to upgrade software regularly and one quarter of consumers do not know why to update software. Available at: http://about.skype.com/press/2012/07/survey_finds_nearly_half_fail_to_upgrade.html [Accessed October 19, 2015].

Walters, R., 2013. Bringing IT out of the shadows. Network Security, 2013(4), pp.5–11. Available at: http://linkinghub.elsevier.com/retrieve/pii/S1353485813700497 [Accessed November 22, 2013].

Webster, J. & Watson, R.T., 2002. Webster and Watson literature review. MIS Quarterly, 26(2), p.11.

Wilkinson, S., 1997. Focus group research. In D. Silverman, ed. Qualitative research: Theory, method and practice. London: Sage Publications Ltd.

Yun, H., Kettinger, W.J. & Lee, C.C., 2012. A New Open Door: The Smartphone's Impact on Work-to-Life Conflict, Stress, and Resistance, *International Journal of Electronic Commerce*, *16*(4), 121-152. doi:10.2753/jec1086-4415160405

OPTIMIZING DECISION SUPPORT IN BUSINESS PROCESS MANAGEMENT USING OBLIGATION AND PROHIBITION NORMS

Thomas Keller[1] and Bastin Tony Roy Savarimuthu[2]
[1]*Institute of Business Information Systems, Zurich University of Applied Sciences, Switzerland*
[2]*Department of Information Science, University of Otago, Dunedin, New Zealand*

ABSTRACT

Social norms constrain behavior of individuals either through obligating or prohibiting certain types of behavior. Norm-based mechanisms have only recently found applications in enhancing decisions of knowledge workers in an automated business process management context. While previous work on such social BPM has focused on the use of prohibition norms based approach for norm inference, this paper extends the work by combining both prohibition and obligation norm based approaches to provide a holistic approach of norm inference. The norms inferred in the context of business process executions are then recommended to users so as to enable them to make informed decisions. The previous work on prohibition norm inference focused on identifying failure cases, which is now complemented by first inferring norms from the successful process execution cases (i.e. obligations) and then inferring prohibition norms. This approach based on considering social feedback (i.e. inferring what is obliged and prohibited from history logs of process execution) shows encouraging results under uncertain business environments. Using simulation results the paper demonstrates that using the norm based mechanism results in reduced failure rates in the decision making of a knowledge worker while still providing maximum flexibility for the user to choose from a range of actions to execute.

KEYWORDS

Operational Decision Support, Norm Inference, Process Mining.

1. INTRODUCTION

Automation in many domains based on business process models has progressed rapidly during the last few years. The rate of penetration differs from industry to industry and is still today led by manufacturing and supply chain management. The reason for a widespread penetration across diverse domains may not just be the maturity [4] of the respective industry but the reason also lies in the type of business processes [9]. Highly standardized processes and well-defined supportive processes are conducive for automation. However, there remain the vast majority of processes that still need a knowledge worker in the loop to make decisions. The support that can be provided to these knowledge workers [6] in the respective context using a social norms approach is the topic of this paper.

Norms are expectations of behavior observed in human societies [22]. Norms provide guidance about how one has to behave in a certain situation (e.g. tipping in restaurants). However, there is also the possibility of violation. This is the freedom enjoyed by the individuals through their autonomy. There are different types of norms followed by societies such as prohibitions, obligations and permissions and these are often called as deontic norms [14].

In this paper, we are interested in prohibition and obligation norms because these norms specify which actions are prohibited and obliged in a society (e.g. not littering a park and the obligation to buy a ticket when using the public transport). Prior research in human societies [9] shows that there are more prescriptive norms (i.e. obligations) than proscriptive norms (prohibitions). However, proscriptive norms were found to be stronger than prescriptive norms.

2. RELATED WORK

Our work in this paper is related to works in several areas [9]. Related work can be found in the areas of a) decision support systems, b) process mining (a specific application of data mining), and c) agent based systems and d) business process management. We describe the related work in these areas in the rest of this section.

Decision support systems integrated in a business process management context can mainly be found in engineering design and manufacturing [13]. The manufacturing area has shown that decision support and operational processes need to be properly integrated [25]. Such a decision support system writes process related data to a knowledge base which is then used by subsequent applications by implementing respective rules and user constraints. This can include robots or other devices in a highly automated production environment. The generated data is fed back to the decision support system which then provides insights into changes to be made. Hence, the feedback loop is closed (i.e. data produced by the system leads to insights which then are implemented as rules in the system). The work presented in this paper differs in that the scope comprises decisions that are not formally describable by rules and conditions and are therefore intrinsically human based.

In less structured situations a decision might not just be the result of applying rules. Therefore decision makers try to adapt old solutions which have shown successful results, to slightly different problem situations. This approach is well known as case based reasoning (CBR) [12] and can be found, for example inthe health industry. For example in [3], chronic disease prognosis and diagnosis is done by integrating CBR with data mining technology. CBR is used for knowledge inference, refining and sharing. An example for business process analysis in the Health Care industry is described in [17]. A general overview of clinical decision support systems in the US can be found in [15], and a specific application for a surgery theatre planning is described by [2]. The work in here is suitable to extend the solutions presented in the above examples from a human-oriented perspective.

Process automation as proposed in [16] aims at substituting human knowledge by artificial (inferred) knowledge. The motivation is to lower cost and time. To ensure decision quality the integration of business data must be ensured while making sure that the data quality remains high. Our approach aims at supporting human decision, not to substitute it. The introduction of decision support in business processes is also described in [26], which is in-line with the higher level goal of this work. Domain specific rules are expected to be available and are then applied on the available process data. Our approach differs in that prohibition and obligation norms are first inferred (i.e. not available ahead of time as in [26] in the form of rules) and then applied.

Process simulation as described in [19] comes closest to our focus. Process mining is used to extract knowledge from log files produced by the process engine which is complemented by actual data of the respective process instance. However, our emphasis is on showing the impact of a changing business environment and the power of norm inference as known in the multi agent systems field [20,21].

Successful business process automation relies on well-defined processes that are stable and have ideally no variations [6]. As soon as business processes comprise ill-structured business cases decisions need to be human based. Our approach aims at supporting these decisions by inferring norms, which are inherently human-based.

3. EXPERIMENTAL SETUP

3.1 Motivation

In multi-agent systems, researchers have investigated mechanisms for norm inference based on observing actions of agents (i.e. software entities) and their interactions. For example, in a multi-player online game, based on chat logs and the record of actions individual game players undertake, social norms can be inferred. A sample norm could be that an agent that was helped by another agent to slay a dragon is obliged to reciprocate help when the other agent is in need. These identified norms can then form the basis of decision making (which actions are forbidden and which actions are obligated). Researchers have developed two norm identification algorithms to identify prohibition [20] and obligation norms respectively [21]. In this paper, we present the case that the applications of norms, where knowledge inferred through the identification of obligation and prohibition norms is key to support knowledge workers in their complex business tasks. Also, we suggest that the norm-based approach shows enough flexibility to adapt to changing business environments.

3.2 Process Model

The process model shown in Figure 1 is an abstraction of a two phase work arrangement as it occurs for releasing documents to appropriate stakeholders or a scenario involving the treatment of a patient involved in an accident at the emergency department. The first phase consists of an assessment of the input (either a document or a patient) and based on this assessment the best alternative is chosen. There is a choice of three alternatives for our simulation[1]. The assessment of the input is considered to be a human task for a knowledge worker like a medical doctor. In our work, we assume that one of the alternatives is the best and will mostly result in a satisfactory output. In a real -environment the assessor will have a certain probability to choose the right (most suitable) alternative. For simulation purposes we replace a human assessor by a random generator which equates to the worst possible scenario (i.e. to start with decisions made at random[2]).

The result of the choice made is evaluated by a control gate (control gate 1 shown in Figure 1). The control gate is a placeholder for any possible imaginable way to evaluate the result of the antecedent steps in the process. It may be a qualitative social feedback system (e.g. based on historical data of past acceptances and rejections of waiting times for similar cases) or an evaluation by an expert (e.g. whether or not the waiting time was deemed appropriate by the expert). The simulation system models the evaluation of the choices made by the human knowledge worker.

Table 1. Success criteria for different input domains and alternatives available

		Alternatives		
		D	E	F
Input domain	A	Pass	Fail	Fail
	B	Fail	Pass	Fail
	C	Fail	Fail	Pass

The second phase consists again of three alternatives and works analogously.

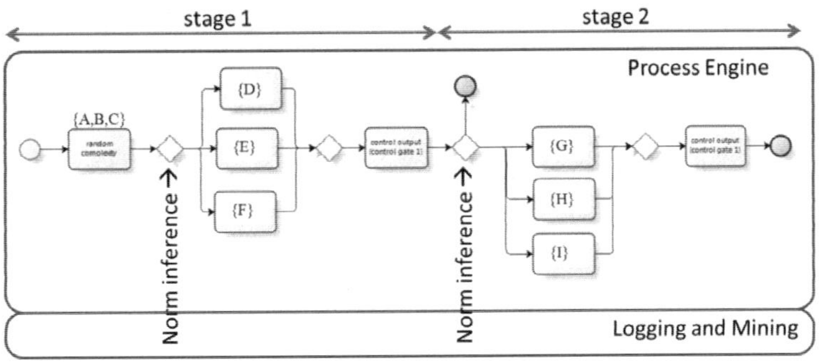

Figure 1. Important aspects of norm inference in the context of an abstract business process

[1] However, in theory, there are no limitations in the number of alternatives.

[2] There is an even worse situation imaginable when an assessor on purpose chooses the wrong alternative. Since we consider this as unnatural this is not further considered.

3.3 Uncertainty

The introduction of uncertainty models human behavior. Human behavior is inherently non deterministic and features errors. The uncertainty is introduced by the two decision points in the process model. Uncertainty means that a good case is accidentally judged as a bad case or a bad case is accidentally judged as good case. An uncertainty given in 'u%' means that u% of cases are erroneous cases (false negatives and positives).

We can now distinguish between two scenarios. A sequence is already identified as an obligation (a good case) but a later observation of the same sequence is now labelled as a bad case. One possible reasoning is that the bad case is erroneous and must be ignored. Another reason could be that the obligation norm is now obsolete and must be replaced by a respective prohibition (e.g. action A was originally obligated but now is prohibited).

We have examined two approaches that take into consideration the execution sequence of successful cases and failure cases. The first approach is based on the simple majority rule [9] and the second one is based on the Bayes rule [2]. We conducted simulations with both these approaches and found that these approaches yield the same results[3]. The results reported hereafter were obtained by using the simple majority approach that is based on weighting the historic data. The reasoning is based on the fact that the knowledge of 'u' can only be anticipated (i.e. not known prior, while the simple majority rule can be easily computed based on historical data).

3.4 Controlling the Time Window

In this paper we claim that our approach can handle a changing business environment, and also can accommodate changing social behavior in case of social feedback mechanisms and employee turnover. For example, it could happen that action A originally obligation might turn out be a costly due to changing circumstance, hence now has to be prohibited. Or, action A may have to be prohibited because the employee who carried out this activity has been replaced by a junior staff member who isn't effective, yet.

In order for a system to meets its goals in terms of keeping below the to-be error rate, it should constantly monitor the current error-rate. If the current-error rate is high, it must undergo changes so as to minimize the difference between the two with the ultimate goal of keeping the error rate under the to-be rate. To facilitate this adaptability in the system, we introduce a controller.

The controller shown in Figure 2 sets the time window based on a given failure rate comparing it to the as-is (current) failure rate and makes appropriate adjustments (increases or decreases it).

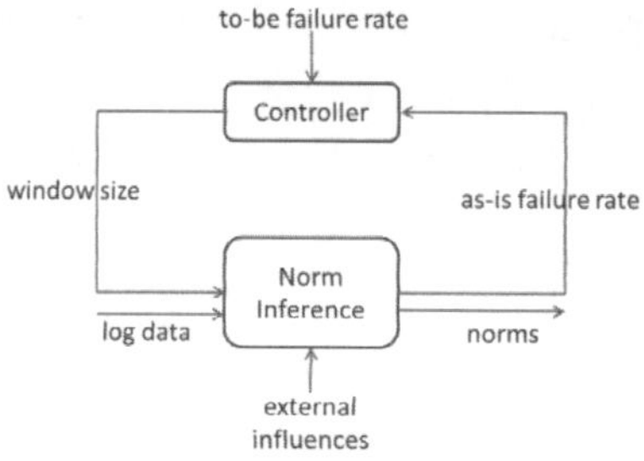

Figure 2. Schematic diagram of the controller and norm inference system

We assume that the shorter the sliding time window (L) the higher the resulting failure rate (f). This is because shorter time windows capture fewer evidences of successses and failure instances, resulting in not so precise inferences. Based on this assumption the controller derives the length of the window size for the subsequent iteration using the following equations:

[3] It does not mean that they may not show different behavior by changing other parameters not considered herein.

$$L_{window}(t_{i+1}) = \begin{cases} L_{window}(t_i) + k_1 * \frac{df}{dt} + k_2, \; if \; \frac{df}{dt} > 0 \; and \; f(t_i) > f_{to-be} \\ L_{window}(t_i) + k_1 * \frac{df}{dt} - k_2, \; if \; \frac{df}{dt} \leq 0 \; and \; f(t_i) \leq f_{to-be} \end{cases} \quad (1)$$

3.5 Hypotheses

In our work, instances of the business processes shown in Figure 1 are generated with random input. Each input fits exactly one alternative in phases 1 and 2. Process instances only terminate successfully when input matches the chosen alternative. This leads to a failure rate of 8/9 respectively to a success rate of 1/9. Note that out of 27 cases that are possible, only three cases (ADG, BEH or DFI) will succeed.

Our hypothesis is now that in a context with a *given uncertainty 'u', norm inference can bring the as-is (current) failure rate 'r' in the system down to as low as the uncertainty* (Hypothesis 1 (H1)). A lower value below 'u' is theoretically not possible because the uncertainty produces these failures that cannot be avoided. However, achieving a failure rate 'r' as low as the uncertainty 'u' means that the erroneous cases do not have a negative impact on norm inference (i.e. the norm inference mechanism is sound). In other words, we claim that our approach is able to identify erroneous cases correctly even in the presence of uncertainty.

Furthermore we argue that *with the active controlling of the time window we can reduce the window size depending on the gap between the to-be failure rate 'z' and the uncertainty 'u'* (Hypothesis 2 – (H2)). If uncertainty is larger, we need a larger window size to minimize to-be error. On the other hand if environment changes fast (e.g. action A now is prohibited), we need a smaller window size. So, there is a trade-off between the to-be failure rate 'z' and the adaptability of the system which should be balanced at the system level.

4. EXPERIMENTAL RESULTS

The results are organized along the two hypotheses H1 and H2. They consist of graphs with associated summary tables. All the graphs below show on the x-axis the number of instances simulated. The y-axis shows the to-be failure rates achieved.

Our hypothesis H1 states that we can bring down the actual failure rate as low as the uncertainty is. This is achieved by using an adequately long time window for norm inference. The following table demonstrates this, based on the result of a simulation series with different fixed time windows (100, 200, 500 and 1000) and three different uncertainties (0, 5 and 10). The duration of the simulation is fixed to 5000 iterations. The output variable is the actual failure rate in the system (shown as an average value in column 3).

Table 2. Failure rates in dependence on time window and uncertainty

#	Time window [#]	uncertainty [%]	Failure rate [%]
1	100	0	10
2	100	5	18
3	100	10	22
4	200	0	6
5	200	5	12
6	200	10	17
7	500	0	2
8	500	5	7
9	500	10	13
10	1000	0	2
11	1000	5	7
12	1000	10	12

A graphical visualization of the figures in Table 1 as shown in Figure 3 makes the results easier to interpret.

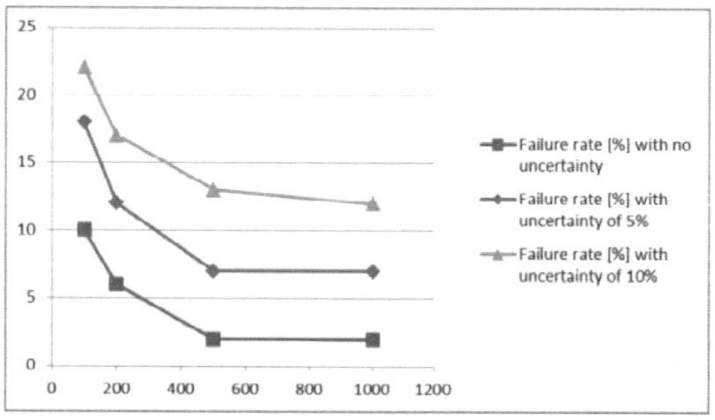

Figure 3. Visualization of the failure rate in dependence of the time window and uncertainty

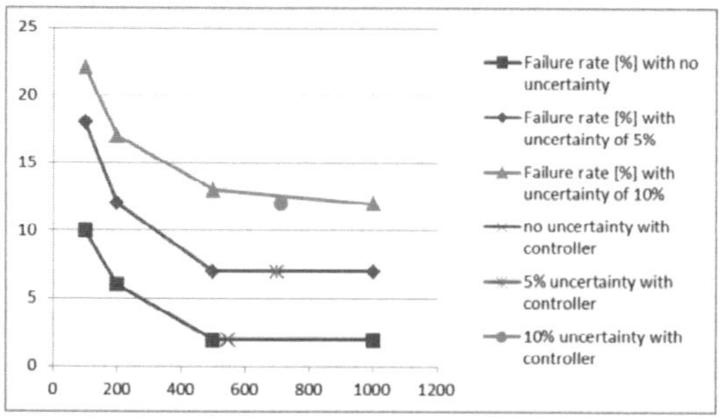

Figure 4. Visualization and comparison of failure rates

There are two main observations that can be made from Figure 3 (and Table 2). First, when uncertainty is increased within a time window, the failure rates increase (see cases 1, 2 and 3). Second, when uncertainty is kept constant and the time window is increased, the failure rates decrease (see cases 1, 4, 7 and 10). So, to achieve the same failure rates under increased uncertainty, one needs to increase the window sizes.

In cases with no uncertainty (cases 1, 4, 7 and 10) point towards the minimal failure rate that can be achieved by the system through norm inference, for a given time window. In our case it is 2% provided that the fixed time window is long enough (see runs 4 and 7). The best result under no uncertainty is achieved for a time window of 500.

The other two cases include an uncertainty of 5% and 10% respectively. The result for failure rate in these cases is related to the case with no uncertainty. The resulting failure rate is the sum of the failure rate at no uncertainty plus the introduced uncertainty, again provided that the time window is sufficient long. For example, the failure rate for time window 1000 for uncertainty five is 7%. This is the failure rate for run 10 plus the uncertainty for run 11 (2+5=7).

The above findings support hypothesis H1. It should be noted that our norm inference approach still leaves us with a minimal failure rate of 2%. However, it should be noted that introducing uncertainty does not add any additional failure rate produced by our norm inference system (i.e. the failure rate observed is a function of uncertainty plus the base failure rate when there is no uncertainty as demonstrated in the example above). This implies that the norm inference is stable against uncertainty.

Note that the time window is fixed in the results shown in Table 1. Towards validating the second hypothesis (H2), the controller is activated which varies the time window. The new parameter that needs to be scrutinized in this context is the to-be failure rate shown in column 3 Table 3 which is compared against the actual failure rate shown in column 5. As we now know from the previous simulation results that we need to allow a minimal failure rate of 2% as a premium on top of the uncertainty.

Table 3. Window size and failure rate in dependence of uncertainty and to-be failure rate

#	Uncertainty [%]	To-be failure rate [%]	Actual window size [#]	Actual failure rate [%]
1	0	2	548	2
2	0	5	207	5
3	0	10	87	10
4	5	7	250 - 700	7
5	5	10	180 - 330	10
6	5	15	70 - 125	15
7	10	12	275 - 710	12
8	10	15	120 - 340	15
9	10	20	50 - 160	20

Two observations can be made from the results shown in Table 3. A first and important observation is that the controller is able to adjust the window size in such a way that the current failure rate (in column 5) matches the to-be failure rate (in column 3). This is true for all cases 1 to 9 of the above table.

Now let's have a look at cases 1, 4 and 7 and compare them with the results from Table 2. It can be noticed that these match (approximately), cases 7, 8 and 9 respectively in Figure 3. To further elaborate this, Figure 3 has been updated by these additional 3 cases and is shown in Figure 4. The resulting window sizes obtained (denoted as a dot, asterisk and a cross in Figure 4), lie on the curves of the first simulation series which again proves the correct and consistent simulation results.

A second observation is that the bandwidth of the controlled window size can be considerably large. It grows with the uncertainty. This can be inferred by comparing three sets of cases 4 and 7, 5 and 8 and 6 and 9. This has to be carefully interpreted because the controller has not been fine tuned. It is most likely that the bandwidth can be optimized by adjusting the parameters of the controller. However, this is not further investigated as it is outside the scope of this paper.

The results from Table 3 support hypothesis H2. The controlled window size is reduced when allowing a higher failure rate. For example, the range of window size (70-125) for case 6 involving a high to-be failure rate is lower than cases 4 and 5 involving lower failure rates. Note that this behavior is independent from the uncertainty. Comparing cases 4 to 6 against 7 to 9 support this statement (i.e. they show decreased range of window sizes as the to-be failure rates increase). This finding is important because the smaller the window size the higher the adaptability for a changing business environment. This clearly demonstrates that one needs to find a suitable tradeoff between adaptability and failure rate. In the context of an example, if action A is now prohibited, then a shorter window time is beneficial (since it accommodates the changeability), however if A is still obligated, one needs sufficiently large window size to keep the current failure rate below the to-be failure rate.

5. CONCLUSION

The overarching implications of our work are three-fold to the area of Business Process Management. First, the notion of obligation and prohibition norms has seldom been considered in the BPM field. We believe it is important that a socially-based BPM system should consider these features as norm-based thinking is ingrained in human societies [10]. Second, we have demonstrated that even in the presence of noise (uncertainty), we can improve the decision making in an organization by recommending the right actions to do (i.e. norm recommendation), by minimizing failures, based on inferring norms (obligations and prohibitions) from historical data. Third, the norm-based approach allows for a human user to override the recommendation (i.e. the recommendations from the system can be still overridden based on the contexts), thus preserving their autonomy and providing maximum flexibility.

We believe our work here has a range of real world applications. For example, the norm inference module can easily be integrated into existing BPM suites, where human decision making capability can be assisted through making the reasons for failures apparent (i.e. if you choose actions AEF to complete a process, then the chances of failure is 75% for the complex case that is being dealt with currently). This can be easily achieved by embedding our norm inference system to the business activity monitoring.

There are several avenues for future work. First, while human societies are used to the notion of obligations and prohibitions, different cultures may prefer one more than the other. For example, prohibition norms may be more effective in Asian countries whereas obligation norms may be more effective in Western World. So, depending upon the culture in question, the same norm can be worded differently (e.g. A is prohibited 90% of the time vs. B is obliged 90% of the times, assuming B is the most suitable alternative for A). This will have consequences for the design of a social BPM providing these recommendations. This forms the focus area for our future study using a questionnaire instrument. Second, we intend to investigate the use of our system in real BPM deployments in organizations. The nature of the type of norms we target will depend upon the cultural make-up of an organization.

This paper demonstrates how a social norms based approach can be beneficial in the context of providing flexible support for knowledge workers involved in complex decision-making in an organization. This paper proposes a social BPM where social norms can be extracted from business process execution instances (prohibition and obligation norms) which can be presented to the users so that they can make informed decision-making. Using simulation results the paper shows how the inferred norms can be used to reduced failure rates in the presence of uncertainty, while still providing maximum flexibility for the knowledge worker to choose from a range of actions to execute.

REFERENCES

1. Artstein, Zvi, "Discrete and continuous bang-bang and facial spaces, or: Look for the extreme points". 1980, SIAM Review 22 (2). pp. 172–185
2. Bessière, P, Mazer, E, Ahuactzin, JM and Mekhnacha, K (2013), Bayesian Programmin, CRC Press.
3. Dahanayake, A., Welke, A. J., Cavalheiro, G., Improving the understanding of BAM technology for Real-Time Decision Support
4. De Bruin, T., & Rosemann, M. (2005). Towards a business process management maturity model.
5. Gomes, C., Sperandio, F., Borges, J., Almada-Lobo, B., Brito, A., A Decision Support System for Surgery Theatre Scheduling Problems, ENTERprise Information Systems, Communications in Computer and Information Science Volume 221, 2011, pp 213-222
6. Grünert, D., Brucker-Kley, E., Keller, Th. (2014). oBPM – An Opportunistic Approach to Business Process Modeling and Execution. International Workshop Series on Business Process Management and Social Software
7. Hofstede, G. (2011). Dimensionalizing Cultures: The Hofstede Model in Context. Online Readings in Psychology and Culture, 2(1)
8. Huang MJ, Chen MY, Lee SC (2007) Integrating data mining with case based reasoning for chronic disease prognosis. Expert Syst Appl 32:856–867
9. Inada, Ken-ichi. "The simple majority decision rule." Econometrica: Journal of the Econometric Society (1969): 490-506.
10. Jasso, Guillermina, and Karl-Dieter Opp. "Probing the character of norms: A factorial survey analysis of the norms of political action." *American Sociological Review* (1997): 947-964.
11. Keller, Th., Savarimuthu, B., (2015), A social norms based approach for enhancing decision support in business process execution
12. Kolodner J (1993) Case-based reasoning. Morgan Kaufmann Inc., California
13. Liu, S., Duffy, A. H. B., Whitfield, R. I., Integration of decision support systems to improve decision support performance, Knowledge and Information Systems, March 2010, Volume 22, Issue 3, pp 261-286
14. Meyer, J-JC, and Roel J. Wieringa. "Deontic logic: A concise overview." (1993).
15. Musen, M.A., Middleton, B., Greenes, R.A., Clinical Decision-Support Systems, Biomedical Informatics, 2014, pp 643-674
16. Niedermann, F., Maier, B., Radeschütz, S., Schwarz, H., Automated Process Decision Making Based on Integrated Source Data, Lecture Notes in Business Information Processing Volume 87, 2011, pp 160-171
17. Rebuge, A., Ferreira, D.R., Business process analysis in healthcare environments: A methodology based on process mining, Information Systems, Volume 37, Issue 2, April 2012, Pages 99-116
18. Rivera, D. E., Morari, M., & Skogestad, S. Internal model control: PID controller design. Industrial & engineering chemistry process design and development, 1986, 25(1), 252-265.
19. Rozinat, A., Wynn, M.T., van der Aalst, W.M.P., ter Hofstede, A.H.M., Fidge, C.J., Workflow simulation for operational decision support, Data & Knowledge Engineering, Volume 68, Issue 9, September 2009, Pages 834-850
20. Savarimuthu, B.T.R., Cranefield, S., Purvis, M.A and Purvis, M.K, "Identifying prohibition norms in agent societies", Artificial Intelligence and Law, Volume 21, Issue 1, pp 1-46, 2013.
21. Savarimuthu, Bastin Tony Roy, Stephen Cranefield, Maryam A. Purvis, and Martin K. Purvis. "Obligation norm identification in agent societies." Journal of Artificial Societies and Social Simulation 13, no. 4 (2010): 3.
22. Ullmann-Margalit, Edna. The emergence of norms. Oxford: Clarendon Press, 1977.
23. Xu, Hongyun, Bastin Tony Roy Savarimuthu, Aditya Ghose, Evan Morrison, Qiying Cao, and Youqun Shi. "Automatic bdi plan recognition from process execution logs and effect logs." In Engineering Multi-Agent Systems, pp. 274-291. Springer Berlin Heidelberg, 2013.
24. van der Aalst, W.M.P.: Process Mining: Discovery, Conformance and Enhancement of Business Processes. Springer, Berlin (2011)
25. Vahidov R, Kersten GE (2004) Decision station: situating decision support systems. Decis Support Syst 38:283–303
26. Van Putten, B.-J., Romeiro, C., Azevedo, L.G. (2011). Decision Support by Automatic Analysis of Business Process Models. Proceedings of the 19th European Conference on Information Systems (ECIS), June 9-11, 2011, Helsinki, Finland

INVESTIGATING THE SOURCES OF DIFFICULTIES IN MANAGING PROJECT INTERDEPENDENCIES: A STUDY OF IT/IS PROJECT PORTFOLIOS

Sameer Bathallath, Åsa Smedberg and Harald Kjellin
Department of Computer and Systems Sciences, Stockholm University
Borgarfjordsgatan 12, Postbox 7003, 164 07 Kista, Sweden

ABSTRACT

Interdependencies between projects have come to play a more active role in the decision on Information Technology/Information Systems (IT/IS) portfolios and their constituent projects. However, managing these interdependencies can be a complex task, especially when there is a high degree of uncertainty and many interdependencies between the projects. In times of unexpected events, portfolio managers may face challenges not only from handling the impact on the projects but also from handling the subsequent effects on the interdependencies of these projects. This may threaten the project portfolio from achieving its final goal. This paper presents an exploratory study aimed at investigating the sources of difficulties and challenges associated with the implementation of project interdependencies. We conducted a qualitative study using semi-structured interviews with managers from four leading organizations in Saudi Arabia. The findings reveal three main categories of factors that increased the difficulty of managing project interdependencies in IT/IS project portfolios: 1) Insufficient understanding of human responsibilities in the whole portfolio, 2) Environmental change and 3) Technology constraints.

KEYWORDS

Project portfolio management; project interdependencies management; IT/IS projects; multi-project management; complexity.

1. INTRODUCTION

Although there is much research addressing how to capitalize on inter-project interdependencies, there are still many questions to be solved concerning how to handle these interdependencies. Several studies on project portfolio management (e.g. Kundisch & Meier 2011; Heinrich et al. 2014) have stressed the role and contribution of project interdependencies in arriving at greater benefits than if a number of projects are carried out separately. As an example of these benefits, sharing of an IT infrastructure between several projects may lead to a considerable cost saving in each of these projects and hence, a cost reduction at the entire portfolio level. In this sense, well-planned and effectively managed project interdependencies can determine how well a project portfolio performs (Dwivedi et al. 2015; Killen & Kjaer 2012; Dahlgren & Soderlund 2010; Zapata et al. 2008; Bardhan et al. 2006; Müller et al. 2015). However, managing projects and their interdependencies within a portfolio is not trouble-free; it involves coping with various uncertainties and constraints (Martinsuo et al. 2014) such as availability of resources and changing of priorities. As a consequence, existing projects can be repeatedly changed, and hence, reprioritization and rescheduling of the projects and their dependencies are likely going to occur. This could add more pressure on the management team to overcome the subsequent effects of unforeseen changes in project interdependencies. A major source of this pressure is due to managerial efforts of maintaining the ultimate goal by which the projects were initially selected, grouped, and interlinked with other projects. For instance, an unexpected change in the information security policy of a company will definitely going to impose some change requirements on the related projects and hence their corresponding interdependencies. As a result, new project interdependencies might be added while existing ones might be removed, modified or just kept unchanged. In such cases, and to ensure minimum impact on the project portfolio goal, managers might be required to deal with different complexity issues. This is not well documented in the literature about interdependencies. Although many studies have paid attention to project interdependencies, only a few studies have highlighted the managerial challenges that may arise while handling these interdependencies. For instance, one study found that lacking of proper inter-project learning and absence of specialized methods may create difficulties in managing project interdependencies (Killen & Kjaer 2012). Another empirical study showed that ineffective inter-project processes and incompetent multi-project management can present a challenge while managing project interdependencies (Patanakul & Milosevic 2009).

This study aims to bring to light the managerial issues and difficulties in handling project interdependencies within IT/IS project portfolios. The research questions addressing this problem are: what factors could increase the managerial difficulties in handling project interdependencies of IT/IS project portfolios, and how can the difficulties be overcome?

Next, in section 2, the research method for the study is discussed, followed by a brief literature overview in section 3. The results from the study is presented in section 4 and discussed in section 5. Conclusions are presented in section 6, and, finally, in section 7, future research work is outlined.

2. RESEARCH METHOD

The research is driven by an interest to find the causes of difficulties in managing project interdependencies in IT/IS project portfolios. The research is explorative in nature as it calls for capturing people's views and perspectives on certain aspects that were most problematic to deal with. How this can be done is described in Yin (2011). The qualitative approach helps to understand problems' real contexts and settings through people who have experienced these problems (Creswell 2012). In qualitative research, interviews are rich sources of information and most preferred technique for collecting in-depth information in the informants' own words. Semi-structured approach for conducting the interview is found to be appropriate for the data collection since it gives freedom for emerging questions during the interview (Myers 2009). To undertake the semi-structured interviews with more efficient measures, we formulated multiple themes of questions as follows:

- Perceived utility of project interdependencies
  - What makes you believe that project interdependencies are important?
  - What are the benefits that you have come by through project interdependencies?
- About project interdependencies' types and forms of interaction
  - Describe the structure of these interdependencies
  - How do the interactions between projects/ subprojects/ tasks take place?
- The planning approach of project interdependencies
  - How are these interdependencies thought out and planned in advance?
- What kind of difficulties have you encountered while handling project interdependencies, and how have you dealt with each case?
- Describe the approach(s) that you are using for handling project interdependencies.

The selection of key informants has taken into consideration the criteria recommended by Myers (2009). For the study, we based our selection of the participants on the following: 1) their managerial position and degree of involvement in deciding upon IT/IS project interdependencies and 2) their total years of management experience. Each interview was planned to take place in each interviewee's office where one-hour meeting was scheduled with each interviewee. There were some variations in the length of the interviews but the mean time was about 80 minutes. All interviews were recorded, and informed consent was provided for each participant. This procedure has helped to build a trust with the participants and fulfilled the ethical obligations of the research (Denscombe 2010). The various parts of the transcribed interviews were classified into a system of codes in order to enable a systematic interpretation of the acquired data. Four organizations in Saudi Arabia were chosen from a pool of leading organizations with a sizable IT infrastructure and based on purposeful sampling (Richards & Morse 2013). Among these, two (a bank and a telecom company) were from the service providers sector with over 2.0 million customer base each, and the remaining two represent a petrochemical company with a multinational presence and a specialized government entity for IT turnkey solutions. By considering the competitive market conditions in Saudi Arabia, the organizations are deemed leaders in their industries.

3. BACKGROUND

In this brief review of the literature, first we provide a comprehensive overview on the concept of project portfolio management and its importance in the field of managing multiple IT/IS projects. Next, we bring the focus on the importance and benefits obtained from having project interdependencies. The difficulty of managing project interdependencies can increase for many reasons, which is highlighted in this section.

3.1 An Explanation of the Concept of IT/IS Project Portfolio Management

In today's intensely competitive markets, IT/IS projects are taking an active role in the advancement of many industries (e.g. telecommunication and financial services). Increasingly, companies need to handle their projects in more efficient and cost-effective ways. Project Portfolio Management (PPM) is a well-known method for prioritizing projects and deciding on the composition of the portfolio (Levine 2005). Among the factors that makes PPM a reliable method there is its emphasis on value creation through an efficient grouping and alignment of projects that fits the strategic desire of the organization (Kundisch & Meier 2011; Meier 2013; Schindler & Eppler 2003; Heinrich et al. 2014; Levine 2005). Another factor is related to various economic and strategic benefits that companies can exploit be using synergistically interrelated projects. For example, introducing a new banking service (e.g. mobile banking service) would entail carrying out multiple hardware, software and integration projects to introduce that service successfully. In real-life, probably the bank is going to introduce a bundle of services to satisfy its customers' needs. In this case, it can be more cost-effective to manage such projects through a project portfolio management approach.

3.2 Types of Project Interdependencies

In connection with the previously explained concept of IT/IS project portfolio management, this section provides an overview of project interdependencies as an important aspect of raising a project portfolio. As a starting point, project interdependencies can be considered as crucial interrelationships between projects that facilitate a progress of one or more projects (i.e. when "the success of a project depends upon another project(s)" (Killen & Kjaer 2012)). In practice, interdependencies between projects may have different setups including tasks, objectives, project and alliances (Rungi & Hilmola 2011; Rungi 2009; Rungi 2010). For instance, the implementation of a data warehouse project might involve handling a range of tasks and agreements with other related projects. Thompson (2011), distinguished between three forms of interdependencies between interdependent organizational parts: pooled, sequential and reciprocal. A pooled form of interdependence between different organizational parts implies that unless each part performs well the total organization may fail. However, each part might still be independent of other parts (Thompson 2011). Contrary to a pooled interdependence is sequential interdependence which involves certain level of interaction between two or more organizational parts (i.e. a progress in one project is influenced by a progress in another project(s)). While, in a reciprocal interdependence, two or more organizational parts have to synchronize their activities (or part of it) in a mutual manner (i.e. the outputs of two or more project are important as inputs for the same projects) (Thompson 2011). The difficulty of managing these forms of interdependencies will vary because "they contain an increasing degree of contingency" Thompson (2011, p.55). In the sequence presented above and based on Thompson's (2011) view, managing a pooled form of project interdependencies is simple compared to a sequential form which tends to be complicated and difficult to manage. However, a reciprocal form is much difficult and complex to manage.

3.3 Difficulty Aspects of Project Interdependency Management

This subsection provides an overview over the managerial aspects of handling project interdependencies. It also involves highlighting the inherent difficulty from the total portfolio system. Only a few studies on project portfolio management have paid attention to managerial aspects of handling inter-project interdependencies. Among those studies, an explorative study aimed to examine issues leading to effectiveness in multiple projects management. The study highlighted two factors that may affect the management of project interdependencies including inter-project processes and managers' competencies of coordinating multiple projects (Patanakul & Milosevic 2009). Another study has found that insufficient inter-project learning and absence of specialized methods may impact project interdependency management (Killen & Kjaer 2012). The difficulty of managing project interdependencies can always be influenced by factors internal to the project portfolio. In this respect, a change in the decision regarding one of portfolio's projects can simultaneously affect other projects in the portfolio and thereby specific interdependencies between projects may arise (Gear & Cowie 1980). However, another source of increased difficulty can be attributed to factors external to the project portfolio. This can be due to unexpected change in the market conditions that, in turn, may impose additional challenges on the project portfolio and hence other projects and project interdependencies in the portfolio (Gear & Cowie 1980).

4. RESULTS FROM THE STUDY

A total number of four interviews with senior managers from leading organizations in Saudi Arabia were conducted between the period of February 2015 and July 2015. The interviewed managers are all responsible for managing more than 50 IT/IS projects in a portfolio and handling IT investment decisions. Two of them manage portfolios of more than 200 projects. Table 1 provides background information about the interviewed companies and the managers.

Table 1. Summary of interviews

	Industry	Employees	Projects	the role of the interviewee
Org.1	Banking and Finance Services	>7000	>200 (four sub-portfolios)	Head of Project Management Office
Org.2	Government Agency	>2000	>50 (four programs)	Senior project portfolio manager
Org.3	Petrochemical Company	>3500	>70 (two sub-portfolios)	Head of global IT solutions
Org.4	Telecommunication Service Provider	>9000	>250 (seven programs)	IT project portfolio manager

In the following subsections, each interview result is presented, and a summary of the results is provided.

4.1 Org1: Banking and Finance Services Company

4.1.1 Organization Background

The enterprise is one of the largest banking and finance service providers in Saudi Arabia with a customer base exceeding 2.0 million customers. The interview was conducted with the Head of Project Management Office (PMO) who is responsible for managing a major project portfolio consisting of four sub-portfolios with more than 200 IT/IS projects in total. Each sub-portfolio has its standalone organization with a portfolio manager overseeing its operations. The PMO is mainly responsible for developing and introducing new banking services and handling change requests for existing services as well.

4.1.2 Difficulties of Handling Project Interdependencies

The interviewee emphasized the importance of project interdependencies and considered them a value-add for the project portfolio. He stressed that "different projects have had an advantage of sharing a feature or a software release offered by another project."

Concerning how project interdependencies are thought out and planned in advance, the interviewee mentioned: "any formation of interdependencies between projects should, at least, consider one of the following factors: a time-saving factor or a resource optimization factor or both." However, he indicated that only a few project interdependencies can be identified during the planning phase of the project portfolio. He attributed this problem to the dynamic nature of the market and the competitors' moves which make it difficult to anticipate project interdependencies beforehand. To reduce the impact of this problem, the interviewee indicated that they try to involve all concerned parties during the planning phase.

The interviewees highlighted different reasons of project interdependencies being difficult to handle while projects are progressing. In this regard, the interviewee pointed to three factors: 1) formal project management processes are not complied with; 2) ill-considered project requirements, and 3) inappropriate documentation of projects. In the first factor, the interviewee mentioned: "not abiding by the formal project management process could distort the progress of one project and hence other dependent projects can be affected as well". The second factor is about initial business requirements being misdirected by the project manager. As a consequence, the interviewee mentioned: "this would create a situation of misalignment with the initial business requirements and would affect the related interdependencies". The third factor is about project managers not doing appropriate documentation for their projects that in return could obstruct tracking the changes in these projects and changes in their interdependencies as well. Also, the interviewee pointed to a situation of project interdependencies being readjusted to cope with a scope change of a project. He described the situation in the following way: "During the implementation of a complaint handling project, new requirements from different business units were added to the project, which has created a conflict with the existing project scope. The project has already been interlinked with various projects in other sub-portfolios. This has forced a project scope to change and accordingly this has required extra resources and extra management efforts by the sub-portfolio managers. Meantime, this has increased the number of interdependencies between other projects and increased the amount of the required work in the interdependent projects as well." To overcome this problem, the interviewee explained: "I stopped the project for the reason that it will be difficult for each sub-portfolio manager to handle the new requirements under the same organizational arrangements. We ended with a large project scope which was difficult to be treated as the original project. Instead, we assigned a program manager to be responsible for managing the project and its interdependencies".

4.2 Org2: Government Agency for Developing IT&S Turnkey Solutions

4.2.1 Organization Background

The interviewee described a specialized government agency (project management office) responsible for developing Information Technology & Services (IT&S) turnkey solutions for customers from 18 government agencies. A major part of its responsibilities is to serve the demand of new IT services and solutions such as e-government portal, performance management, complaint handling, etc. The interview was conducted with the senior project portfolio manager who is responsible for managing a project portfolio consisting of four programs with more than 50 IT/IS projects in total. Amongst other duties, the manager is responsible for planning and negotiating the strategic decisions at the project portfolio level with the top management.

4.2.2 Difficulties in Handling Project Interdependencies

The interviewee considered project interdependencies an important aspect in an effectively developed project portfolio. He justified his opinion by indicating the importance of sharing human resources between the projects in the portfolio.

Concerning how project interdependencies are planned, the interviewee indicated that interdependencies are first assessed based on their contribution to human resource optimization. On the second level, they are evaluated based on their contribution to the business objectives. With regard to difficulties of planning project interdependencies, the interviewee mentioned: "we faced a difficult issue regarding sharing of human resources among different projects in the portfolio. This was attributable to some project managers who were not able to specify their projects' demand of human resources. Therefore, it was difficult to reflect the actual demand for human resources in the project portfolio plan". The interviewee indicated that by raising the awareness level of resource interdependencies they were able to reflect the actual demand for human resource in the project portfolio plan.

In the course of implementing projects, the interviewee highlighted a problem of centralized decision-making process. He further indicated that this problem keeps recurring and as consequences projects and project interdependencies are usually affected. The other situation was about a difficulty caused by a delay in a software project that was responsible for delivering a web-based application. In effect, another project, in the same portfolio, was stopped due to its high dependability on the first project.

4.3 Org3: Petrochemical Company

4.3.1 Organization Background

The company is a growing oil and gas cooperation with a footprint in some parts of the world. Last year the company went through several reforms and mergers to improve its competitiveness and remain profitable. In response to these changes, the project office is expected to take the lead in maintaining IT capabilities that serve to meet the business goals. The interview was conducted with the head of global IT solutions who has more than eight years of experience in IT project management. The project organization is mainly responsible for managing a project portfolio consisting of 70 projects on average. The projects are divided between two sub-portfolios based on two categories (i.e. infrastructure projects and application projects).

4.3.2 Difficulties in Handling Project Interdependencies

The interviewee emphasized the important aspect of project interdependencies as an important aspect of maintaining high-performance project portfolio. In this regard, he mentioned: "we use project interdependencies as a driver for time efficiency and cost efficiency."

Concerning how these interdependencies are planned, the interviewee indicated that they spend a long time in deciding upon project interdependencies. In this regard, he mentioned: "project interdependencies require enormous planning efforts because they are like a chain if one link is affected then the rest will be affected as well." However, the interviewee highlighted two obstacles that had always distressed the planning of project interdependencies. The first obstacle is dealing with different technology areas and standards, which end up in a wrong assessment of projects' relatedness and hence project interdependencies become difficult to anticipate. To avoid having this kind of problems, the interviewee mentioned: "we usually base our selection of projects on technologies that are renowned as being best practices." The second obstacle is about having different technology providers (for collaborative projects) which make it less cost-effective to negotiate interdependencies among these providers. To overcome this obstacle, the interviewee found it more cost and time effective to reward technology providers that can handle interdependent projects at once. In this regard, the interviewee mentioned: "we used a technique of offering the same vendor more projects if he is going to take the interdependent projects because there will be more negotiation power over the projects' prices and implementation times."

In the course of implementing project interdependencies, the interviewee highlighted two kinds of problems that can affect project interdependencies: 1) the impact of a project delay and 2) the impact from insufficient business engagement in projects. Regarding the first problem area, the interviewee mentioned: "we usually have a tight timeline for implementing the projects and whenever there is a delay in one project, this would likely impact the workflow in the interdependent projects as well". To deal with such problem, the interviewee indicated that they should immediately raise the attention on the defected interdependencies. This can be done by having more control over these interdependencies and by ensuring that all stakeholders are properly engaged. In the second problem area, the interviewee highlighted the impact from insufficient business engagement in projects. In this regard, the interviewee mentioned: "failing to gain business buy-in on the project might end up in having a delay in one project and consequently other dependent projects as well." To handle such problems, the interviewee pointed to three techniques: "first we try to convince the business owner by explaining the added value from the project and how he can benefit from the project to achieve his business goals. Second, we highlight the expected risk on the business if the project fails to achieve its strategic objectives. The third is that we let the business owner, sometimes, drive the project instead of IT department being the sponsor".

4.4 Org 4: Telecommunication Service Provider

4.4.1 Organization Background

The company is one of the leading telecommunication service providers in Saudi Arabia and among the top three telecommunication service providers in the middle-east. The interview was conducted with the head of the Project Management Office (PMO) who is responsible for managing a project portfolio consisting of seven programs with more than 250 projects in total. The company operates under high pressure from the competing market. At least 30-40 new services have to be launched every year.

4.4.2 Difficulties with handling project interdependencies

As regards the drivers of embracing project interdependencies, the interviewee stressed the importance of project interdependencies and considered them a driver for cost optimization and crucial part in integrating projects into the platform.

Regarding the planning difficulties of project interdependencies, the interviewee provided a general description of how interdependencies being drawn from projects. As he said: "interdependencies are either determined by technology guidelines such as connecting different systems through IP connections (e.g. connecting a network access device to a core network) or determined by the requirements of new telecom services". However, the interviewee raised two difficult aspects concerning these determinants. For the interdependencies determined by technology guidelines, it is usually difficult to identify project interdependencies that deal with legacy components. Under such constraints, the interviewee indicated how difficult and time-consuming it is to evaluate project relatedness with another project(s), not to mention the high cost of implementing such interdependencies. To reduce this difficulty, the company implemented a migration plan from legacy to NGN (Next-Generation Network). For interdependencies determined through new service requirements, the interviewee indicated how difficult it is to decide upon project interdependencies under unanticipated service's needs. To deal with this difficulty issue, managers from the business units are often asked to participate in the project planning workshops. The interviewee explained that: "This had enabled us to understand better the business requirements of new services but have never eliminated the problem of fully identifying project interdependencies".

In the course of implementing projects, the interviewee raised a concern of two main reasons where project interdependencies being difficult to handle: 1) Legacy network constraints: the legacy network problem was highlighted in the discussion about planning difficulties. This time, the interviewee indicated that (legacy network) is a continue-to-appear kind of problems and it usually disturbs the workflow of projects and consequently the interactions with other projects. To deal with this kind of problems, the interviewee mentioned: "first we isolate the project area affected by the problem from other project activities, and then we create a separate team to handle the problem." 2) Inappropriate coordination of interdependent projects. In this problem area, the interviewee shared an example of project interdependencies being ill-coordinated. As he mentioned: "we faced a situation of four projects being implemented in parallel, and all were requested to be closely coordinated. Three out of four projects were to install more than 500 network elements (nodes) distributed over many sites. The fourth project is an IT project to establish links between the nodes through an IP network. A major part of the test operation has involved conducting more than 4500 tests between the network nodes. Every test has involved adjusting a set of network parameters at each node and then the test results has to be sent (through the IP links) to a database by the IT project. After completing 50% of the test, we realized that many test records were improperly transferred through the IP links". To deal with this problem, the interviewee mentioned: "we decided to reinitiate the test to prevent facing a quality issue. We then assigned a coordinator from each project team to keep track of the test records and immediately response to any error".

4.5 Summary of Results

To provide a basis for the discussion part and respond to the research question, we took into consideration the lifecycle of each project portfolio at each organization. We found that the four interviewed organizations have had, in common, two distinct portfolio phases, whereas project interdependencies were highlighted most during the interviews. These phases are: 1) the planning phase of the project portfolios and 2) the implementation phase of the project portfolios; this often involves the deployment of projects and their interdependencies. A total number of 16 factors were identified and grouped based on their relatedness to the previously mentioned portfolio phases. These factors are listed in Table 2.

Table 2. Factors attributed to increasing difficulty of handling project interdependencies

	factors that related to planning of the portfolios	factors related to implementation of the portfolios
Org.1	1. inability to identify the right set of project interdependencies since the design schemes of the new services are difficult to foresee	7. not abiding by the formal project management process can distort the progress in one project leading many project interdependencies to run off-course 8. misdirected project requirements may divert project interdependencies from achieving its original objectives 9. inappropriate documentation of projects makes it less possible to keep track of the changes in the projects and their interdependencies 10. a change in a project scope may lead to substantial changes result in consequential changes on its interdependencies
Org.2	2. less attention to resource reservation for a set of projects make it difficult to share human resources in an optimized way	11. a schedule slippage in one project can put other dependent projects on hold 12. a centralized decision-making effects the progress of projects leading project interdependencies to run off-course
Org.3	3. dealing with different technology areas and standards make it less possible neither to assess the right combination of projects nor assessing their interdependencies 4. having different technology providers reduces the negotiation power over the costs and times involved in the interdependencies between the projects	13. a schedule slippage in one project can affect the completions date of other dependent projects 14. insufficient business engagement with projects may put projects and their interdependencies off-course
Org.4	5. inability to identify the right set of project interdependencies since the design schemes of the new services are difficult to foresee 6. project integration with legacy network components is difficult to anticipate	15. lack of project interoperability with legacy network components stood against implementing interdependencies 16. inadequate coordination of interdependencies among projects forced reworks on these interdependencies

5. DISCUSSION

In this section, we will discuss the results presented in previous section. We focus on understanding the managerial difficulty of handling project interdependencies within large IT/IS project portfolios within four project organizations. The discussion involves highlighting various kinds of project interdependencies and the factors that led to increasing difficulty of managing these interdependencies throughout the portfolios' lifecycles. The research results in Table 2 revealed several factors that imposed further complexity on handling project interdependencies, particularly during the planning and implementation phases of the project portfolios. In a review of these factors, a number of themes stood out which drew our attention to three broad categories including 1) factors that relate to insufficient understanding of human responsibilities in the whole portfolio, 2) factors that relate to changing business environment, and 3) factors that relate to technology constraints. These factors and their implications on the management of project interdependencies and on the portfolio as whole are further presented and discussed in the following subsections.

5.1 Difficulties of Handling Project Interdependencies in the Planning Phase of the Portfolios

During this phase, projects typically undergo a decision-making process to specify projects that can be strategically aligned with the business objectives. Included in this phase, potential interdependencies between projects are also specified. For instance, interdependencies between two (or more) projects might be decided within a portfolio in order to produce a set of new software products.

The first category of factors (Table 2: factor [2]) is about insufficient understanding of human responsibilities in the whole portfolio. The manager from Org. 2 had difficulty obtaining correct information about the projects' demand of human resources. This resulted in an inappropriate scheduling of scarce resources between the projects in the portfolio. In effect, many projects in the portfolio suffered from major delay due to resource shortages. This difficulty can be traced to lack of accurate information about project requirements of human resources. Patanakul & Milosevic (2009) asserted that success in multiple project management hinges on several influencing factors including the ability to lead individual project and to coordinate among projects. To deal with this problem, the manager indicated that they managed to increase the awareness level of project resource planning among the project managers.

The second category of factors (Table 2: factors [1 and 5]) is about environmental change. The managers from the service provider companies (i.e. Org.1 and Org.4) had difficulty identifying project interdependencies during the planning phase of the portfolios (Table 2: factors [1, 5]). They attributed the problem to the dynamic (and competitive) nature of the services market that makes it difficult to assess the demand of projects and the project interdependencies beforehand. In such innovative environments (i.e. new product/service development), projects undergo on-going revisions and change. Because of this, future project needs are hard to anticipate and plan ahead of time (Söderholm 2008). To deal with this problem, the manager in Org.4 suggests hosting of brainstorming sessions with the key decision-makers.

The third category of factors (Table 2: factors [3, 4 and 6]) is about technology constraints. The manager from Org.3 reported two difficulties. The first difficulty (Table 2: factor [3]) is the inability to make the right selection of technology for the projects in the portfolio, since there are many technology domains and different standards of each. Because of this, it becomes hard to identify the right set of projects and specify the relationships and interdependencies among the projects. The second difficulty (Table 2: factor [4]) is that the company has to deal with different technology partners for the projects. Because of this, it becomes less possible to negotiate the price and the implementation time of the projects especially when the projects come to be more interrelated and assigned to different technology-providers. The manager form Org. 4 faced a difficulty of anticipating project interdependencies that may arise from the interactions between the candidate projects and the existing platforms. Because of this, it was difficult to come up with a correct assessment of the projects, their interdependencies, and the portfolio as whole.

5.2 Difficulties of Handling Project Interdependencies in the Implementation Phase of the Portfolios

In the implementation phase of the project portfolios, projects are carried out by teams using a project management approach alongside other cross-project activities (interdependencies) to fulfill their goals and their portfolio goal as well.

The first category of factors (Table 2: factors [7, 8, 9, 12, 14 and 16]) is about insufficient understanding of human responsibilities in the whole portfolio. The manager from Org. 2 made reference to three root causes of increased difficulty with managing project interdependencies. Regarding the first factor, not abiding by the formal project management process, this matter can impact the progress of one project and consequently many project interdependencies may run off-course. For the second factor, misdirected project requirements, this matter may divert projects and, hence, interdependencies from achieving their original objectives. The third factor, inappropriate documentation of projects, can make it less possible to keep track of the changes in the projects and their interdependencies. It can be detected that the three factors emphasized the role of the actors involved in the project management process especially project managers. These aspects were emphasized by findings of Patanakul & Milosevic (2009). The study indicates that the competencies of multi-project manager and the process dealing with individual projects and intra-project dependencies can impact multi-project management effectiveness. In a similar vein, the remaining factors (Table 2: factors [12, 14 and 16]) under the same category have reflected on different kinds of stakeholders at different portfolio levels. Among those factors, the impact that the top management commitment can bring on the flow of work throughout the whole portfolio (Table 2: factor [12]). This key role is emphasized by (Patanakul & Milosevic 2009), who stated that "the project commitment has to come from top management and has to be supported by every level of the organization". Project owner commitment is also crucial to portfolio success. This factor (Table 2: factor [14]) was raised by the manager from Org.3 who stressed the importance of project owner engagement in the project to streamline the communication between the business unit and the PMO. This will help to keep the project on track and therefore it will reduce the impact on the interdependencies. The last factor in this category is related to coordination effectiveness between projects. The manager from Org.4 indicated that inadequate cross-project coordination of the interdependencies between the projects, at different programs, has forced reworks on the same interdependencies. Chiang & Nunez (2013) emphasized that the need for coordination between interrelated projects may arise due to dependencies between projects assigned to different programs.

The second category of factors (Table 2: factors [10, 11 and 13]) is about environmental change. The manager from Org.1 indicated how a change in a project scope lead to increases in the magnitude of resource requirements and in the number of interdependencies between a set of interrelated projects within different sub-portfolios (Table 2: factor [10]). The impact that interdependent projects can have from changing the scope of one project was emphasized by Gear & Cowie (1980) as they indicated that a change in project scope can affect the resource requirements and timing of other projects within the portfolio. This applies to the factors (Table 2: factors [11 and 13]) where a schedule slippage in one project leads to an impact on the other interrelated projects.

The third category of factors (Table 2: factor [15]) is about technology constraints. The manager from Org.4 pointed to a difficulty that emerged during the implementation of a project when the interoperability of the project with a legacy network element stood against completing the work with the project.

In summary, managing multiple interdependent projects within IT/IS portfolios (e.g. new product/service development portfolios) tends to be a rather complex task especially when many optimization activates have to be clearly described and effectively carried out. Uncertainties from the external/internal environment and from single projects may give rise to negative consequences, not only at the project level, but also at the interdependence level between the projects (Martinsuo et al. 2014). As shown in the study, uncertainties can emerge from different sources and can be a source for complexity in managing project interdependencies. In specific, we identified a total number of 16 factors that were mainly responsible of different kinds of complexity at the project interdependencies level, both in the planning and in the implementation phases of the portfolio.

6. CONCLUSION

Effectively managed project interdependencies have shown to be essential for maintaining high-performance project portfolios. In large IT/IS project portfolios, project portfolio managers should realize the difficulty aspects of handling project interdependencies especially when the uncertainty level is high. In this paper, we have presented and discussed results from semi-structured interviews with managers of IT/IS portfolios in four leading organizations in different industries in Saudi Arabia. The managers were selected because of their responsibility for managing large IT/IS project portfolios and handling IT investment decisions. The study draws the attention to the managerial difficulties of handling project interdependencies in IT/IS project portfolios. The study shows that managers have to deal with different types of difficulties in relation to interdependencies in both the planning and the implementation phases of their project portfolios. By providing a number of examples of how project interdependencies arise and should be handled, we have argued for the crucial importance of managers assuming a certain type of responsibility. The research findings, that contribute to the field of IT/IS project portfolio management, are essentially pinpointing three main sources of difficulty in managing project interdependencies: 1) Insufficient understanding of human responsibilities in the whole portfolio, 2) Environmental change and 3) Technological constraints.

7. FUTURE RESEARCH

In this paper we have drawn conclusions concerning the interviewed managers' perception and experiences of the causes of project interdependencies and which type of responsibility they need to take. In the next papers concerning the topic of project interdependencies we will describe social, technological and environmental issues related to project interdependencies. We will also analyze and propose a number of formal methods for 1) diagnosing project portfolios in order to secure that all possible interdependencies are found, 2) developing methods for classifying each possible interdependency into a type of interdependency in order to be able to register them in an index of possible interdependencies, 3) analyzing and proposing formal methods of how to manage a database of registered possible interdependencies and 4) discuss which levels and which roles in the organization should be responsible for handling the ever changing interdependencies.

REFERENCES

Bardhan, I.R., Kauffman, R.J. & Naranpanawe, S., 2006. Optimizing an IT project portfolio with time-wise interdependencies. In *Proceedings of the 39th Annual Hawaii International Conference (HICSS'06), Kauai, Hawaii.* IEEE, p. 168b.

Chiang, I.R. & Nunez, M.A., 2013. Strategic alignment and value maximization for IT project portfolios. *Information Technology and Management*, 14(2), pp.143–157.

Creswell, J.W., 2012. *Qualitative Inquiry and Research Design: Choosing Among Five Approaches*, Sage.

Dahlgren, J. & Soderlund, J., 2010. Modes and mechanisms of control in Multi-Project Organisations: the R&D case. *International Journal of Technology Management*, 50(1), pp.1–22.

Denscombe, M., 2010. *Good Research Guide : For small-scale social research projects (4th Edition).*, Berkshire, GBR: McGraw-Hill Education.

Dwivedi, Y.K. et al., 2015. Research on information systems failures and successes: Status update and future directions. *Information Systems Frontiers*, 17(1), pp.143–157.

Gear, T.E. & Cowie, G.C., 1980. A note on modeling project interdependence in research and development. *Decision Sciences*, 11(4), pp.738–748.

Heinrich, B., Kundisch, D. & Zimmermann, S., 2014. Analyzing Cost and Risk Interaction Effects in IT Project Portfolios. *Banking and Information Technology*, 15(2/2014), pp.8–20.

Killen, C.P. & Kjaer, C., 2012. Understanding project interdependencies: The role of visual representation, culture and process. *International Journal of Project Management*, 30(5), pp.554–566.

Kundisch, D. & Meier, C., 2011. A new Perspective on Resource Interactions in IT/IS Project Portfolio Selection. In *Proceedings of the 19th European Conference on Information Systems (ECIS 2011), Helsinki, Finland, 2011, Paper 174.*

Levine, H.A., 2005. *Project Portfolio Management A Practical Guide to Selecting Projects, Managing Portfolios, and Maximizing Benefits*, John Wiley & Sons: San Francisco, CA.

Martinsuo, M., Korhonen, T. & Laine, T., 2014. Identifying, framing and managing uncertainties in project portfolios. *International Journal of Project Management*, 32(2014), pp.732–746.

Meier, C., 2013. Identifying Output Interactions Among Is Projects -A Text Mining Approach. In *ECIS 2013 Research in Progress. Paper 20.*

Müller, M.P. et al., 2015. Interactions in IS Project Portfolio Selection - Status Quo and Perspectives. In *Proceedings of the 12th International Conference on Wirtschaftsinformatik, Osnabrück, Germany, 2015, Paper 50.*

Myers, M.D., 2009. *Qualitative Research in Business & Management*, SAGE Publications.

Patanakul, P. & Milosevic, D., 2009. The effectiveness in managing a group of multiple projects: Factors of influence and measurement criteria. *International Journal of Project Management*, 27(3), pp.216–233.

Richards, L. & Morse, J.M., 2013. *Readme first for a user's guide to qualitative methods*, SAGE Publications.

Rungi, M., 2009. Managing resource and technology interdependencies in project portfolio A case-study results. In *IEEE International Conference on Industrial Engineering and Engineering Management, Hong Kong*. pp. 1508–1512.

Rungi, M., 2010. Success rate and resource consumption from project interdependencies. *Industrial Management & Data Systems*, 110(1), pp.93–110.

Rungi, M. & Hilmola, O.-P., 2011. Interdependency management of projects: survey comparison between Estonia and Finland. *Baltic Journal of Management*, 6(2), pp.146–162.

Schindler, M. & Eppler, M.J., 2003. Harvesting project knowledge: a review of project learning methods and success factors. *International Journal of Project Management*, 21(3), pp.219–228.

Söderholm, A., 2008. Project management of unexpected events. *International Journal of Project Management*, 26(1), pp.80–86.

Thompson, J.D., 2011. *Organizations in action: Social science bases of administrative theory*, Transaction publishers: New Jersey.

Yin, R.K., 2011. *Qualitative research from start to finish*, The Guilford Press.

Zapata, J.C., Varma, V.A. & Reklaitis, G. V., 2008. Impact of tactical and operational policies in the selection of a new product portfolio. *Computers and Chemical Engineering*, 32(1), pp.307–319.

ONTOLOGY LEARNING FOR OPEN SEMANTIC TRIZ IN SOFTWARE ENGINEERING

Vanja Bevanda[1], Giorgio Sinković[2] and Marko Turk[3]
[1]*Full Professor,* [2]*Associate Professor,* [3]*PhD Student*
Juraj Dobrila University of Pula,
Zagrebačka 30, 52100 Pula, Croatia

ABSTRACT

TRIZ (the theory of inventive problem solving; an acronym for the Russian phrase "*Teoriya Resheniya Izobretatelskikh Zadatch*") is a broad title representing a collection of methodologies, tools, knowledge bases, and model-based technologies for generating inventive ideas and solutions. It has been developed for over 65 years to support engineers and natural scientists solving problems in the fields of physics, chemistry and mechanical systems by using knowledge of former inventors.

In today business environment, new technologies and competitions force business organizations to invest additional resources in order to continuously improve their business models, products, processes, services, management, information system and knowledge of employees. As a part of these efforts, appears an exigency for strengthening the importance of inventive solving problems capabilities in area of software engineering, supporting innovative aspects of business organizations in extremely changing environment.

Although the software engineering (SE) is "a branch of computer science that deals with the design, implementation, and maintenance of complex computer programs", the existing research shows that only a part of the available TRIZ toolkit is applicable to this specific field. The current literature records numerous attempts made in different directions in order to fulfil a prominence need for adjustment, widening or upgrading existing TRIZ methodology to SE domain. This article synthetizes those efforts and proposes the development of semantic portal for open TRIZ in supporting collaborative software engineers` inventive problem solving process. As a part of this development process, authors have offered a solution for facilitating the ontology acquisition activities using inductive learning.

KEYWORDS

TRIZ inventive principles, software engineering, open innovation, semantic web, ontology learning and collaborative knowledge management platform.

1. INTRODUCTION

TRIZ (the theory of inventive problem solving; an acronym for the Russian phrase "*Teoriya Resheniya Izobretatelskikh Zadatch*") is a broad title representing a collection of methodologies, tools, knowledge bases, and model-based technologies for generating inventive ideas and solutions. It is being developed for over 65 years to support engineers and natural scientists solving problems in the fields of physics, chemistry and mechanical systems by using knowledge of former inventors. TRIZ involves a systematic analysis of problem to be solved and the application of a series of guidelines for the generation of solution alternatives (Altshuller, 1994). Their methods are being drawn from analysis of the most innovative inventions in different industries, technologies and fields of engineering and integrate system approach, function analysis and function modeling.

The idea of TRIZ is to provide a problem solver with easy access to a wide range of experience and knowledge of former inventors and use it for solving new problems or it can be said: "somebody someplace has already solved similar problem and it is necessary to find that solution and adapt it to specific problem".

Altshuller found that often the same problems have been solved over and over again using one of the fundamental inventive principles and that over of 95% of the problems engineers faced had been solved somewhere before, inside or across industries and sciences. The fundamental principle behind this method is to find contradictions in a system and to eliminate them by using TRIZ tools such as the 40 Inventive

Principles (IPs), Contradiction matrix, separation principles, 76 standard solutions, substance-field analysis and ARIZ- algorithm of inventive problem solving. Supporting TRIZ problem solving process, practitioners developed a comprehensive, well proven, toolkit. Using those tools, problem solver can view a problem from different perspectives, can combine them or use in isolation, individual or as a team.

In the IEEE collection of standards, software engineering (SE) is defined as :"(1) The application of a systematic, disciplined, quantifiable approach to the development, operation and maintenance of software, i.e. the application of engineering to software. (2) The study of approaches as in (1)" (IEEE 610.12, 1991). SE can be considered as "a branch of computer science that deals with the design, implementation, and maintenance of complex computer programs. The existing research shows that only a part of the available TRIZ toolkit is applicable to SE`s specific field. The current literature records numerous, domain related attempts made in different directions in order to fulfil a prominence need for adjustment, widening or upgrading existing TRIZ methodology to SE domain. This paper synthetizes those efforts by developing the portal for open TRIZ in order to support collaborative software engineers` inventive problem solving processes. As a part of the open semantic TRIZ portal development process, authors have offered a solution for facilitating the ontology acquisition activities using C4.5 algorithm of inductive learning.

After an introduction, the authors will continue with a brief description of the main characteristics of a TRIZ problem-solving tool. In the same part, based on a literature overview, there were several attempts analyzed to suit TRIZ principles to specific requirements of SE domain. As a result, in the third part, we propose the development of open TRIZ semantic portal in order to integrate efforts on collaborative upgrading TRIZ to the problems in the SE. Finally, the conclusion contains the suggestions for future work and limitations of proposed solution.

2. TRIZ METHODOLOGY IN SOFTWARE ENGINEERING

2.1 TRIZ Innovation Methodology: Brief Overview

Following steps describe the problem solving process with TRIZ: The problem solver analyzes specific, factual problem in details, matches their specific characteristics to an abstract, conceptual problem, searches for an abstract, conceptual solution and transforms this abstract solution into a specific one. This process may vary in the levels of abstractions and in the number of loops, which the problem-solver can pass through.

Central to TRIZ methodology are the conceptual solutions for engineering problems. These are about 100 in number, derived from the overlap of the 40 inventive principles, 8 trends of technical evolution and 76 standard solutions (Gaad, K. 2011). To apply these, a specific and factual technical problem would need to be reduced to its essentials and stated in a conceptual or generic format. The conceptual problem can afterwards be matched with one of the conceptual solutions. The important aspect of translating the specific and factual problem into its conceptual format achieved by asking the right questions and drawing out its key functions and features. The second important stage is the translation of the found conceptual solution into specific, factual solutions.

Altshuller by analyzing patents found that (Kluender, 2011):

- Innovation emerges from the application of a relatively small set of strategies, so called *Inventive Principles* (IPs),
- The strongest solutions actively seeks out and destroys the conflicts or *contradictions* most design practices assume to be fundamental,
- They also transform unwanted or harmful elements of a system into useful resources,
- Technology evolution trends are predictable.

Problems can be characterized as contradictions, and one of TRIZ`s objective is to remove these contradictions. The process of resolving contradiction without compromise (optimization) launched approximate ideal condition of system. In practice there can be identified 39 standard technical features leading to conflict within the technical system and 40 principles through which most contradictions may be resolved. The 40-IPs are 40 basic methods of eliminating contradictions. They became popular because of the "contradiction matrix", where the principles and the contradiction are placed in a format easy to handle for beginners.

The diversity of available, contemporary methods, techniques and tools supporting activities of problem solving process steps followed to solve a problem describes Ilevbare, I. et al, (2012.) in Figure 1.

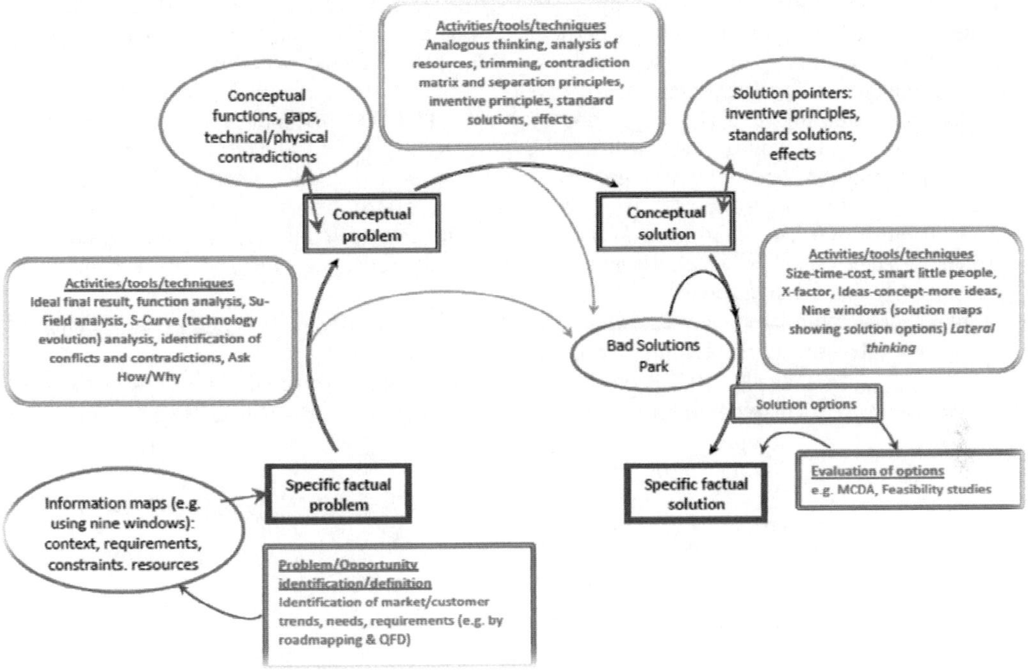

Figure 1. Techniques and tools supporting TRIZ problem solving process (source: Ilevbare, I. et al, 2011.)

After identification, the specific problem translated or modeled into its conceptual form by applying tools or concepts such as ideal result, function analysis, Su-Field analysis, Ask How/Why, identification of conflicts and contradictions that will further help to understand the problems. A contradiction matrix, inventive principles and separation principles would be required for the step of finding conceptual solutions to the conceptual problems. To complete process, the final step is translating the conceptual solution into a set of factual solution options applying the nine windows, size-time-cost analysis or using other creativity tools such as smart little people. "Bad solutions" which might have been identified during the course of solving the problem might also be applicable here for identifying the required solution. Based on feasibility studies or application of multiple-criteria decision analysis (MDCA), it can be decided about the final choice of the specific solution.

2.2 TRIZ in Software Engineering

In the IEEE collection of standards, software engineering (SE) is defined as :"(1) The application of a systematic, disciplined, quantifiable approach to the development, operation and maintenance of software, i.e. the application of engineering to software. (2) The study of approaches as in (1)" (IEEE 610.12, 1991). The main problem SE deals with is requirement to develop a software to satisfy the needs of some users or clients. It is not sufficient to reach the final goal of having the desired software, but the project has to be done at low cost, in low cycle time, and deliver high-quality software.

Tekinerdogan and Aksit, 2006. determined that SE is in essence a problem solving process. These authors approach to SE from a problem solving perspective that consists of five concepts for the certain context of problem: Need, Problem Description, Solution Domain Knowledge, Alternative, Solution Description and Artefact (solution). They consider that "In SE, an explicit problem analysis process does not exist, solution domain analysis is still not fully integrated in software design processes, and alternative management is usually done in an implicit manner and is practically missing. Obviously, synthesis is an useful concept in mature problem solving and it is worthwhile to integrate this in software engineering." According to Shaw and Garlan, 1996., in "software practice, knowledge about techniques that work is not shared effectively with workers on late projects, nor is there a large body of software development knowledge organized for ready reference". In terms of TRIZ methodologies, for SE`s problem solving is characteristic the existence only one fragment of the process that is searching for specific, factual solution for specific, factual problem. The results of SE activities remark dependencies on the context and the changing user requirements, the lack of existing conceptual problems and solutions knowledge base and the possibility of creating a knowledge base only for the domain specific problems.

All mentioned above may lead to the conclusion that the full application of TRIZ problem-solving approach to software engineering scientific discipline, at the present stage of their development, is unsuitable due to numerous reasons. Some of them refer to core purpose of SE that is developing a software to satisfy users` needs, with low cost, short time and high-quality software. As a support of this view is work of Wang, 2011. saying that "there is no need to put all the TRIZ principles on the problem, we should identify the problem, decide when, in which phase of SE process use TRIZ and then put corresponding principle on particular problem need to solved.

In recent literature can be noticed some emerging efforts of TRIZ customization in SE domain related to:

- Inventive principles in order to:
    - adapt TRIZ Inventive Principles to service oriented context in order to enhance the delivery of services to the customer (Gazem & Rahman, 2014.);
    - interpret Inventive Principles (IP`s) in Software Engineering (Rea, 2005; Fulbright,2004; Nakagawa, 2004.);
    - add new inventive principles related to information systems and technology (called TRIZ-PINE) (Fulbright, 2004.);
    - interpret IP`s in specific domain related context such as structured programing (Nakagawa, 2004);
- develop complete new TRIZ methodologies tailored for SE domain (Mann, D. 2004);
- complement different innovation tools in SE domain and use TRIZ only to overcome the difficult problems of software design. The reason for using an innovation toolkit combination relay on fact that the TRIZ cannot be used to identify a customer`s need or compile the requirements (Bonnema, 2011.; Wang et al. 2011.);
- develop a collaborative software environment supporting individual or group problem solving in specific engineering domain (Yan et al., 2015.; Cavalluci et al.,2011.; Liou et al., 2011.) which is web based or semantic web based with common ontology for domain knowledge acquisition.

According to Mann, 2004., most of them, if not all of the TRIZ tools, methods and strategies originally are configured for use in solving technical problems and they have direct or analogous application in a non-technical or software context. In combination with other problem definition and solving methods, it offers a uniquely powerful systematic innovation methodology. A significant amount of work is still required to develop and deploy the methodology in non- technical or specific related fields like software engineering. In 2005. the initiative for implementation TRIZ for SE (called T4S) was recorded, but ten years after, there are no published or shared results of the work on this initiative.

From all mentioned above previous researches, it can be concluded that use of Inventive principles is appropriate in SE problem solving and there is an evident lack of conceptual problems` knowledge base related to specific SE domain. Cavallucci et al. (2011.) contribute to TRIZ progress building the software prototype for knowledge acquisition using ontology as a base for communication mediation between TRIZ experts and domain experts. We think that application of the open innovation ideas on software engineering community that are practicing TRIZ solving problems, integrated with automatic ontology learning, may contribute to an integration, sharing and co-working on TRIZ application in SE domain thereby avoiding communication gaps between different actors.

3. OPEN SEMANTIC TRIZ FOR SOFTWARE ENGINERING

Open Innovation (OI) is a term promoted by Henry Chesbrough and defined as "a paradigm that assumes firms can and should use external ideas as well as internal ideas, and internal and external paths to market, as the firms look to advance their technology". OI founded on the fact that, in a world of widely distributed knowledge, companies cannot afford to rely entirely on their own research, and consequently should rely on the outside sources and buy or license processes or inventions. As a one of software solution supporting OI processes is a Web based portal, which serves as a module or standalone platform with idea management tools allowing an easy integration of external contributors and problem solvers into the innovation process. It connects customers, partners, users and researchers to an innovation community, and gives access to "Crowd Wisdom". The main features of open web portals are: configuration of different rating criteria for evaluating ideas in the different phases, tracking ideas through multiple stages in its lifecycle, supporting different discussions and voting schemes and ideas that can be clustered in different ways, presented in various kinds of reports, portal pages, and integrated with databases. It is possible to easy adopt open web portal functionality (portlets) to requirements of TRIZ methods practiced by specific community. Adding semantic content to this portal seems to be logical and natural solution that could provide adequate knowledge management support for SE TRIZ community.

The essence of Semantic Web (SW) is to develop ontology-based semantics in term of some standards, thereby making information given formal, explicit meaning and thus machine understandable. SW is coordinated by W3C Sematic Web working group and is based on XML (eXtensible Markup Language), RDF (Resource Description Framework) and OWL (Ontology Web Language).

Open sematic web portals are designed to allow users to access and utilize the rich source of data, information and knowledge stored in different forms, but also to support knowledge creation, transfer and continuous learning of the people in a specific field. Information and knowledge must be shareable between users, but also must be represented in the machine-understandable form for software agents` communication. For this reason, the architecture of open SW portal is consisted of four integrated layers: structured and unstructured data source (data source layer), ontology layer, communication layer and layer of different applications (Figure 2.).

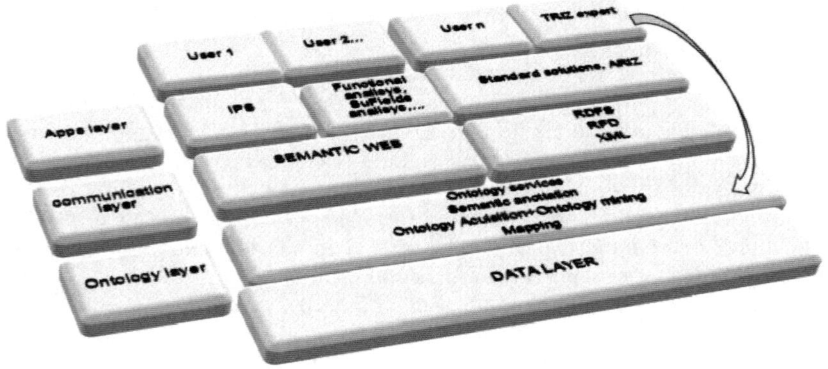

Figure 2. Ontology layer in Open Semantic Portal

The mapping process enhance the semantics of data source layer by providing additional ontological entities. Ontology layer should reference source data and create the information in RDF form on demand. The ontology should be computed once and recomputed only if database schema is changed. There is a need to produce two sorts of files from ontology: one file containing ontology and another containing instance that refers to RDF schema. XML files must contain a reference to their ontology descriptions. The process in which semantic information is added to the web document is called semantic annotation.

Ontology is a “specification of the conceptualization and corresponding vocabulary used to describe a domain”. It is clamed able to provide a shared and common understanding of a domain, so that people and various application systems can communicate across the widely spread heterogeneous sources (Maedche and Staab, 2001). In the highly changing environment, there is a need for constant ontology development and maintenance and manual activities can easily fail because of the dynamic nature of related domain or availability of domain experts. Knowledge engineers create standardized ontology that domain experts can use to share and annotate information in their fields. Like in the development of other knowledge-based systems, ontology development process consists of two phases: acquisition and representation of acquired, explicit knowledge. Ontology acquisition activities are: to find common attributes that could contain all classes from source systems, define properties that describe chosen attributes, and then search for their values and adapt and refine ontology in order to capture differences in related knowledge/ information sources. For the OI field, Riedl et al., 2009. introduced ontology to represent ideas for service innovations and they provided a common language to foster interoperability between tools and to support the idea life cycle. We identified three types of ontology sources, which could be treated in the acquisition process: TRIZ expert knowledge, existing ontology as a cases and results of applying ontology discovery (data mining) techniques.

Bergman and Schaaf, 2003. showed a strong relationship between ontology-based and case-based reasoning (CBR) with respect to the technological and methodological issues. According to them, ontology development and maintenance approach could take advantage of experience with real world CBR application.

3.1 Ontology Learning for Open Semantic TRIZ in Software Engineering

Cunningam and Bonzano, 1999. give the elements of a CBR system: „ the knowledge representation used, the cases themselves; the similarity metric used in identifying cases to be reused and the mechanism for adapting solution, if any." Cases can be anything that we can describe from important aspects. In symbolic logic, it is done with attributes and their values. One value of every attribute is assigned to each of the cases that form logic rules. Cases described with the same rule are consider similar. Therefore, the case base is used to extract rules from experience. As it goes from the particular experiences towards the general rules, it is called induction. Induction can be based on C4.5. algorithm introduced by Guinlan, 1992. All cases form a disordered set, where the order is defined as homogeneity by benchmark values (value of outcome attribute), which means that cases in one subset have the same benchmark value. The attribute is searched, which contributes the most to the order. Their strength in making order is measured by an entropy-gain calculating algorithm. Determining informativity (I_b) of attribute b is as follows: Let C be the set of cases in node, a the benchmark, $a_1 ... a_n$ its values, and $w_{a1} ... w_{an}$ ($\sum_i w_{ai} = 1$) their rates in set C. Then entropy of benchmark in set C can be written:

$Ec = - \sum w_{ai} \log_n w_{ai}$. Let $b_1 ... b_n$ be the values of attribute b, β is a set of them. Disjoint β into not empty subsets $\beta_1 ... \beta_m$. Then Ui $\beta i = \beta$. Disjoint C into subsets $C_1 ... C_m$ being attribute b of all elements of C_i in β_i for each i. Let w_i be the weight of C_i in C ($\sum_i w_i = 1$). Then $I_b = E_C - \sum_i w_i E_{Ci}$, or informativity is an increment of entropy resulted from disjoining $\beta 1 ... \beta m$. Real output of computing is I_{bmax} of optimal selection. The most informative attributes are chosen and this first level of subset values are further divided using the same algorithm until all subsets are homogenous by benchmark values. The result of this cases classification appears in the form of decision tree that can be converted to production rules.

For exploring possibilities of supporting TRIZ ontology learning in software engineering domain, we use a little domain ontology with available resources describing IPs cases. Ontology consists six attributes with values:

- Inventive principle (Segmentation, Extraction, Local condition, Asymmetry, Consolidation, Universality and Nesting), describes several IPs used in SE domain;
- Specific problem parameter (overlap of flows, simple maintenance, complex procedures, account management, software quality, project management, user requirement), describe one of the parameters of the artefact involved in the contradictions (Yan, W. et al, 2015);
- Generalized problem parameter (subroutines, modular programming, multiple functions, the most important function alone, user self service, customization, differentiate users, parallel development, provide service package, one service for different situation, embedded advanced technologies) describes one of the possible generalized parameter that we pair from existing cases found in literature. All parameter have been used under the specific SE context;
- SE field (programming, network, software quality, web apps design, software development) describe context of individual case;
- Form (article, case, example, UML diagrams, code) describes in which presentation form learning material is available;
- Resources (www.triz-journal.com, www.ccsenet.org, www.idationtriz.com, www.innovation-triz.com, www.xtriz.com) are available ontology resources or paths where can be find it.

A small pilot ontology base consists of thirteen examples (cases) founded in literature, describing the use of IPs in the SE area (Table 1.).

Table 1. Attributes with values in IPs ontology

	IPs	Specific problem par	Generalized problem parametar	SE field	Form	Resources
c1	Nesting	overlap of flows	subroutines	programming	case	www.triz-journal.co
c2	Segmentation	simple maintenance	modular programming	software development	article	www.triz-journal.co
c3	Universality	simple maintenance	multiple functions	software development	article	www.triz-journal.co
c4	Segmentation	complex procedures	modular programming	programming	case	www.triz-journal.co
c5	Extraction	complex procedures	the most important functione alone	programming	case	www.triz-journal.co
c6	Extraction	account management	user self service	network	article	www.xtriz.com
c7	Local condition	software quality	customization	software quality	article	www.innovation-triz
c8	Local condition	software quality	customization	web apps design	example	www.ccsenet.org
c9	Asymetry	software quality	differentiate users	web apps design	article	www.ccsenet.org
c10	Nesting	software quality	embeded advanced technologies	software development	article	www.ccsenet.org
c11	Consolidation	project management	parallel development	software development	UML diag	www.ccsenet.org
c12	Consolidation	project management	provide service package	software development	example	www.idationtriz.con
c13	Universality	user requirement	one service for different situation	software development	example	www.innovation-triz

After applying induction algorithm on those values, we got the induction tree (Figure 3.)

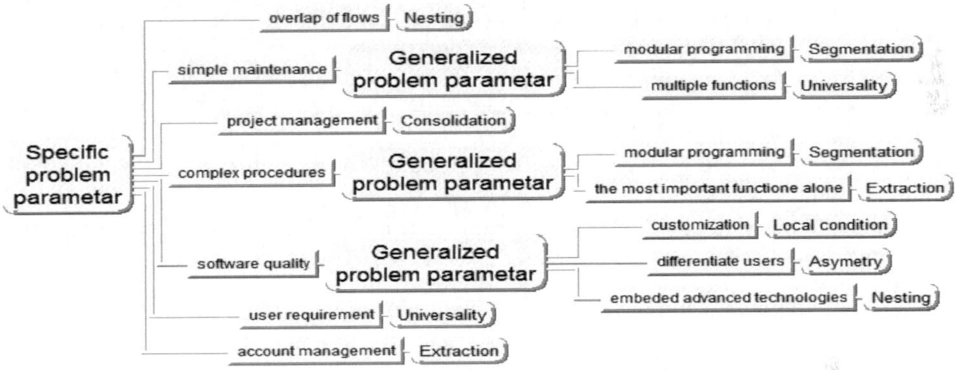

Figure 3. Induction tree for ontology learning

Resulting induction tree can be interpret by "If- Then" rules. For example: If attribute "Specific problem parameter" has a value "Overlap of flows" then attribute "Inventive principle" has a value "Nesting". Cases addition, deletion or some kind of modification will described by different induction tree.

4. CONCLUSION

In this paper, the authors have attempted to review different research conducted in the area of TRIZ methodology applicability to a specific SE domain and they outline how open semantic portal can become an umbrella for fragmented empirical and theoretical streams of software engineering community. Development and maintenance of an ontology, as a central point of that portal, requires continual effort to evolve the ontology over time. For that reason, a possibility of inductive reasoning was explored on how to produce the most informative attribute, generate rules in the domain ontology and in that way to enable TRIZ ontology learning. Its successful implementation depends on the user involvement and requires a change in the culture of software engineering community. The results is a domain of discourse that can be basis for further transformation to XML or RDF form needed in software agents` communication and for refinement from community of interest.

REFERENCES

Altshuller, H., 1994. *The art of inventing (and suddenly the inventor appeared)*. Technical Innovation Center, Worcester, MA 12.

Bonnema, G.M., 2011. The engineers` innovation toolkit. *Procedia Engineering 9,* 345-354.

Bergman, R. and Schaaf, M., 2003. Structural Case-Based Reasoning and Ontology Knowledge Management. A perfect match? *Journal of Universal Computer Science*, Vol.9, No. 7, 608-626.

Bevanda, V. and Turk, M, 2011. Exploring Semantic Infrastructure Development For Open Innovation. *Proceedings The 5th International Scientific Conference "Entrepreneurship and Macroeconomic Management: Reflections on the World in Turmoil"* Pula, Croatia, March 24-26, 2011, Vol 1.

Breslin, J. G. et al, 2010. Semantic Web computing in industry. *Computers in Industry 61 (*2010) 729–741, Available at: www.elsevier.com/locate/compind, accessed at 1.11.2010.

Cavalluci, D. et al, 2011. An ontolgy for TRIZ. *Procedia Engineering 9,* pp. 251-260.

Chesbrough, H., 2003. *Open innovation, the New Imperative for Creating and Profiting from Technology*. Harvard Business School Press. Boston, MA.

Cunningam, P. and Bonzano, A., 1999. Knowledge Engineering Issues: Developing a Case-Based Reasoning Application. *Knowledge-Based Systems,* Vol.12, 371-379.

Fulbright, R.D., 2004. TRIZ and Software Fini. *The TRIZ Journal*.

Gaad, K., 2011. *TRIZ for Engineers: Enabling Inventive Problem Solving*. John Wiley & Sons, Ltd.

Gazem, N. and Rahman, A.A., 2014. Intrepretation of TRIZ Principles in a Service Related Context. *Asian Social Science*, Vol. 10, No 13, pp. 108- 130.

Gruber, T.R., 1993. A Translation approach to portable ontologies. *Knowledge Acquisition*, Vol. 5, No.2, 199-220.

IEEE Std 610.12, 1991. *IEEE Standard Glossary of Software Engineering Terminology*, Corrected Edition, February

Ilevbare,I. et al, 2011. Integration of TRIZ and roadmapping for innovation, strategy, and problem solving. Available at: http://www.ifm.eng.cam.ac.uk/uploads/Research/CTM/Roadmapping/triz_dux_trt_phase1_report.pdf (accessed 5.11.2015.).

Kluender, D., 2011. TRIZ for software architecture. *Procedia Engineering*, Volume 9, 2011, Pages 708–713

Liou, Y. et al, 2011. Using Collaborative Technology for TRIZ Innovation Methodology. *International Journal of Electronic Business Management,* Vol. 9, No. 1. pp. 12-23.

Maedche, A. and Staab, S., 2001. Ontology Learning for the Semantic Web. Available at: http:// computer.org (accesed 20.04. 2010)

Mann, D., 2004. *TRIZ for Software Engineers*. IFR Press.

Mishra, U., 2010. *TRIZ Principles for Information Technology*. Umakanta Mishra.

Moehrle, M.G., 2005. What is TRIZ? *From Conceptual Basics to a Framework for Research Creativity and Innovation Management*, Volume 14, Issue 1, pages 3–13, March 2005.

Nakagawa, T., 2004. Software Engineering and TRIZ: Structured Programming Reviewed with TRIZ. Presented at *Mitsubishi Research Institute Users' Study Group Meeting*, Sept. 17, 2004 (J); TRIZ Home Page in Japan, Sept. 2004

Quinlan, J.R., 1992. *C4.5. Programs for Machine Learning*. Morgan Kauffman.

Rousselot, F. and Renauda, J., 2015. On TRIZ and Case Based Reasoning synergies and oppositions. *Procedia Engineering* 131 (2015) 871 – 880.

Rea, K.C., 2001. TRIZ and Software 40 Principles Analogies. Part 1. and Part 2. *The TRIZ Journal.* Sep, 2001. Internet: http://www.triz-journal.com/ archives/2001/09/e/index.htm

Riedl, C.et al, 2009. Managing Service Innovations with an Idea Ontology. *Proceedings of XIX International RESER Conference Budapest*, Hungary, p. 876-892.

Shaw, M. and Garlan, D., 1996. *Software Architecture: Perspectives on an Emerging Discipline*. Pearson.

Sommerville, I., 2004. *Software Engineering*. Addison Wesley, 7th edition.

Tekinerdogan, B. and Aksit, M., 2006. Integrating the Concept of Synthesis in the Software architecture Design Process. *Transactions of the SDPS*, Vol. 7, No. 4, pp. 1-11

Wang, S. et al, 2011. Software Development and Quality Problems and Solutions by TRIZ. *Procedia Computer Science 5,* 730-735.

Yan, W. et al, 2015. A Method for Facilitating Inventive Design Based on Semantic Similarity and Case-Based Reasoning. *Procedia Engineering 131* (2015) 194 – 203

Yan, W. et al, 2015. IngeniousTRIZ: An automatic ontology-based system for solving inventive problems. *Knowledge-Based Systems*, Volume 75, February 2015, pp. 52-65.

DECOMPOSING ERP SUCCESS DYNAMICS: A PROPOSAL FOR A MEASUREMENT MODEL

Pierluigi Zerbino, Davide Aloini, Riccardo Dulmin and Valeria Mininno
Department of Energy, Systems, Territory and Construction Engineering, University of Pisa
Largo Lucio Lazzarino, 56122 Pisa, Italy

ABSTRACT

Defining success in ERP implementation projects is a relevant, complex, and still unsolved endeavor. To our best knowledge, existing proposals are neither comprehensive nor univocal. Thus, extant ERP success models may be incomplete, flawed, and misleading.
This work delimits and redefines ERP success in most of its dimensions, initially drawing upon theories about IS failure. Through a rigorous logical shift, we attempt to model ERP success as a third order factor. Results overcome the literature gaps and potentially open the way for further developments such as revisiting ERP success / implementation frameworks for addressing ERP success in a more systematic, complete, and hence correct way.

KEYWORDS

ERP, Success, Failure, Measure, Conceptual model, Information Systems.

1. INTRODUCTION

To our best knowledge, empirical and theoretical ERP literature lacks a formal, shared, and comprehensive definition of success. In order to cope with this shortage, ERP success has often been defined and measured by means of proxies like User Satisfaction (*i.e.* Wu and Wang 2006; Law and Ngai 2007). In other cases (*i.e.* Zhang et al. 2005; Ifinedo 2006; Bento and Costa 2013) ERP success models do not consider all the typical dimensions (technological, organizational, project) as a whole, different points in time (*i.e.* Häkkinen and Hilmola 2008), and / or pertinent stakeholders. Empirically, ERP success has often been measured through the achievement of some benefits (*i.e.* Panorama Consulting Solutions 2014). Nevertheless, such an approach is misleading because it focuses on the outcomes of an ERP implementation and not upstream, on what ERP success is. Kronbichler et al. (2010) found that some of the most important measurement models of ERP success "*might be limited in scope and do not suit for every practical case*". In fact, ERP success models have often been borrowed, partially or totally, from the context of information systems (ISs) without an adequate contextualization. Such a contextualization is mandatory due to several ERP systems peculiarities, detailed and classified by Markus and Tanis (2000). A direct merger of existing approaches to ERP success could fill up some of the single gaps above but it would result in an ineffective and too much broad solution.

From a theoretical perspective we aim to provide a sound, comprehensive, and compact definition of ERP success that could overcome these gaps. We want to handle this definition to steer the construction of an ERP success framework. From a practitioners' perspective, the ERP success framework could increase the control of on-going and future implementations by enhancing management capabilities in driving them to success. Then, the multidimensionality of success must be addressed through controllable and integrated measures. The ERP success framework could explain what variables define success and what mechanisms perform its achievement. In addition, the integration of the framework with determinants and impacts of ERP success may delimit better what could be an input for success and what success could likely imply.

In this paper, we develop a definition of ERP success and the corresponding construct within an ERP systems success chain. The structure of this work is: literature review; objectives, methodology and modeling phase; discussion of the resulting ERP Success construct; conclusions and future implications.

2. THEORETICAL BACKGROUND

The literature review was started from the general concepts of IS success and failure and it was integrated with a theoretical and empirical perspective on ERP success and failure. Most important evidences are in table 1 and 2. Then, the review was briefly extended on the fit between processes and technology because it is a known relevant aspect within ERP implementations. For each stream, one or two papers that we consider the most relevant to our research were selected and discussed separately, as follows.

2.1 IS Success and Failure

IS success has been challenged in different ways by researchers, in order to catch up its complexity and multidimensional nature. DeLone and McLean (henceforth D&M, 2003) analyzed criticisms and recommendations suggested in literature about their 1992's work and they proposed an update of their IS success model. D&M (2003) explained IS success through specific relationships among System Quality (SQ), Information Quality (IQ), Service Quality (SQ), Intention to use / Use, User Satisfaction (US) and Net Benefits. Respectively, these constructs describe quality on a technical and semantic level, attitude toward using the system / use (behavior) of the system, users' reaction to the use of IS output, net benefits from using the system. D&M applied a holistic approach to Net Benefits and Use (U): benefits should be identified for the various stakeholders through a multi-cause and multi-effect perspective; U includes frequency measures but further evaluations too, *i.e.* who uses the system, nature and appropriateness of use.

Table 1 shows further pertinent evidences we have analyzed in literature.

Table 1. Evidences from literature about IS success and failure

Stream	References	Evidences
IS success	Raymond (1990)	He conceptualized IS success as a combination of US and online/offline system Usage; IS success is hypothesized as directly influenced by organizational context, on one side, and managerial and technical sophistication in implementing/using the IS, on the other side.
	D&M (1992)	They developed an IS success model on the basis of a comprehensive review of the IS success measures used in literature. Within the model, SQ and IQ affect Use (U) and US. U and US are linked by a mutual influence and they are direct antecedents of Individual Impact (InI). Finally, InI could yield some Organizational Impact (OI).
	Seddon and Kiew (1994); Seddon (1997)	They questioned formalization of constructs and nature of relationships of the D&M (1992)'s model.
	D&M (2003)	Fully discussed in the body of the paper.
	Petter et al. (2008)	They reviewed 180 papers about IS success for the period 1992-2007. They examined 90 empirical studies for verifying pairwise associations among the IS success constructs by D&M (2003), highlighting not univocal findings.
	DeLone (2009)	He evaluated the support of determinants of success on the IS success model by D&M (2003) through a literature review on 600 studies and a deep data analysis. He found a strong support for task-technology fit, user attitudes, user involvement.
IS failure	L&H (1987)	Fully discussed in the body of the paper.
	Sauer (1993)	He criticized the IS failure model by L&H (1987) due to its plurality. Differently, he argued that an IS results in a failure if a development termination occurs. An already operating IS turns into a failure if it does no longer attract commitment and resources.
	Flowers (1996)	He stated that an IS is a failure if at least one of the following conditions occurs: (I) the system does not perform as intended or there is a gap between the overall desired performance and the effective performance; (II) the IS is rejected or underutilized by the users due to its hostility; (III) development costs are higher than the benefits achievable with the system during its whole useful life; (IV) the IS development is prematurely abandoned due to the complexity of the system or problems in managing of the project.

IS failure has not been investigated as deeply as IS success. Lyytinen and Hirschheim (henceforth L&H, 1987) proposed the most complete and widespread empirical taxonomy of IS failure consisting in four major failure domains. (I) *Process failure*: the planned IS is not workable at all, often due to problems in IS design, implementation or configuration; or, more frequently, the system development process exceeds budget and / or time schedule; (II) *correspondence failure*: IS design objectives are not met; (III) *interaction failure*: users reject the system or do not use it as intended; (IV) *expectation failure*: the IS fails to meet requirements, expectations or values of one or more of the stakeholders groups that are typically involved in IS development. Drawing upon this taxonomy, L&H (1987) built an IS failure framework consisting in sixteen IS failure classes that cover both the IS development and the IS use.

2.2 ERP Success and Failure

Success in ISs is a multidimensional concept and its complexity increases in the ERP environment due to specific features and issues. Usual project management hurdles and challenges become more tough and a general approach to IS implementation may not be appropriate. Markus and Tanis (2000) defined a process theory of Enterprise Systems success in four phases: chartering, project, shakedown, onward / upward. For each phase, they suggested activities, common problems or errors, possible outcomes, conditions and recipe for success. They recommended to assess ERP success on different dimensions (financial, technical, and human) in different points of the project lifecycle through a set of balanced metrics that should include, at least: project metrics; early operational metrics (shakedown); longer-term business results (onward / upward).

Markus et al. (2000) gathered data, results, problems, and outcomes of ERP implementations from 16 ERP-adopting organizations finding that the adopting companies differed in the definition of success. They noticed that some companies achieved an early success but resulted in a failure on subsequent measures. They also found early failure that turned into later success. Moreover, due to different reasons, several companies were unable to say if they have achieved business benefits in the onward and upward phase.

Table 2 depicts further ERP success evidences in literature, according to the three main logics of analysis by which scientific literature approaches ERP success.

As literature lacks models measuring the ERP failure, we addressed ERP failure through the analysis of implementations that have gone wrong (*i.e.* Barker and Frolick 2003; Perepu and Gupta 2008). Besides other relevant reasons, different ERP implementations failed mainly due to a low fit among system and business processes (CIO Magazine 2004; Xue et al. 2005; Chen et al. 2009) or reject of the system (Scott 1999).

Table 2. Evidences from literature about ERP success

Logic of analysis	References	Evidences
ERP success theories developed according to the phases of an ERP implementation	Markus and Tanis (2000)	Fully discussed in the body of the paper.
	Bento and Costa (2013)	They enriched the IS success model by D&M (2003) and contextualized it in the ERP environment. They developed four versions of the model, one for each phase of an ERP life cycle they suggested: selection / acquisition, implementation / use, stabilization, decline.
Empirical perceptions of ERP success according to different stakeholders and points in time	Larsen and Myers (1997)	They found that an ERP implementation could results in an early success and a later failure, they highlighted how the meaning of success can change if examined from different points of view or in different points in time.
	Markus et al. (2000)	Fully discussed in the body of the paper.
Explaining ERP success by means of proxies	Hong and Kim (2002)	They considered ERP success as the extent of the achievement of expected project goals, *i.e.* compliance with budget and scheduling, system performance targets, expected benefits. About 24% of the implementation success variance was explained by the organizational fit.
	Gable et al. (2003, 2008)	Gable et al. (2003) found that ERP success might be a second order factor, measured by four first order factors: IQ, SQ, InI, and OI. Gable et al. (2003, 2008) questioned the utility of both U and US in explaining ERP success.
	Ifinedo (2006)	He extended the model by Gable et al. (2003) adding two further dimensions: Vendor / Consultant Quality and Workgroup Impact. He found that ERP success could be a third order factor.
	Chien and Tsaur (2007)	They developed a partial extension and re-specification of the D&M's model in the ERP context. They tested the framework involving three high-tech firms in Taiwan. They found that the most relevant constructs in explaining ERP success are SQ, Service Quality (SrQ), and IQ.
	Law and Ngai (2007)	They measured ERP success through US. They found that ERP success and the extent of business process improvement (BPI) have a mutual influence and positive association with the organizational performance.
	Moalagh and Ravasan (2013)	They drew and tested a fuzzy approach considering the six dimensions by Ifinedo (2006). They found SQ and IQ as the most important dimensions in explaining ERP success, while OI ranked least.

2.3 Technology Acceptance and Organizational Fit

ERP success and failure heavily depend on the organizational dimension. In fact, "*it is often said that ERP implementation is about people, not process or technology*" (Bingi et al. 1999). Thus, an ERP system can be rejected or underutilized by users whether or not it performs as hypothesized. For instance, people who do not have a positive attitude toward the ERP system will not likely use it; they could also hinder its use. In literature, perceptions that could shape the attitude toward using an IS have been addressed through the Technology Acceptance Model (Davis et al. 1989; Venkatesh and Davis 1996) and its evolutions (Venkatesh and Davis 2000; Venkatesh and Bala 2008). Despite the empirical importance of technology acceptance in ERP implementations, according to the literature we consider such perceptions as determinants of success and not as potential dimensions of success. Therefore, in this paper, their relevance is negligible.

Rejection, underutilization, or low performance of the ERP system may also be the result of a low fit between the package and the business processes of the adopting company: people could not be able to work and to perform tasks by means of the system. Such a scenario can undermine the whole implementation and could lead to severe business disruption. In order to optimize the organizational fit, performing a Business Process Reengineering (BPR) is typical. A formalization of the organizational fit is the Task-Technology Fit (TTF) introduced by Goodhue and Thompson (1995) in their Technology-to-Performance Chain (TPC) model. The TPC model asserts that an IT could exert a positive impact on individual performance if: (I) the technology is utilized; and (II) the fit between technology and the tasks it supports is good. TTF describes the degree of correspondence among task requirements, individual characteristics, and the functionality of the technology that supports the specified tasks. The authors hypothesized TTF as a direct determinant of the individual performance impacts. They tested a simplified version of the model, finding a moderate support.

2.4 Evidences from the Literature Review

According to our literature review, we find out some points of weakness in extant analysis of ERP success:

- Often, there is a substantial overlap between what ERP success is and what a successful implementation could imply and this leads to ambiguous and misleading evaluations. In our opinion, the ERP success dimensions should unravel and measure how the transition to success may occur. Consequences and outcomes of an ERP implementation, that we label as ERP impacts, are an aftermath of such transition and, then, they are an indirect and imprecise measure of success. The information they could witness is not sufficient to shed light on ERP success, which still remains a black box. For example, US is sometimes considered as an ERP success dimension (*i.e.* Gable 2003; Moalagh and Ravasan 2013) but this may be a flawed approach. Adequate US (ERP positive impact) could be caused by using an ERP that did not change at all the previous way of working, but this may happen due to generally undesirable decisions that could undermine ERP success, *i.e.* too many customizations or absence of BPR.

  ERP success is often measured even through individual or organizational impacts (i.e. Hong and Kim 2002; Ifinedo 2006) or by benefits from use (*i.e.* Chien and Tsaur 2007). Actually, such factors are ERP impacts, which are subsequent to an ERP implementation. An implementation implies impacts, likely positive if the implementation has been a success: thus impacts, similarly to US, cannot be a dimension of ERP success but only a possible consequence.
- Frequently, the multidimensionality of ERP success is not challenged adequately. In fact, the assessment of ERP success through a snapshot from a single perspective is partial and little useful: in the best case, such an approach may only highlight a local sub-optimization. Most works we analyzed (table 2) do not catch the whole complexity of the problem. For example, ERP success is often conceptualized as a trade off: pleasing only some stakeholders (usually management and users); aiming to the best possible outcome in a specific point in time and not in an overall perspective; simply ignoring relevant aspects of an ERP implementation (*i.e.* adequacy of business processes). Consequently, failure or partial success are the most frequent judgments about ERP implementations.
- Markus and Tanis (2000) classified the management of stakeholders like vendors, consultants, internal human resources, as a necessary condition for ERP success in the project phase. Instead, we believe that the stakeholders' management could be a success dimensions and not a factor, if adequately extended to the whole implementation and to each relevant stakeholder that has a legitimate interest towards the implementation. For instance, even expectations of a partner or a provider may be involved in the

mechanisms that explain ERP success. In fact, Markus et al. (2000) included "*success as viewed by ERP-adopting organization's customers, suppliers, and investors*" as a dimension in their assessment of ERP success. Markus et al. (2000) provided a matchless empirical overview about ERP adopters' experience on almost all the relevant aspects about ERP success, integrating the ERP success model by Markus and Tanis (2000). Nevertheless, literature still lacks an ERP success model that encompasses all the shortages we identified above and that formalizes them within a thorough framework.

3. OBJECTIVES, METHODOLOGY AND DEVELOPMENT

3.1 Objectives

On the basis of gaps highlighted through the literature review, this research aims to three main objectives:

1. To determine a comprehensive, integrated, and sound definition of ERP success;
2. To formalize an ERP success framework;
3. To structure an ERP success construct within the framework.

"*In general, companies that do not deliberately set out to achieve measurable business results do not obtain them (or do not realize that they have obtained them)*" (Markus et al. 2000, p. 259). We believe that this is true for ERP success too: if you do not set out a measurable success, you may not achieve it. Thus, practitioners need for a framework that should explain how ERP success is formed during time and that should measure ERP success according to the above objectives. Such measures of ERP success of on-going or ended implementations may enhance the control of future ERP projects, like rollouts, and may improve the occurrence of the possible impacts. Then, we set out four kinds of expected contributions the ERP success framework should enable: (a) to define when measuring what for evaluating ERP success; (b) to address ERP implementations toward success; (c) to allow objective comparisons among ERP implementations; (d) to exert a control function under a learning perspective, linking results to performed actions.

3.2 Methodology

According to the three main objectives, we followed a two-step methodology:

1. An in-depth literature review was performed in order to clarify boundaries and position of ERP Success within a determinants-impacts success chain. Then, assumptions for developing both the ERP success definition and a raw basis of the construct were argued.
2. The architecture of the ERP Success construct was refined according to the success chain's structure.

3.3 Seeking for the Definition of ERP Success

According to the Structural Equation Modeling conventions (Ullman and Bentler 2003), figure 1 depicts the overall framework architecture.

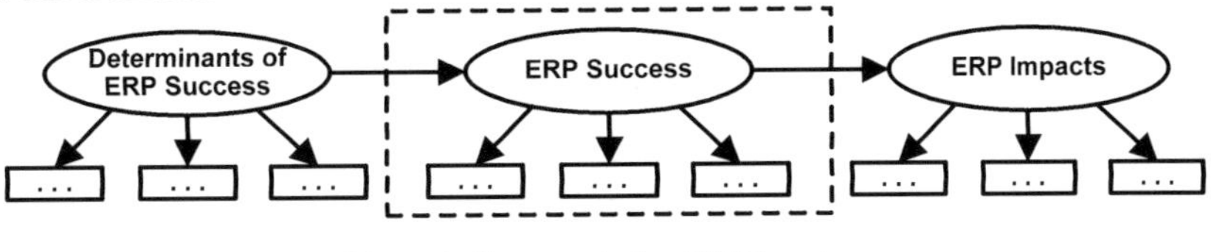

Figure 1. Success chain of ERP systems

Determinants of ERP success gather critical success factors (CSFs). ERP success should explain how the transition to a positive judgment about the implementation occurs and how subsequent impacts may be generated in a holistic view. Its operationalization must measure the goodness of an on-going or a completed ERP implementation. ERP impacts define where, how, and how much an ERP implementation affects the adopting company, *i.e.* benefits from automation.

In general, ISs are not as pervasive and binding as an ERP system. Then, the implementation of a generic IS hardly results in a partially positive outcome. Instead, empirical evidences show that the coexistence of success and failure in the ERP context is quite frequent: ERP partial success is typical. Despite this, failure and success are not totally specular, even in the ERP environment. First, while it is possible to "*reconstruct a systematic pattern of events that led to the failure*" (L&H 1987), this is not necessarily true for success. Second, CSFs and Critical Failure Factors (CFFs) are not always dual. For example, poor top management support is a well-known CFF in ERP implementations, but an excessive or unreasonable support can result in a dangerous escalation, *i.e.* FoxMeyer Drugs (Scott 1999). Third, failure is more dynamic than success: it may propagate in a gradual domino effect (L&H 1987), while success does not.

On this basis, we argue two basic assumptions:

1. The status of an ERP implementation is a combination of success and failure. Such a combination is dynamic because it changes continuously depending on the progress of the implementation. L&H (1987) pointed out that, in a continuous domain, the transition from IS failure to IS success is a gradual shift. Instead, in the ERP context an early success (failure) can result in a later failure (success): *i.e.* in a specific point in time, failure can overcome success but such a configuration could capsize afterwards. We conceptualize these dynamics as a fluctuation of the status of an on-going ERP implementation between two extremes: complete failure, that excludes any form of success; flawless success, an ideal and theoretical situation that excludes any failure.
2. The above dynamic behavior is defined by a set of dimensions operationalized through some variables. Then, these variables are able to describe both ERP success and ERP failure. Depending on the determinants in input, such variables behave and interact among them differently realizing the dynamic combinations of success and failure.

L&H (1987) empirically built their IS failure taxonomy through the declension of four dimensions: process, correspondence, interaction, and expectation. A declension within the success environment is possible too; in fact, most existing ERP success dimensions fall into those categories: *i.e.* compliance with budget and / or scheduling (*i.e.* Hong and Kim 2002) in the process dimension; SQ and IQ (*i.e.* Ifinedo 2006; Chien and Tsaur 2007) in the correspondence dimension; U (*i.e.* Bento and Costa 2013) in the interaction dimension; success viewed by different stakeholders (*i.e.* Markus et al. 2000) in the expectation dimension.

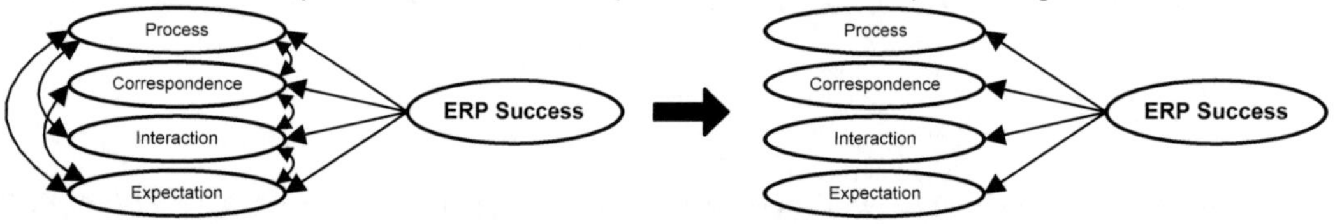

Figure 2. Raw basis of the ERP success construct

Then, in our opinion, an adequate declension of the four dimensions above is able to define ERP success too (figure 2), but with some peculiarities respect to the failure environment. First, L&H recognized the existence of a strong correlation among the four failure notions, which justifies the potential domino effect among them. For instance, if the ERP system does not comply with some explicit requirements (correspondence failure), it can be rejected because users cannot work as intended (interaction failure). However, empirical evidences show that this effect in success is not as probable as in failure, *i.e.* the ERP system can still be rejected due to interaction problems even if it complies with all the explicit requirements. Therefore, we set out the simplifying hypothesis of no correlation among the four dimensions (figure 2). Second, the four dimensions do not have the same weight. Nevertheless, setting general weights can be misleading because they are context-specific, according to the differences among ERP implementations.

3.4 Modeling the ERP Success Architecture

According to figure 2, we have contextualized each construct within the ERP success environment. The *Process* construct requires that: (I) there are not irresolvable problems in designing, implementing, or configuring the ERP system; (II) the ERP project does not exceed budget and / or time. The first requirement is typically challenged upstream through an adequate management of determinants of success (figure 1). We have formalized the second requirement as a dichotomy: time and / or budget overrun does / does not occur. Within the project phase, delays and / or additional expenses could hinder compliance with time or budget. Often, success on project metrics is forced through inappropriate actions, like the cut of end-user training, implying negative effects downstream on measures concerning the shakedown phase. Then, project and shakedown metrics should be integrated, and not assessed independently from each other.

According to the *Correspondence* construct, system / design explicit objectives, requirements, and specifications have to be met. We have operationalized this construct according to SQ and IQ by D&M (2003). SQ represents the technical quality of the ERP system. IQ describes the characteristics of the system outputs. A comparison between measures of SQ and IQ on one side and system objectives / specifications on the other side provides the extent of the correspondence.

The *Interaction* construct requires that the ERP system is not rejected by its users. Hence, the system is used as intended and users' attitude toward it is positive. Such a positive attitude is explained through the technology acceptance, which can be managed upstream through the determinants of success (figure 1). We have operationalized *Interaction* by means of TTF, Output Quality (OQ), and Use.

Finally, the *Expectation* construct requires that the ERP system meets requirements, expectations, or values of the stakeholders groups. Expectations can refer to technical, political, economic, personal, or social dimensions (L&H 1987) and they are often not verbalized or explicitly expressed / identified. Stakeholders are people interested in the implementation and that are not considered within other constructs. Then, a stakeholder is someone that has a legitimate interest in the ERP, even if s/he does not interact with the system either directly or indirectly: *i.e.* a shareholder, a provider, a partner, an operational manager, a project sponsor. The choice of relevant stakeholders is critical. It is function of the implementation scope and of characteristics of the adopting firm. The decision-making process may show that no other stakeholders are relevant besides direct users, management, and project team, which are considered within other constructs.

4. DISCUSSION

The ERP Success construct we propose (figure 3) does not include US because we consider US as a possible ERP impact (figure 1). However, the *Interaction* construct comprehends several drivers of US: if TTF is fine, if the user utilizes the ERP system adequately, and if s/he perceives a good OQ, then s/he could be satisfied.

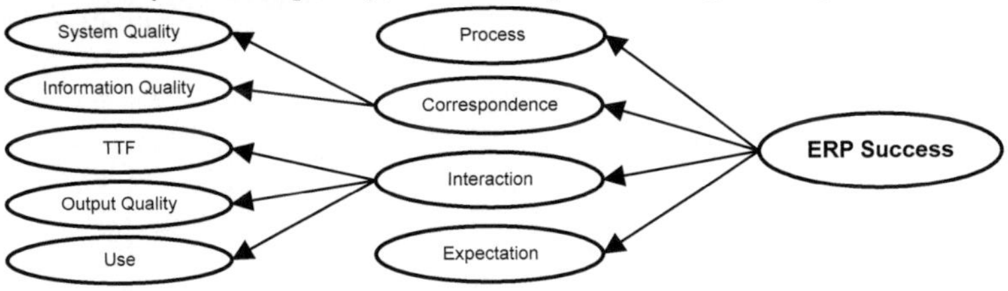

Figure 3. The ERP Success construct

In addition, a user might be even more satisfied if s/he is aware about success on other dimensions, *i.e.* correspondence success and so on. We consider the probable achievement of benefits as part of ERP Impacts (figure 1) and not of ERP Success because they are the most desirable consequence of a good management of the success mechanisms we have defined. Instead, according to Smyth (2001) and unlike DeLone (2009), we consider TTF as a success dimension and not as a determinant. Empirically, BPR is linked to the dynamics of an ERP implementation so deeply that the organizational fit cannot be an enabling factor. TTF was formalized as the fit among characteristics of the tasks in their theoretical to-be version, characteristics of the ERP package – including its best practices –, and characteristics of individuals that will perform tasks by means of the system. An adequate TTF measures a positive alignment among technological, process, and individual dimensions. We believe that a high value of TTF exerts an effect on some impacts, but only if utilization is objectively adequate and not at any given level of use. No benefits can be achieved if the system is not used and is not used appropriately, even if it does perform an acceptable organizational fit.

OQ is a user's judgment about the effective quality of the system. Thus, it differs from Perceived Output Quality by Davis (1985) and from Output Quality by Venkatesh and Davis (2000). Measures of OQ should be repeated in different points in time.

Use describes how (*i.e.* dependence from use; appropriateness and purpose of use) and how much users utilize the ERP system. Frequency of use is secondary because a low level of use can be used as a proxy for failure, but a high level of use does not measure success. Degree of use should be measured only to assess if it is high enough to deny underutilization. In our opinion, ERP systems are so tightly linked to business processes that a distinction between mandatory and voluntary use is not relevant: not using the system means to not perform business processes. Perceptions of constraints in using the ERP system could be overcome upstream through success determinants, *i.e.* organizational readiness or change management.

5. CONCLUSIONS

On a theoretical level, this paper meets the objectives we set out:

1. We define ERP success as success in the four following dimensions, contextualized within the ERP environment: process, correspondence, interaction, and expectation. This definition accurately delimits what ERP success is and is not; it combines an empirical and a theoretical approach; it dynamically considers all the most relevant dimensions of success in different points in time; it keeps into account ERP peculiarities; it gathers, integrates, and formally improves the extant definitions of ERP success.
2. The ERP success chain we have built show a clear role of ERP success, distinguishing it from what causes it and from what it could imply.
3. ERP Success was depicted as a third order factor.

On a managerial level, these results enable the future expected benefits we have hypothesized: (a) practitioners may measure ERP success in a complete and holistic view, distinguishing the time frame of each measure; (b) the ERP Success construct defines a goal which each ERP implementation should tend to, focusing on what is ERP success and, consequently, potentially reducing the waste of resources; (c) the comprehensive nature of the framework could allow a complete comparison of punctual measures concerning different ERP implementations; (d) the integrated sets of measures may identify weak points and both local and global sub-optimizations of an ERP implementation. Linking the management of the determinants of success to the mechanisms that form success might reduce the variability of the ERP potential impacts: in a nutshell, it may enhance the results of an ERP implementation, especially in a roll-out perspective.

Future research steps may be to: (I) validate the theory-building through a case study; (II) define and validate reliable measurement items for each construct; (III) empirically test and validate the framework.

REFERENCES

Essential references are listed below. Further references available on request to the authors.

DeLone, W. H. and McLean, E. R., 2003. The DeLone and McLean Model of Information Systems Success: A Ten-Year Update. *Journal of Management Information Systems*, Vol. 19, No. 4, pp. 9–30.

Goodhue, D. L. and Thompson, R. L., 1995. Task-technology fit and individual performance. *MIS Quarterly*, Vol. 19, Issue 2, pp. 213–236.

Law, C. C. H. and Ngai, E. W. T., 2007. ERP systems adoption: An exploratory study of the organizational factors and impacts of ERP success. *Information and Management*, Vol. 44, Issue 4, pp. 418–432.

Lyytinen, K. and Hirschheim, R., 1987. Information systems failures - a survey and classification of the empirical literature. *Oxford surveys in information technology*. Oxford University Press Inc., New York, pp. 257–309.

Markus, M. L. and Tanis, C., 2000. The Enterprise System Experience - From Adoption to Success, in *Framing the Domains of IT Management: Projecting the Future Through the Past*, pp. 173–207. Pinnaflex Educational Resources Inc., Cincinnati, Ohio.

Markus, M. L. et al, 2000. Learning from adopters' experiences with ERP: Problems encountered and success achieved. *Journal of Information Technology*, Vol. 15, Issue 4, pp. 245–265.

Moalagh, M. and Ravasan, A. Z., 2013. Developing a practical framework for assessing ERP post-implementation success using fuzzy analytic network process. *International Journal of Production Research*, Vol. 51, pp. 1236–1257.

MOTIVATIVE COMPUTING: AN INTERDISCIPLINARY ANALYSIS AND DESIGN FRAMEWORK

Deborah A. Gears[1], Carla Lorek[2], Keli DiRisio[1] and Alexander Goldberger[1]
[1]*Rochester Institute of Technology*
[2]*Boolean Shore, LLC*

ABSTRACT

Competition for funded research continues to tighten around the globe with awards granted to higher impact projects. While sharing of ideas generally occurs in pockets, it becomes crucially necessary to advance collaborative engagement among researchers. At a growing research university, interdisciplinary methods were applied to gain deep understanding of the scholar's world and to develop an engaging platform for collaboration. User-centered design, systems analysis and design, object-oriented analysis and design, and psychology theory facilitated a multidimensional view of the problem domain. A critical finding revealed that faculty did not know about the skills, knowledge, and interests of others across campus. Curiosity, honor, and idealism were found to intrinsically motivate researchers that provided an empirical basis for creative design.

Analysis findings, along with aesthetic and game elements, informed a solution designed to energize and direct self-determined participation—elements missing in classic systems development processes. Scholar Trading Cards™—the locus of purposeful and serendipitous interaction—mobilized researcher acumen in digital and non-digital spaces. Digital card data published on the university Intranet allowed for searching and sharing of information useful to collaborators, administrators, and staff. Paper-based cards facilitated face-to-face interactions. The platform is showing promise in bridging interpersonal gaps to improve the flow of scholar information across campus. We introduce a contemporary systems framework and information platform that is demonstrating a positive effect on campus-wide collaboration.

KEYWORDS

Systems, collaboration, psychology, motivation, games, interaction.

1. INTRODUCTION

Competition for research funding continues to plague scientists, with no relief in sight (Howard & Laird 2013). Shrinking grant awards in nationally supported programs, along with flat public and private sector money, leaves researchers feeling discouraged and some programs at risk. The scientific community and university administrators recognize that traditional models are ineffective in keeping pace with fiscal limitations and continue seeking alternate means to sustain external research (Howard & Laird). Collaborative proposals along with improved communication and networking are among the growing strategies needed for success in funded projects.

Amid global tensions for research survival, Rochester Institute of Technology (RIT) increased faculty requirements for scholarship, namely externally funded research. Of the many challenges encountered in the multi-year transition, collaboration–a critical success factor–was found to occur in pockets highlighting the problem of weak collaborative pathways. At the time, gamification–the use of game elements in non-game contexts (Deterding, et al. 2011, p. 2)–was touted as a bellwether to energize and direct volitional behavior (Hamari, et al, 2015). Recognizing a parallel between volitional engagement in games and collaboration this research emphasized the need to understand more about what motivates researchers.

Funded by RIT's Sponsored Research Services, the overarching goal of this research project was to improve interdisciplinary collaboration (interaction between people or organizations directed toward a common and mutually beneficial goal (Miner, et al. 2011)). We approached the problem of weak collaborative pathways using the Methodopoly™ analysis and design framework. Methodopoly™ evolved from a previous study (Gears & Braun 2013) that considered motivating factors of key players to solve a business problem. We extended that framework more formally in this research by designing a framework that integrates interdisciplinary methods, psychology, game design, and aesthetic elements, with creativity during analysis and design (Deterding et al. 2011).

Our study addressed four research questions: 1) Are there common intrinsic desires among researchers that can be used in systems design to motivate engagement? 2) Can a solution using the Methodopoly™ framework be designed to engage volitional participation and increase collaboration? 3) Can the inclusion of game elements in a goal-oriented user-experience be taken seriously by a research community? 4) Will the solution result in increased scholarship (grant proposals and awards, publications, and increased graduation rates for thesis-bearing degrees)? In this paper, we will introduce the Methodopoly™ framework, our solution, and the results of our work still in-progress.

2. THEORETICAL FOUNDATIONS

Energizing behavior through motivation design has demonstrated prolonged behavioral engagement and achievement of desired outcomes (Rigby 2014; Rigby et al. 2011). A study of employee behavior in an open enterprise wiki (a socially open technology facilitating collaborative content development and information sharing) (Gears, 2011) highlights the role motivation (an internal state, need, or desire that energizes and directs behavior (Deci & Ryan 1985; Reber & Reber 2001; Reeve 2005)) plays in contextually-bound collaborative environments (Gears 2012; Gears 2011). Two motivation theories guided understanding of psychological factors prompting wiki participation; positive and negative affect (emotion) were also found to be predictors of engagement (Rigby 2014; Rigby & Ryan 2011; Ryan and Deci 2000). The Theory of 16 Basic Desires contributed to understanding the innate human desires of individuals. The Self-Determination Theory (Deci & Ryan 2000; Deci & Ryan 2011) identified internally regulated action along a spectrum of extrinsic and intrinsic motivation. Collaborative engagement patterns describe contextual conditions, emotions, and motivational elements that contributed to positive and negative participation behaviors (Gears et al. 2013).

2.1 Theory of 16 Basic Desires (Sensitivity Theory)

The theory of 16 basic desires (Reiss 2004, 2000) a psychological content theory of motivation, provided utility for analyzing and predicting human behavior. Reiss' model, derived from Maslow's (Maslow 1954) theory of human needs, and William James' (James 1950) theory of internal desires, describes basic desires for: Order, Power, Independence, Curiosity, Acceptance, Saving, Idealism, Honor, Social Contact, Family, Status, Vengeance, Romance, Eating, Physical Activity, and Tranquility. The manner in which humans act upon these desires is shaped by the intensity of each desire, cultural influences, and individual experiences. An individual's intensity for each of the 16 basic desires can be measured using Reiss' Profile of Fundamental Goals and Motivational Sensitivities Assessment (Reiss 2000).

2.2 Self-Determination Theory (SDT)

The self-determination theory (Deci & Ryan 2000, 1985; Ryan et al. 2000a, 2000b) framed a motivation model that explains what and how human behavior is initiated and regulated (Deci et al. 2000; Ryan et al. 2000a, 200b). The SDT recognizes social and environmental conditions that affect personal volition and engagement in activities. The SDT combines both content (psychological needs) and process (cognition) motivation describing needs for autonomy, competence, and relatedness. An individual's motivation for action is defined along a spectrum of amotivation, extrinsic motivation, and intrinsic motivation measured by perceived locus of causality (external to internal regulation). Needs for autonomy and competence allow the "prediction of the social circumstances and task characteristics that enhance versus diminish intrinsic motivation" (Deci et al. 2008, p. 233).

Quality of extrinsic and intrinsic motivation contribute to explanations for why individuals engage (Rigby 2014; Rigby et al. 2011). The SDT also describes psychological principles in gamification design that sustain user engagement, satisfaction, and behavioral change. In gamification design, goals are not necessarily directed towards the experience of "fun," rather goals are more closely related to personal value and avoidance of pressure and control (Rigby 2014). Deep understanding of the psychological needs of individuals is deemed necessary to motivate desired outcomes (Rigby 2014).

2.3 Collaborative Engagement Patterns (CEP)

In a study of corporate wikis (Gears et al. 2013), four collaborative engagement patterns explained contextual conditions and internally regulated psychological factors contributing to wiki participation decisions. When required by managers, projects, or teams, *Conformists* interacted (lurk, add, minor edits) when required by their managers, a project or team—emotions changed from negative to positive (liking the wiki) and positive to negative (because interaction was required). *Embracers,* initially experiencing negative emotions interacted (lurk, add, edit, explore) when their manager shared a positive attitude and offered time to explore. *Collaborators* actively interacted (lurk, add, edit, collaborative content development, wiki discussions) describing perceived value [of the wiki], confidence in appropriate interactions of others (corporate conscience), and positive affect. *Traditionalists*, deeply rooted in a traditional corporate culture, expressed negative affect and would not change other employees' words in the wiki. These patterns provide empirical evidence of technology facilitate collaboration inside organizational boundaries.

3. ANALYSIS AND DESIGN APPROACH: METHODOPOLY™

Classic systems development processes lack explicit inclusion of interdisciplinary methods that address emotion, motivation, artistry, and creativity. Considering the upswing in web-based information systems and the competition for participation in social platforms, we tested the Methodopoly™ framework designed to energize and direct (motivate) participation. Formal methods (user-centered design, structured and object-oriented analysis and design) and psychology theory (motivation and emotion) were integrated synergistically with game design, visual arts, and creativity. The framework depicts an interdisciplinary, iterative, incremental, and improvisational analysis and design framework (refer to Figure 1). Formal methods were applied in concert with analysis of the data (study hall), design ideation (visits to the drawing board), collaboration (collaboration corner), and resting the mind for creativity (take-a-walk). Methodopoly™ was not partitioned in phases or executed in sprints. The step-by-step model allows team members to take two steps forward and three steps back; budget, schedule, and final decisions left to the principal investigator.

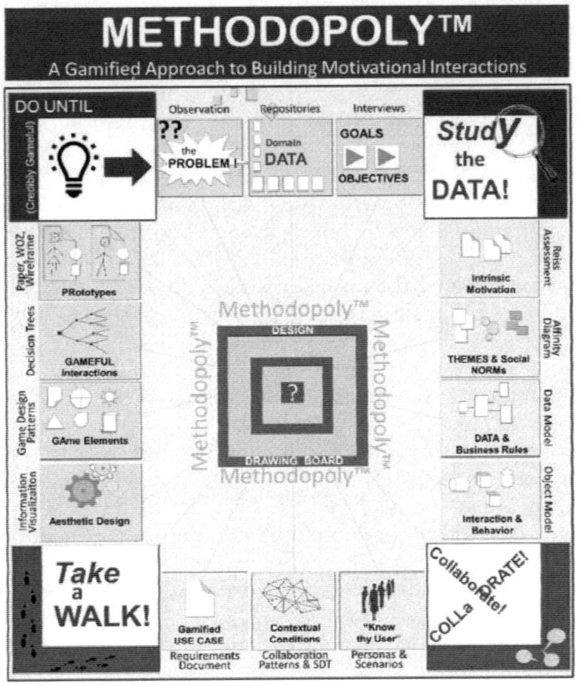

Figure 1. Methodopoly Framework

3.1 Analysis Activities

Study participants (24 researchers), varying in research abilities and experiences, working in different disciplines, were selected through purposive sampling. Researcher experience ranged from "interested in research, haven't done much and need to", to "significant, research has been my career." Qualitative methods were applied where participants were interviewed in their working environment. Analysts captured descriptive (record of details) and reflexive (subjective reflections) (Bogdan et al. 2003) field notes from interviews and observations.

The Reiss Motivation Sensitivities Assessment (Reiss 2000) was administered to all participants through an anonymous web-based instrument. The survey replicated Reiss' protocol to assess intensity of the 16 basic desires that motivated each researcher. Data were analyzed in the aggregate (refer to Figure 2).

Structured and object-oriented methods, collectively known as software engineering, e.g., data, process, object, sequence, state diagrams, logic models, etc., were integrated to flesh out requirements and for design (Constantine et al. 1999) . User-centered design (from human-computer interaction discipline) were also applied to gain deeper understanding of researcher needs, wants, personas, and contextual conditions. Synergistic application of methods and study of the data facilitated a deep understanding of the domain necessary to test the boundaries of what could be possible in design (Coleman, 2005).

Table 1.Excerpt of findings

Business/Institute Problems
• Weak collaborative pathways • Research skills vary across institute • Student and external involvement a lost opportunity • Difficult finding faculty and students to work with • Departmental silos interfere with collaboration • Sharing takes effort when domain language not understood
Researcher Norms
• Like to share and expect acknowledgement for their work • Prefer to choose with whom they collaborate • Very busy with limited direct contact availability
Business Rules
• Researchers may be faculty or students • Faculty are expected to, and evaluated for, their research • Research requirements vary by faculty position • Researchers may be associated with many affiliations

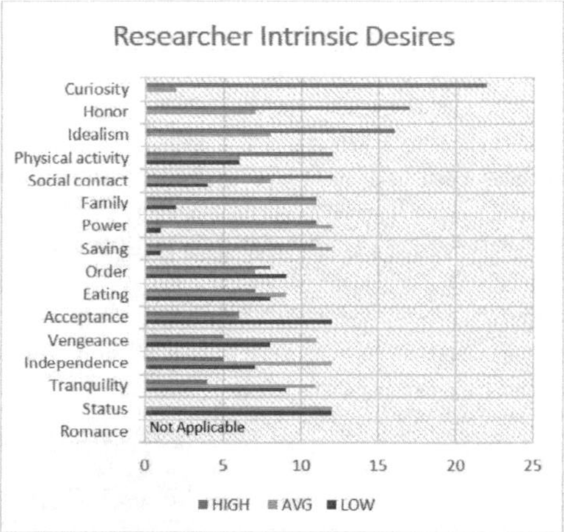

Figure 2. Researcher Intrinsic Desires

Interpretation and field notes taken from interviews provided a basis for card sorting and affinity diagramming (Holtzblatt et al. 1997)—revealing key themes in the data (refer to excerpt in Table 1). Personas and user scenarios mapped actor characteristics, behavior, expectations, processes, value perceptions, and more.

Participant's intrinsic motivational tendencies were analyzed along the continuum of the 16 basic desires described by Reiss (2000). Data indicated that *Curiosity* (the desire to explore and learn) ranked highest on the motivational spectrum for all researchers. *Honor* (the desire to be loyal and a credit to ancestry) and *Idealism* (the desire to make the world a better place) followed and were also highly scaled with no desires for avoidance (low importance). Acceptance, Tranquility, and Status ranked low indicating they held little motivational value. Refer to Figure 2 for distribution of all 16 basic desires.

Analysis findings were aligned with research questions and use cases were created to include goals and objectives for the system under study. Based upon factors that enable collaborative engagement in organizations (CEP), pre-conditions included the need for egalitarian governance, time for participation, value proposition, and conditions that would not affect pay or performance measures, to create an environment conducive for community engagement.

In parallel with analysis, we studied an array of game design elements (Bjork et al., 2004; Burke, 2014; McGonigal 2011; Reeves et al. 2009; Ryan et al. 2000a; Schell 2008; Werbach et al. 2012) throughout analysis and design. A shared understanding of game elements—their behavior, use, and parameters—provided a common language for discussion and mental bookmarking of game-oriented building blocks. We wanted to build on the positive aspects of game play (without delivering a game) by leveraging known motivational tendencies that might prompt action.

3.2 Design Activities

Platform design involved recursive study of the data, functional design proposals, and evolution of analysis models to design models. We studied characteristic of intrinsic desires wondering how, when, and where they could be leveraged to pique (and sustain) curiosity, and invoke feelings of honor and idealism (Reiss 2004; Reiss 2000). We studied scaling of extrinsic motivators described in the SDT (Dec et al. 2000; Rigby 2014; Ryan et al. 2000a) searching for means to foster feelings of autonomy, competence, and relatedness. Motivational characteristics, game element conditions, and contextual study data weaved through our thoughts throughout design.

To clear our mindset from reality and shift to possibilities of invention we deliberately transformed our thinking about system objects e.g., Employee, College, to *Players* and *Playing fields*. This facilitated a more open flow of design ideas during joint application design sessions and independent reflection. A project wiki facilitate sharing of design ideas when they were sparked by individuals. Visual effects and prototypes facilitated the acting out of complex design concepts. Design ideas were play tested with the research community and helpful in dispositioning, i.e., throwing out or building up.

Over time, a feasible design solution emerged and provided a basis for momentum to build in system design. The entity relationship diagram then served as a central design model for connecting use case interaction rules, constraints, and system data. All requirements and design specifications were collectively documented in *gamified* use cases. Each use case indicated actor behaviors, values, beliefs, contextual norms, data, rules, constraints, game elements, motivators, contextual conditions, and normal course of interaction.

3.3 Creativity

Wallas' (1926) four stages of creativity were explicitly called out as the anchors to the novel combination of structured methods, domains and disciplines. The Preparation stage served to demarcate and clarify the problem statement through immersion: gathering approaches and collaborating with others. Frequent walks and time away from the problem itself facilitated a period of unconscious and involuntary Incubation where new patterns and insights were generated. Potential ideas emerged in the design space: some like flashes of insight, others like progressive bytes of knowing (Wallas; Czikszentmihalyi 1996). These were the "aha's" of the Illumination stage. The building of physical prototypes tested the validity of the problem solution in the Verification stage.

Czikszentmihalyi (1996) suggested that the creative process is more recursive than linear, requiring multiple iterations, loops, and insights. Both the genesis and attributes of Methodopoly™ paralleled this recursive nature. While the design process portrays a simplified organization of the numerous methods used, the game play was designed to "Do Until" a credible and gameful solution was completed.

3.4 Approach Summary

An unscripted process framework–Methodopoly™ guided synergistic application of interdisciplinary methods for systems analysis and design. Brainstorming of design ideas (Schell 2008) focused on means to energize intrinsic motivators of curiosity, honor, and idealism found to motivate scholars. User-centered design, structured, and object-oriented methodologies, motivation psychology, game design, and aesthetic design were linked through creativity. A plausible design solution emerged following an improvisational sequence of action directed by the Principal Investigator.

4. SOLUTION

Scholar Trading Cards™ were implemented as the locus of intrinsically motivated interaction in digital and non-digital spaces. Pocket-sized to emulate historical sports artifacts, card fronts featured a professional photo, QR code for digital sharing, contact information, and a campus-wide tie strength indicator. Card backs highlighted credentials useful in finding collaborators: academic degrees, skills, domains, research interests, research methods, affiliations, fun facts, publication keywords, and a trending moniker (refer to Figure 3).

The *Scholar Trading Card*™ is directed at researcher's (scholar's) intrinsic desire for Honor—incentive to feel pride, meaning, and self-worth (Epley 2014; Reiss 2000)—and Idealism—motivation to get involved and contribute to the betterment of the academic community by attending to the significance of what they do (Epley 2014; Reiss 2000). A web-based platform facilitated digital manipulation (tap and transfer of cards) by viewing (flipping), searching, and collecting cards. This appealed to the intrinsic desire for curiosity (explore, learn, and analyze information). Printed (touch and trade) cards allowed free-play with known and unplanned uses. Students, faculty, staff, and alumni had the freedom to participate and feel part of the academic community (autonomy & relatedness.)

Figure 3. Scholar Trading Card Example (front and back)

A Dedicated Facilitator assisted scholars with development of their card content due to scarcity of researcher time (CEP) and inability of most researchers to succinctly articulate key accomplishments. Content patterns were based upon scholar personas (developing researcher, practicing researcher, established researcher), department colors (reflection of Honor to the university's academic discipline), along with unique professional or personal attributes.

Each new card owner received a limited number physical cards to distribute as desired; the digital card was immediately published to the web upon scholar approval. According to the Law of Scarcity (Hogan, 1998), the value of physical cards will increase over time given limited supply in circulation. Additional physical cards were earned by growing the network through scholar referrals, scholar card acquisitions, special events, and more. In alignment with Hamari, et al. 2012, we found that users found their own value for the cards. For example, academic advisors allow students to add digital cards when recommending faculty to put a face to a name.

Any digital card could be added to a user's collection of cards directly through the web or by scanning the QR code on a physical card. Collectors were asked about their connection to the scholar to analyze effectivity in bridging structural holes (Burt, 1992) and social network growth over time. "How do you know a scholar?" questions were directed at quantity of interactions, not quality of a relationship. For example, card acquirers must indicate their tie-strength as the final step in card acquisition: 1) Never interacted, 2) Been introduced, 3) Interacted with infrequently, and 4) Frequently interacted with.

Card design focused on brand recognition, presentation of information, and appeal to intrinsic motivators. Integrating color and contrast according to Gestalt Theory (O'Connor 2005) provided structure and consistency for visual perception of information (O'Connor). The combined selection of typography, color, contrast, proportion, and balance contributed to a coherent and comprehensive design (O'Connor; Tufte 1990).

The study of game elements (indicated in italics) in games provided a thought-provoking pallet of discrete building blocks used to gamify the user experience. According to Bjork, et al. (2004), cards were considered *memorabilia* for *social interaction* allowing for *gain ownership, collecting, reward, and game element trading.* New players experience *player created game elements* when, with the help of a *dedicated game facilitator,* they create their card. *Unnecessary obstacles* (McGonigal 2011) were inserted to provide some level of challenge leading to a sense of competence. Rules governing the use of physical cards were left open for opportunistic and serendipitous interaction.

5. RESULTS

The *Scholar Trading Card*™ platform was deployed in grassroots fashion beginning with one small group presentation (approximately 50 faculty, staff, and students), a digital briefing in the daily university news, and word-of-mouth exchanges. Ten printed digital trading cards were play tested for a period of three months while web development and design continued. During the play test period, the number of new scholar cards increased to 30 published cards representing an estimated 6% of research faculty. Serendipitous uses for the cards are also surfacing among students, staff, and faculty.

Early indicators suggest that the inclusion of game elements in goal-oriented systems design can be taken seriously by a research community (research question 3). Engagement (types of interaction with the digital system) included: card requests, face-to-face card exchanges (metrics unknown), website views, digital cards collected, and referrals. Over a nine-month period dating from late November 2014 to late August 2015 (including three academic break months), a total of 51 cards have been requested, with 261 unique users, and 650 views.

A measure of tie-strength indicated that 136 digital cards were added to individual collections between May 2015 and August 2015. Of the digital cards collected, 40% were made among people who had *Frequently Interacted*, 29% among people who had *Been Introduced*, 26% among people who had *Infrequently Interacted*, and 5% who had *Never Interacted*. Increases in scholarly activity (rises in grant proposal, awards, publications, and graduation rates for thesis bearing degrees is not know at this writing (research question 4). Longitudinal data collection be collected over time to measure the impact on scholarly activity among the research community.

6. CONCLUSION

Systems development projects involving motivation psychology, game elements, and creativity, go beyond the phased borders of traditional systems development lifecycles or agile development. This research introduced a framework, Methodopoly™ that resulted in a platform designed to improve weak collaborative pathways. Interdisciplinary building blocks were called upon when needed to understand the user's world, leverage motivating factors of key players, test organizational boundaries, and to create an environment that fostered volitional participation. Early results demonstrate an increase in user connections across a university campus.

ACKNOWLEDGEMENTS

Sincere gratitude is extended to Rochester Institute of Technology, Dr. Marc Marschark, Dr. Ryne Raffaelle and Sponsored Research Services, Dr. Lynn Wild and The Wallace Center, and RIT MAGIC Center for their support of this project. Sincere appreciation is extended to individual contributors Dr.'s Ronald Vullo and Christopher Egert, Lisa Mauro, Keli DiRisio, Paige Satterly, Alexander Goldberger, Ravitega Gunda, and Betty Hillman for their knowledge, creativity, dedication, and collaborative efforts.

REFERENCES

Bjork, S., Holopainen, and Jussi, H., 2004. *Patterns in Game Design*, Hingham, Charles River Media, MA, USA.

Bogdan, R. and Biklen, S. K., 2003. *Qualitative Research for Education: An introduction to theories and methods*, Pearson Education Group, New York.

Burke, B., 2004. *Gamify: How Gamification Motivates People to do Extraordinary Things*, Bibliomotion, Inc., Brookline, MA, 2014.

Burt, R. S., 1992. *Structural holes: The social structure of competition*, Harvard University Press, Cambridge, MA.

Coleman, D., 2005. "Dimensions of interactive software requirements: Synergistic opportunity", *IEEE SoutheastCon 2005*, pp. 397-405.

Constantine, L. L. and Lockwood, A. D., 1999. *Software for Use: A practical guide to the models and methods of usage-centered Design,* Addison-Wesley, Reading, MA.

Czikszentmihalyi, M., 1996. *Creativity: Flow and the Psychology of Discovery and Invention*, Harper Collins Publishers.

Deci, E. L., and Ryan, R. M., 2000. "The "what" and why" of Goal Pursuits: Human needs and the self-determination of behavior", *Psychological Inquiry,* 11(4), pp. 227-268.

Deci, E. L., and Ryan, R. M., 1985. *Intrinsic Motivation and Self-determination in Human Behavior*, Plenum Press, New York.

Deterding, S., Dixon, D, Khaled, R., and Nacke, L. E., 2011. "From game design to gamefulness: Defining gamification", *MindTrek.*

Epley, N., 2014. *Mindwise: How We Understand What Others Think, Feel, and Want*. Knopf, New York.

Gears, D. A., and Braun, K., 2013. Gamification in Business: Designing motivating solutions to problem situations. *CHI Gamification Workshop*, http://gamification-research.org/chi2013/papers/.

Gears, D. A., 2012. "Corporate Wikis Underground: An investigation of motivation and collaborative engagement", *Academic and Business Research Institute, Journal of Management and Marketing Research*, Vol. 9, pp. 14-33.

Gears, D. A., 2011. *Wiki Behavior in the Workplace: Emotional aspects of content development*. Dissertation published in ProQuest/UMI Dissertations.

Gears, D., and Lorek, C., 2013. "Context Matters: A grounded theory analysis of wiki engagement", *International Conference on Multimedia and Human Computer Interaction*, pp. 47.1 – 47.9.

Hogan, K., 1998. *The Psychology of Persuasion: How to persuade others to your way of thinking*, Pelican Publishing, New York.

Holtzblatt, K., and Beyer, H., 1997. Contextual Design: Defining customer-centered systems, Morgan Kaufmann Publishers, San Francisco, CA.

Howard, D. J., and Laird, F. N., 2013. The New Normal in Funding University Science, *Issues in Science and Technology*, Vol. 30, Fall Issue 1.

Huotari, K., and Hamari, J., 2012. Defining Gamification–A service marketing perspective, *MindTrek,* pp. 17-22.

Hamari, J., Koronen, L., and Alha, K., 2015. "Why do people play games? A review of studies on adoption and use", *Proceedings of the 8th Annual Hawaii International Conference on System Sciences*.

James, W., 1950. *The Principles of Psychology*. Dover Publications, New York.

Maslow, A., 1954. Motivation and Personality. Harper and Row, New York.

McGonigal, J., 2011. *Reality is Broken: Why games make us better and how they can change the world*, The Penguin Press, NY.

Miner, J. T., Miner, L. E., & Griffith, J., 2011. *Collaborative Grantseeking*, Santa Barbara, CA: Greenwood.

O'Connor, Z., 2005. Colour, Contrast and Gestalt Theories of Perception: The impact in contemporary visual communications design, *Color Research & Application,* 40(1), pp. 85-92.

Reber, A. S., & Reber, E. S., 2001. *Dictionary of psychology*, 3rd ed., Penguin Books, New York.

Reeve, J., 2005. *Understanding Motivation and Emotion, 4th Ed.,* John Wiley & Sons, Hoboken, NJ.

Reiss, S., 2004. Multifaceted Nature of Intrinsic Motivation: The theory of 16 basic desires, *Review of General Psychology*, 8(3), pp. 179-193.

Reiss, S., 2000. *Who am I? The 16 Basic Desires that Motivate our Actions and Define our Personality, Penguin Publishing*, New York.

Reeves, B., and Leighton, J., 2009. *Total Engagement: Using games and virtual worlds to change the way people work and businesses compete*, Harvard Business School Publishing, Boston, MA.

Rigby, S., 2014. *Gamification and Motivation*, In S. P. Walz and S. Deterding (Eds.), The gameful world: Approaches, issues, applications, MIT Press, Cambridge, MA.

Rigby, S., and Ryan, R. M., 2011. Glued to games: How video games draw us in and hold us spellbound, Praeger, Santa Barbara, California.

Ryan, R. M., and Deci, E. L., 2000a. Intrinsic and Extrinsic Motivations: Classic definitions and new directions, *Contemporary Educational Psychology*, 25(1), pp. 54-67.

Ryan, R. M., and Deci, E. L., 2000b. Self-determination Theory and the Facilitation of Intrinsic Motivation, Social Development, and Well-being, *American Psychologist*, 55(1), pp. 68-78.

Schell, J., 2008. *The Art of Game Design: A book of lenses*, Morgan Kaufmann Publishers, New York.

Tufte, E. R., 1990. *Envisioning Information*, Graphics Press, Cheshire, CT.

Wallas, G., 1926. *The Art of Thought*, Brace and Company, New York.

Werbach, K., and Hunter, D., 2012. *For the Win*, Wharton Digital Press, Philadelphia, PA, 2012.

METHODOLOGICAL FRAMEWORK FOR THE DEVELOPMENT OF COMPUTATIONAL THINKING AND PROGRAMMING THROUGH EXPERIENTIAL LEARNING: CASE STUDY FROM SCHOOLS JUAN SEGUEL AND ALLIPEN IN FREIRE, CHILE

Marcos Lévano[1], Vanessa Córdova[1] and Andrea Albornoz[2]
[1]*Escuela de Ingeniería Informática*
[2]*Departamento de Lenguas*
Universidad Católica de Temuco
Manuel Montt 56, Casilla 15-D, Temuco, Chile

ABSTRACT

In this study a methodological framework to develop computational thinking in the students' process of developing logical and abstract self-learning in computer programing on epistemic learning based on TICs is presented. The framework is constructed on an experiential learning cycle that allows students increase their skills in an insightful way, in order to develop programing computer since childhood.
From the intervention of Scratch software in the subject of mathematics, the results of the case study were obtained. The study was conducted in two schools from Freire district, Chile: Escuela Municipal Juan Seguel, from the urban sector, and Escuela de Allipén, from the rural sector. We worked with 135 students and their ages ranged from 9 to 13 years old. There were two groups of study, group 1 (rural), from which the following results were obtained when Scrach software was applied 92.5%, motivation 96.2%, creativity 96.2%, and problem solving 77.7%; as from group 1 (urban) the following results were obtained when Scrach software was applied: 79.1%, motivation 100%, creativity 83.3%, and problem solving 95.8%. In the group 2 (rural) the following results were obtained when Scrach software was applied: 72.7%, motivation 72.7%, creativity 63.6%, and problem solving 77.2%; while from group 2 (rural) the following results were obtained when Scrach software was applied: 72.7%, motivation 72.7%, creativity 63.6%, and problem solving 77.2%.
Scratch is software used as a pedagogical resource. It allows students to develop some skills like logical thinking, so they can express ideas concerning generation of algorithms in order to solve problems in a consistent way. It also strengthens the personal relationship between teachers and students and builds knowledge and self-learning within a social environment. Through the activities carried out with the software, a type of learning called "learning by doing" was developed in theory and in practice. The main purpose of the implementation of this type of learning was to enhance the motivation and participation of students during class. In addition, by implementing Scratch, peer collaboration was generated, which is useful to carry out projects of greater and lesser complexity.

KEYWORDS

Methodological Framework, Scratch, Computational Thinking, Metacognition, Knowledge, Epistemic Learning.

1. INTRODUCTION

Nowadays, computational thinking is encouraged since pre-school stages to motivate students to engage in the future in areas related to computer technologies. Some countries like England, United States, Finland, Estonia, Japan and Singapore have been focusing on the development of computational thinking since early school stages, as a way of leading the global digital revolution (Atilano et al., 2014), (Wing, 2006). In fact, the basics needed to prepare creative technology developers can be submitted to children from pre-school even without using specific technology (Bilbao-Osorio et al., 2014). Those basic concepts are encompassed in what today is known as "computational thinking" (CT, 2011). In general, computational thinking skills include designing and decompose a problem, process data, create algorithms and generalize them (CT, 2011); (Wing, 2014). The creators of software technologies for domestic or industrial impact, such as applications like email, search engines, meta-search engines and video games use those computer programming skills. Computer programming can solve general problem for us making a sequence of steps of a sequential processes (Knuth, 1997).

The computational and programming thinking is a way of solving problems integrating digital technologies with peoples' ideas (Wing, 2006). For that reason, problems should be formulated so that they can be solved by using computers (Knuth, 1997), and students should be prepared by their teachers, so they can abstract problems, organize data in logical ways, identify and analyze solutions, specify a solution through a series of orderly steps (algorithm), encode solutions in a language understood by the computer (program), and generalize and transfer those solutions to other problems where applicable (Lee, 2014). The objective of this work is focused on developing a pedagogical framework for the development of computational thinking in computer programming through experiential learning (Kolb, 1984) within systematic learning. From the perspective of the logic of learning focused on the student, the development of knowledge in controlled environments, with approaches based on reality, allows students a certain degree of maturation of thought in terms of problem solving. When students are immerse in learning through experience, in receiving knowledge, and when they are able to think about the contents they are learning and apply those contents, it means that they have developed the process of self-learning in an early stage.

This investigation aims to develop computational thinking and computer programming, and it was conducted on students from primary schools from rural and urban sectors from Freire district, La Araucanía region, Chile. One of the purposes of this study was to measure improvements in math class. Some of the questions raised about the problem were: Why do we have to encourage computational thinking and programming in children? How can we motivate student-student and student-teacher interaction in learn by doing focused classes? Can Scratch help to develop computational thinking and computer programming skills?

2. BASIS

The following models and key elements are described to develop the methodological framework:

2.1 Experiential Model of Learning

The experiential model of learning, developed by David Kolb and Ronald Fry (Kolb, 1984), (Kolb and Fry, 1975), in the early seventies, is based on four key elements: concrete experience, reflexive observation, abstract conceptualization and active experimentation. These four elements are the core of a spiral of learning that can begin with any one of the four elements, but typically begins with the concrete experience. Usually this model is known as Kolb's cycle.

2.2 Epistemic Community of Learning

The objective of the epistemic community is to build knowledge collectively. The theoretical perspectives of knowledge construction are designed to achieve intentional learning (Bereiter and Scardamalia, 1989) in the process of developing knowledge (Bereiter and Scardamalia, 1993) and in the process of building a community based on the construction of knowledge in schools (Scardamalia and Bereiter, 1994). Nowadays individuals are able to generate a series of elements to manage their e-villages of knowledge, for example: personal learning networks (Dabbagh and Reo, 2011a), personal learning environments, (Kooken, Ley and De Hoog, 2007), Web 2.0 (Dabbagh and Reo 2011b) and virtual learning community.

2.3 Zone of Proximal Development

According to the work of Lev Vygotsky (Vigotsky, 1930), learning is achieved based on games that generate cognition from early childhood. Cognition can be developed in children with different types of games in first person and in social environments.

2.4 Collaborative Design of Technology Integration

The research done by Mishra and Khoeler (Mishra and Koehler, 2006), suggests that learning is more effective when technological support is used. This idea is based on three main concepts: technology, pedagogy and content; plus the different links between them. Mishra applies the model based on technology, pedagogy, content and knowledge (TPCK). This model was introduced in the field of pedagogy as a theoretical framework designed for teachers to get the knowledge required for working within technological integration. It was built as a pedagogical content knowledge (Schulman, 1986), in which the major complex interrelationships between the knowledge that teachers have about the contents and pedagogy are shown.

TPCK model emphasizes the fact that teachers should consider aptitudes because there is a need of incorporate technology in practical education (Koehler y Mishra, 2008). The key point of TPCK is the integration of multiple areas of knowledge that can support teachers and students (Niess et al., 2011).

3. DEVELOPMENT OF THE FRAMEWORK

3.1 Design of the Framework

In figure 1, the methodological framework developed for the computational thinking and programming is described:

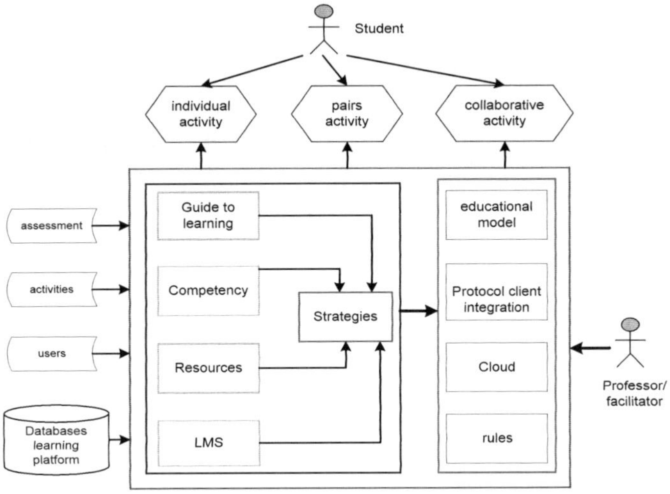

Figure 1. Methodological framework of self-learning on computational thinking and programming

This framework is composed by the following elements: guide to learning, competency, resources and learning management system (LMS). Strategies are defined by the order of integration of technicalities in the educational process to develop computational thinking in the abstraction and logic of programming structures. The instructional design of the activities is adjusted by the following elements: the educational model of each school, the protocol client integration (configuration modes that the user wishes to work with the learning system), the cloud (the way in which the user develops an epistemic community), and the rules (guidelines introduced by the educational institution). These four elements regulate the internal characteristics of the methodological framework. For the framework to operate with student actors, teachers or facilitators, interactions based on individual activity, peer activities and / or group activities occur in four domains (Figure 2): practical domain (PD), which is purely focused in the classroom, under the design of the classroom activities; the external domain (ED) which is developed based on the personal learning environment and that allows us to create social networking communities to build and share knowledge gradually; personal domain (HD) which is planned to make students to develop skills, ethical values and relationships with their peers in a social e-village; and finally consequence domain (CD) which allows the student to increase his/her tendency to face more complex problems, like design software artefacts or scale technological applications.

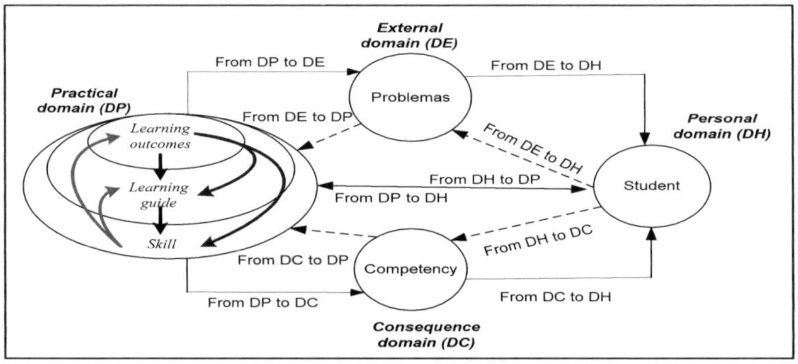

Figure 2. Systemic scenarios based on four domains as are the practical domain (DP), external domain (DE), personal domain (DP) and consequently the domain (DC)

4. RESULTS

The study was conducted in two schools in La Araucanía region, the age range of students was 9 to 13 years old. The intervention was made in mathematics program, by the use of Scratch. We made the intervention in five levels, from fourth to eighth grade of primary school.

Subjects of study

Table 1. Subjects of study in the application of Scratch in schools Allipén and Juan Seguel.

School	Number of students	Study sample	Level	Age
Allipén (rural)	102	49	fourth to eighth grade	From 9 to 11 years old From 12 to 13 years old
Juan Seguel (urban)	369	86	fourth to eighth grade	From 9 to 11 years old From 12 to 13 years old

Design of the pedagogic activities (learning guide student - teacher) applied in both schools.

Table 2. Pedagogical planning of the activities.

Class planning	
Teacher: name of the teacher or instructor	Class: basic level 2 – basic level 4
Time : 2 hours	Date: June 23, 2015
Objective: to awake logical and abstract thinking in order to generate self -learning.	
Topic: programming with Scratch software.	
Previous knowledge: basic mathematics, according to the level of each class.	
Learning objectives	**Contents**
-To develop competences in the students -To develop playful games following the game templates of Scratch. -To generate interaction between pairs	-Concepts: programming with Scratch software, algorithms, abstraction. -Processes: use of Scratch software. -Attitude: interest in the activities, respect, companionship.

Activities of the students	Activities of the teachers
Motivation: Animation, creativity, audio. Activation of previous knowledge: stimulation of abstract thinking. Practical activities: create mathematical games, solve and analyze proposed problems, autonomous working. Closing: survey at the end of the activity.	Motivation: apply positive psychology, apply didactic teaching and activities. Activities to activate previous knowledge: help students with difficulties in the development of each activity. Development: create game samples, generate mathematical problems, and stimulate the competences of students. Closing: questions related to the topic.
Evaluation:	
Type of evaluation (process/product – formative self-evaluation): guideline comparison. Activity of evaluation: activities using Scratch with a mathematical approach. Assessment tool: comparison of the guideline. Guide questions: Did the students understand the activity? (1); Did the student develop the right activities? (2); Did the student work independently? (3); Was the logical and abstract thinking awakened? (4); Where the mathematical skills enhanced? (5); Did the student understand the functioning of the software? (6); Were the Scratch codes well applied? (7).	
Possible modifications : no	
Resources: multimedia projector, computers, Internet, Scratch software, notebooks, sheets of paper.	

Description of each case use: the design of the interaction of the games for the use of scratch is showed in the diagram of case use in figure 3. The case use between teachers and students is showed. The case use "startup of Scratch" begins when the user creates an account and when the configuration of the problem to be solved is made. At the same time, a project for the development of the codifications is predefined. The case use "apply knowledge" serves to provide a set of tools to support the student to face the exercises according to the program of activities of the subject, which in this case is mathematics (see Table 2). The case use "receive information" is a context of the situation faced by the student, like guidelines, descriptions, tools, goals, and objectives. The case use "generating activities" has the function of the teacher developing a series of cases for the development of the class. The case use "corrections" corrects the activities realized by the students, the evaluation is made based on a scale, and the main purpose of this case use is to support, give assistance and provide feedback to students. The case use "evaluation" is designed to evaluate the students, based on rubrics designed for the progress of the learning curve in each session. In figure 3, relationships, extensions and inheritance for the case uses of Scratch are exposed.

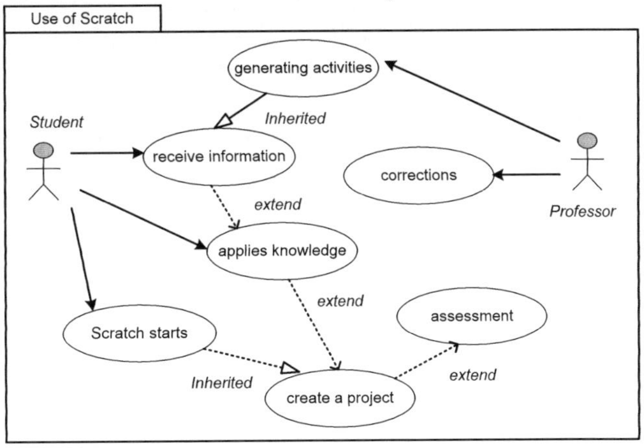

Figure 3. Cases uses between the subjects and Scratch

Example: we have an object, in this case an insect (bee), the exercise consists in moving the bee, by giving it straight movements in steps of 10 to 10 microns, rotations of 20 to 20 sexagesimal degrees (left or right), shifts up or down in steps of 20 to 20 centimeters. The case consists in finding the beehive to reserve food for the winter. There could be four bees to help carry more food; they have to complete the task before 6:00pm. The computing experience makes sense when it is immersed in a real context. That situation can be seen through a logically event-driven programming in which structures such as sequence, repetition, and conditions (Bohm and Jacopini, 1966) are outstanding and they awake the process of computational thinking and programming. This example is focused on arithmetic and algebraic problems. Based on experiments and measured results, students can learn with the heart, which can lead to receive and processing information in a natural way, for continuous learning and education throughout life.

Evaluation: the final sample of students was evaluated with an evaluation guideline, there are thirteen categories that are divided in five criteria (see Table 3 and Table 4). The marks may score up to 20 and at least 5. The evaluation rubric is the same for all the students in both groups. The students were evaluated according to the following criteria: achieved (4); achieved with difficulty (3); moderately achieved (2) and failed (1). The criteria were defined as followed: motivation, participation, creativity, application of the activity, and use of the computer. Based on the level of learning for the sample of 135 students the following results were obtained (see Table 3):

Table 3. The results of both schools, with their respective blocks, show slight differences. However, the urban school had better results in learning level.

criteria	Group 1 rural Allipén	Group 1 urban Juan Seguel	Group 2 rural Allipén	Group 2 urban Juan Seguel
Proper use of the information technologies	59.2%	91.6%	81.8%	100%
Task performance in Office	51.8%	62.5%	77.2%	83.2%
Solving everyday problems	51.8%	59.2%	72.2%	89.4%
Computer games	55.5%	100%	81.8%	100%
Problem solving	77.7%	95.8%	77.2%	97.3%
Following instructions	100%	100%	77.2%	100%
Applies the software properly	92.5%	79.1%	72.7%	94.7%
Difficulties	29%	20.8%	18.1%	21.0%
Motivation	96.2%	100%	72.7%	100%
Creativity	96.2%	83.3%	63.6%	100%
Boredom	3.7%	6.2%	27.2%	0.0%
Fatigue	0.0%	4.1%	22.7%	0.0%
Participation	100%	93.7%	72.7%	100%

Table 4. Example of how to measure motivation, participation and creativity criteria and categories.

Criteria	Achieved (4 points)	Achieved with difficulties (3 points.)	Poorly achieved (2 points)	Not achieved (1 point)
Motivation	The students are motivated and glad with the activities.	The students show disinterest about the activities.	The students show some interest but demonstrate low motivation for collaborating with the activity.	Students do not show motivation, they show fatigue and boredom.
Participation	Students do not show motivation, they show fatigue and boredom.	Students participate in the activity, ask questions with slight distractions.	Students do not participate much in the activity.	Students do not participate, do not ask, do not collaborate with peers.
Creativity	Students use Scratch in a creative and playful way, show originality and dedication in their ideas.	Students develop activities with creative and playful way.	Little creativity and dedication is observed among students.	Students do not demonstrate creativity in activities with Scratch.

The most meaningful finding was that by the logic of computer programming we can help to motivate computational thinking in students (Table 3). The results of this project demonstrate that Scratch is a useful tool for the development of students because it opens creative minds, increase their skills and competences, captures their attention, and as a result it promotes logical and abstract thinking of students. In Table 3, we can see that the fatigue criteria influences learning style (Hayes and Allinson, 1997) because when "learning by doing" was in interaction with Scratch software, students were more motivated and concentrated. How the measurements were obtained in Table 3 is explained in table 4.

The activities implemented through methodological framework have been successfully applied, because positive psychology was used (Seligma and Csikszentmihaly, 2000) as well as the theory of constructivism and the cognitive theory (Cortés and Gil, 1997) in that way, implementation in each school could be achieved. School principals and teachers were satisfied with the results obtained by their students and the software is still installed in their laboratories. Scratch is a new tool and the expected impact was totally achieved.

In the rural sector, the implementation of the software for sixth and seventh grade was better evaluated, while for fourth and eighth grade the students had some difficulties in mathematics and computer skills. The scores obtained in SIMCE 2014 showed the same results as the implementation of Scratch. We can affirm that the procedures and instruments where implemented according to the requirements of the Ministry of Education of Chile. The urban sector was better evaluated in the implementation of the software than the rural, and in the urban sector, seventh and eight where the ones with the highest scores, while fourth grade presented some difficulties in mathematics.

In the process of interaction between different domains (Figure 2), a growth in the interest of facing situations using the computer is observed. The practical domain leads students to interact in other situations, with peers who have more computer proficient. That situation makes students to search in the internet consciously. We can say that the natural development of metacognitive learning in a practical domain towards a consequence domain leads to engage in more complex activities, in order to give answers about the cognitive process in which the student is involved. Practical domain towards personal domain of the student shows a growth in the appreciation, respect, and aptitude towards the way of receiving knowledge of knowing, being and doing (Tobón, 2005).

5. CONCLUSIONS

From the present study, it can be concluded that Scratch enhances computational thinking in order to strengthen abstraction and the systemic development of computer applications. Change the phenomenon of low interest in mathematics in children, can diminish the gap of the learning curve in an experiential context in which they develop a sense of actual use and importance of mathematics.

During recent years, theoretical and abstract works regarding the causes of low academic performance in primary schools have been a growing trend in Chile. Our study is a contribution to the paradigm shift in order to change classroom teaching into an experiential learning integrating math, technology and science.

Early changes in the development of computational thinking performance can be generated by making, for example, Programming Olympics in all levels of primary school, to make systematization tasks an important part of teaching science, biology, physics, chemistry, mathematics, etc.

REFERENCES

Atilano Alvaro, Mercado Jesús and Casanova Helen. Indicadores de Innovación Tecnológica de los Países de América Latina y el Caribe, 2014. http://eventos.caf.com/media/34584/Indicadores_Innovacion_Tecnologica_paises_

America_Latina_Caribe_Version_resumida.pdf

Bohm, Corrado and Giuseppe Jacopini (1966). Flow Diagrams, Turing Machines and Languages with Only Two Formation Rules. *Communications of the ACM* 9 (5): 366–371

Bereiter, C., and Scardamalia, M. (1993). Surpassing ourselves: An inquiry into the nature and implications of expertise. La Salle, IL: Open Court.

Bereiter, C., and Scardamalia, M. (1989). *Intentional learning as a goal of instruction.* In L. B. Resnick (Ed.), Knowing, learning, and instruction: Essays in honor of Robert Glaser (pp. 361-392). Hillsdale, NJ: Lawrence Erlbaum Associates.

Beñat Bilbao-Osorio, Soumitra Dutta, and Bruno Lanvin, Editores. The Global Information Technology Report 2014 – World Economic Forum, 2014. http://www3.weforum.org/docs/WEF_GlobalInformationTechnology_Report_2014.pdf

Cortés, Fernando and Gil Manuel. (1997). *El Constructivismo Genético y las Ciencias Sociales: Líneas Básicas para una Reorganización Epistemológica.* La epistemología genética y la ciencia contemporánea, de Rolando García (coord.). Editorial Gedisa, Barcelona, España.

CT, Computational Thinking, leadership toolkit. Computer Science Teachers Association, International Society for Technology in Education, 2011. http://www.iste.org/docs/ctdocuments/ct-leadershipt-toolkit.pdf?sfvrsn=4

Donald E. Knuth. (1997). *The Art of Computer Programming*, Vol. 1: Fundamental Algorithms, 3rd Edition.

Dabbagh, N., and Reo, R. (2011a). Impact of Web 2.0 on higher education. In D. W. Surry, T. Stefurak, & R. Gray (Eds.), *Technology integration in higher education: Social and organizational aspects* (pp. 174–187). Hershey, PA: IGI Global.

Dabbagh, N., and Reo, R. (2011b). *Back to the future: Tracing the roots and learning affordances of social software.* In M. J. W. Lee, and C. McLoughlin (Eds.), Web 2.0-based e-learning: Applying social informatics for tertiary teaching (pp. 1–20). Hershey, PA: IGI Global.

Hayes, J., and Allinson, C. W. Learning Styles and Training and Development in Work Settings: Lessons from Educational Research. *Educational Psychology* 17, nos. 1-2: 185-193.

Kolb D.A. (1984). *The experiential learning: Experience as the source of learning and development.* NJ: Prentice-Hall.

Kolb D. A. and Fry R. (1975). *Toward an applied theory of experiential learning. in C.* Cooper (ed.), Theories of Group Process, London: John Wiley, UK.

Kooken J, Ley T. and De Hoog R., (2007). *How Do People Learn at the Workplace? Investigating Four Workplace Learning Assumptions*, in E.Duval, R. Klamma and M. Wolpers (eds.): Creating New Learning Experiences on a Global Scale, Springer, Heidelberg, 158-171.

Koehler, M.J., and Mishra, P. (2008). *Introducing TPCK.* In AACTE Committee on Innovation and Technology (Ed.), The handbook of technological pedagogical content knowledge (TPCK) for educators (pp. 3-29). New York, NY: Routledge.

Lee Irene. CSTA Computational Thinking Task Force, 2014. http://csta.acm.org/Curriculum/sub/CurrFiles/471.11CTLeadershiptToolkit-SPvF.pdf

Mishra, P., and Koehler, M.J. (2006). Technological pedagogical content knowledge: A framework for teacher knowledge. *Teachers College Record*, 108(6), 1017–1054.

Niess, M., van Zee, E., and Gillow-Wiles, H. (2011). Knowledge growth in teaching mathematics/science with spreadsheets: Moving PCK to TPACK through online professional development. *Journal of Digital Learning in Teacher Education*, 27(2), 42–52.

Shulman, L.S. (1986). *Those who understand: Knowledge growth in teaching. Educational Researcher*, 15(2), 4–14.

Seligman, Martín and Csikszentmihaly, Mihály. (2000). *Positive Psychology.* American Psychologist, 55 (1), 5- 14.

Scardamalia, M., and Bereiter, C. (1994). Computer support for knowledge-building communities. *The Journal of the Learning Sciences*, 3(3), 265-283.

Simce. (2014). Agencia de la calidad de la educación. [10, dic. 2015] http://www.agenciaeducacion.cl/simce/resultados-simce/

Tobón, S. (2005). *Formación basada en competencias. Pensamiento complejo diseño curricular y didáctica.* Bogotá: ECOE, Colombia.

Vygotsky, L. (1930/1978). *Mind in society.* Cambridge, MA: Harvard University Press.

Wing Jeannette M. (2006). Computational thinking. *Commun. ACM* 49(3), 33-35.

ENHANCING THE QUALITY OF CONFIGURABLE PROCESS MODELS USING ONTOLOGY LANGUAGES

Loubna El Faquih and Mounia Fredj
Ecole Nationale Supérieure d'Informatique et d'Analyse des Systèmes, Mohammed V University of Rabat, Rabat, Morocco

ABSTRACT

Variability management in business process aims at providing solutions to the redundancy problems and enhancing business process reuse. The most widely used approach in this context is the Configurable Process Model solution which consists in representing the variable and the fixed parts together in a unique model. These models become complex and incomprehensible with the increasing number of variants. Therefore, the quality of configurable process models is impacted. Nowadays, producing sound and valid process models still represents a concern for business process designers. Most of research work focus on syntactic quality of process variants. Our contribution consists of a novel method towards syntactic verification and semantic validation of configurable process models based on ontology languages. We define validation rules for assessing the quality of configurable process models. An example in the e-healthcare domain illustrates the main steps of our approach.

KEYWORDS

Configurable Process Models Quality, Semantic Validation, Syntactic Verification, Ontology, Variant Rich BPMN.

1. INTRODUCTION

Business process modeling has become a primordial and critical task for enterprises, since business process models capture the practices of a given organization, and enable enterprises to achieve their business goals. Models are used for documenting, analyzing and redesigning business operations (Mendling et al., 2014). They also provide a communication support within and inter enterprises.

Due to the emergence of business process management field and the frequent use of business processes, companies have faced a problematic issue related to model redundancy. In fact, process repositories exist with many variants for the same business process models. Moreover, new business processes are created from scratch instead of adapting existent processes to meet new business requirements (Schnieders and Puhlmann, 2007). This has motivated the need to manage the variability of business processes.

Variability management in business processes aims at enhancing the reuse of business processes. In the literature, two approaches are used to represent the variability of business processes: single model approach which consists of representing the model and its variants in one single model (Gottschalk, 2009) and multiple models approach which separates the model and its variants (Hallerbach et al., 2009). The approaches based on a separated formalism pose the problem of managing dependencies between reference models and variants models. In this case, the evolution of variants is somewhat difficult. Thereby, the most widely used approach for managing variability in process engineering domain is the single model representation, also called Configurable Process Model (CPM). In this context, several languages have been proposed to represent business process variability: for EPC (Event-driven process chain) models, C-EPC (Gottschalk, 2009) and C-iEPC (La Rosa, 2009) and for BPMN (Business Process Model and Notation) models, Variant Rich BPMN (VR BPMN) (Schnieders and Puhlmann, 2007) and (Nguyen et al., 2014).

With the increasing number of process variants represented in one single model, the configurable process model may become complex and incomprehensible. Therefore, the quality of configurable process models is impacted. Most of the research works in business process variability mainly tackle three domains: i) variability modeling (La Rosa, 2009; Gottschalk, 2009; Schnieders and Puhlmann, 2007; Nguyen et al., 2014), ii) variability resolution (also called configuration) (Hallerbach et al., 2009; Aalst et al., 2010), and iii)

CPM evolution (Ayora et al., 2013). While much attention has been directed towards modeling and configuration, little effort has been given to the quality of CPM. The main contributions in this domain focus on the correctness and the soundness of variants obtained after the configuration phase (Hallerbach et al., 2009; Aalst et al., 2010; Asadi, 2014).

On the other hand, an increasing attention has been paid to the quality of business processes over the last few years (Nelson et al., 2012; Lohrmann and Reichert, 2013; Hammer, 2014; De Oca et al., 2015). According to this latter research work, "The quality of a business process model has a significant impact on the development of any enterprise and IT support for that process". Producing high quality business models still represent a concern for business designers, because a sound process can reduce the performance difficulties resulted from defects in execution (Hammer, 2014). The issue of business processes quality is mainly related to the designers mastery of modeling tools and their involvement in the design task, as to their knowledge of the domain being captured. According to (Reijers et al., 2014), the error rate in business process collections could reach 10 to 20 %. Consequently, the usage of business process models in later phases is impacted. Business process quality is being addressed through two main dimensions (also called types): syntactic quality (also called verification) which consists in verifying that all statements in the model are in conformity with the syntax and vocabulary of the modeling language, and semantic quality (also called validation) which checks whether models make true statements on the real world they aim to capture (Krogstie et al., 1995). Since the CPM is defined as a set of variants, if it contains errors (syntactic or semantic ones), these errors will propagate to the variants as well. In this paper, we aim at verifying and validating the CPM in order to ensure its quality in the modeling phase because detecting and correcting errors at the early stage (modeling) reduces maintenance costs and avoids dysfunctions in the deployment phase. Our contribution is twofold: 1) we propose an approach based on both domain knowledge and variability knowledge to check CPM's quality and 2) we define a set of rules for CPM's syntactic and semantic quality checking. Our proposal is ontology based since ontologies are commonly used to capture a domain knowledge.

The remaining of this paper is organized as follows: Section 2 presents the main concepts regarding the validation of configurable process models; Section 3 examines the related work and Section 4 details our contribution. In Section 5, we conclude and make suggestions for future research.

2. BACKGROUND

This section lays the foundations for semantic quality of CPM. We explain two basic notions related to our work, namely configurable process models and business process models quality.

2.1 Configurable Process Models

Variability is defined as the ability to change or customize a software system (Maßen and Lichter, 2002). It relies on two main concepts: variation point and variant. The variation point represents the variable parts of a given process, and the variants are the specific realizations of this variation point (Gottschalk et al., 2009). A variation point can be optional (which corresponds to the choice of selecting zero or one from one or more variants), alternative (which corresponds to the choice of selecting only one variant) or optional alternative (at last a combination of optional and alternative characteristics must be considered) (Maßen and Lichter, 2002). The choice of a variant may require or exclude another variant. In order to organize the selection of variants, there are two major constraints: Inclusion and Exclusion.

In the next section, we present the main concepts related to CPM's quality.

2.2 Quality in Business Process Engineering

In the ISO 9000 definition, the quality is defined as "the degree to which a set of inherent characteristics fulfills requirements" (ISO, 2015). In other words, a quality model is a model that respects a set of rules and meets the stakeholders' needs. Quality has been a subject of research in different disciplines. In the business process domain, several authors have worked on defining "a good process model" (Krogstie et al., 1995; Ayad et al., 2012; Lohrmann and Reichert, 2013; Reijers et al., 2014; De Oca et al., 2015). A modeling language lies on three main concepts: syntax (modeling elements and structural relationships between them), semantics (relation between the model and the real world to capture) and a notation (specific graphical symbols for the visualization of models) (Mendling et al., 2014). Thereby, business process quality is of two types: syntactic quality and semantic quality.

2.2.1 Syntactic Quality (Verification)

Syntactic quality aims at ensuring that the model respects all the techniques and notations of the modeling language (Krogstie et al., 1995; Nelson et al., 2012; Ayad et al., 2012; Reijers et al., 2014; De Oca et al., 2015). This is related to the vocabulary and the syntax of the modeling language. Syntactic quality is also being referred to as verification. In the context of syntactic quality, two similar subquality aspects can be distinguished: Correctness and Soundness which are defined in the context of CPM variants as follows: a model is said sound if it is correct regarding the reference model (Hallerbach et al., 2009).

2.2.2 Semantic Quality (Validation)

While syntactic quality of models focuses on the respect of the modeling language notations regardless of the real world they aim to capture, semantic quality covers these aspects and relates to check whether the business process model makes true statements on the real world (Krogstie et al., 1995; Nelson et al., 2012; Ayad et al., 2012; Reijers et al., 2014; De Oca et al., 2015). In other words, semantic quality should be checked against a set of rules that are related to the domain in question. Semantic quality is also being referred to as validation.

In the context of semantic quality, two subquality aspects can be distinguished (Reijers et al., 2014):

- Validity: "means that all statements in the model are correct and are relevant to the problem"
- Completeness: "means that the model contains all relevant statements that would be correct".

There are some other quality dimensions cited by (Nelson et al., 2012) such as social quality, pragmatic quality and empirical quality, but they are out of the scope of this paper.

In this paper, we refer to CPM quality as a concept which englobes both syntactic and semantic quality. We use the term verification for syntactic quality and validation for semantic quality.

The next section is devoted to presenting and discussing the research work related to our study.

3. RELATED WORK

Previous efforts on validating configurable process models focus mainly on variants verification. Several algorithms have been developed to ensure the correctness and soundness of CPM during the configuration phase (Hallerbach et al., 2009) (Aalst et al., 2010). The study presented in (Gröner ret al., 2013) proposes a validation algorithm based on description logic to ensure the validation of reused process models with respect to the original process models. While in (Asadi, 2014), the validation is based on feature modeling in order to provide an automatic validation of variants. They proposed a feature-oriented customization approach based on a formal framework (using Description Logic) that enables the validation of customizations of reference process models. Existing approaches related to variants validation are not suitable for CPM validation since they focus on variants correctness rather than the CPM itself. Moreover, despite these multiple approaches, there is no conclusive work about CPM validation in the modeling phase.

Research work about the quality of business processes is numerous. The work of (Nelson et al., 2012) tackles the conceptual modeling domain. The authors proposed a Conceptual Modeling Quality Framework (CMQF) which contains eight quality bases and four ''layers'' containing twenty-four quality type. The work of (Ayad et al., 2012) proposed a semantic framework for business process quality evaluation and improvement. Their proposition relies on domain knowledge and business process meta-models. They also defined validation rules for checking the completeness of BP models. Finally, (Reijers et al., 2014) proposed the Simple Integrates Quality (SIQ) framework, which is built upon three cores: syntactic quality, semantic quality and pragmatic quality. The SIQ framework is meant to provide links to tools, procedures and guidelines to clarify how quality evaluations can take place.

To sum up, quality in CPMs was approached only in terms of soundness and correctness of variants. The quality of the CPM itself is somewhat neglected. We believe that verifying and validating the CPM in the modeling phase is necessary in order to produce high quality models. Distinctly, in this paper we are interested in the following question: Given a configurable process model, how can we affirm whether it is correct syntactically and valid semantically? In this perspective, we propose to use ontologies in order to enhance CPM quality. We propose a hybrid approach which encompasses both dimensions of the CPM quality. In our previous work (El Faquih et al., 2014a), we proposed an ontology based framework to semantically enrich CPM with the objective of enhancing its quality. We explain in the next section our contribution.

4. OUR CONTRIBUTION

By analogy to the quality of business processes, we define the syntactic quality and the semantic quality of configurable process models as follows:

- Syntactic quality of CPM: given a CPM, its syntactic quality relies on verifying whether the model respects the syntax of the modeling language as well as the variability constraints of business processes.
- Semantic quality of CPM: given a CPM, its semantic quality relies on validating the model according to the domain that it's meant to capture.

Our proposal is intended to be hybrid since it combines both semantic and syntactic dimensions of CPM's quality. To the best of our knowledge, no such approach is available. Our objective is also to propose a tool for quality assessment of configurable process models. For a given CPM, the syntactic verification could be established through a set of rules that depends on both the modeling language notation and the variability constraints. Regarding the semantic validation, it mainly depends on the domain being captured by the CPM. Thus, the domain knowledge must be represented and taken in consideration.

Ontologies are suitable for representing a specific domain language since they provide a formal representation of the real world objects related to a specific domain, and also describe the different relations between them. The use of ontologies in business process management is not new. In the context of business process automation, ontologies have been introduced in business process management by endowing business processes with intelligence and make them thereafter accessible to intelligent queries; this concept is called Semantic Business Process Management (Lautenbacher et al., 2008). The main goal behind associating semantic technologies to business processes is to provide automated solutions for querying and manipulating the process space of a given organization. In fact, these tasks could be difficult, time consuming and involve much human intervention (Lautenbacher et al., 2008). Several approaches that cover the whole business process life cycle have been proposed in semantic business process management (Wetzstein et al., 2007). However, the combination of variability and ontologies in business process is still in its early stages.

In our previous work (El Faquih et al., 2014b), we conducted a comparative study on the use of semantics in variability modeling in three domains: product engineering, service engineering and process engineering. We concluded that there is no single standard for modeling variability in business process; different representations are used to express the same variability concept and that there is a low degree of automation. Thereby, we proposed to take advantage from the use of semantics for variability management in both service and product engineering and apply it in the configurable processes domain. Taking advantage of the benefits of the use of ontologies in semantic business processes, we propose to enhance the quality of CPM by providing an automatic approach for syntactic verification and semantic validation of CPM. Our work is based on the semantic enrichment of CPM (El Faquih et al., 2014a). The framework is composed of three main layers: the CPM layer, the CPM ontology layer and domain ontology layer. The latter layers are linked via a set of semantic rules that involves knowledge about the two ontologies. The framework is represented in Figure 1.

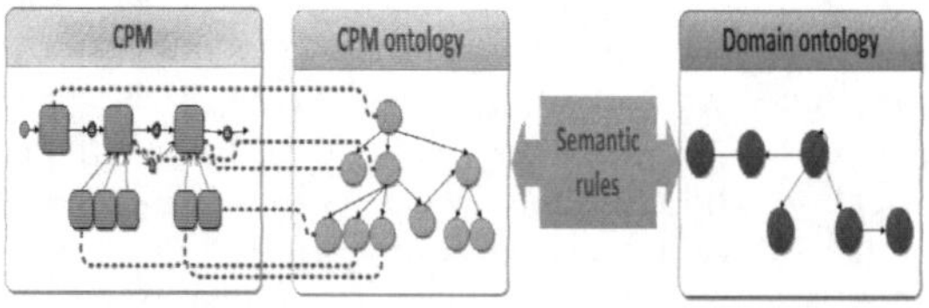

Figure 1. Framework for the semantic enrichment of CPM

In this context, we define a Semantic Configurable Process Model (SCPM) as follows: a SCPM is a configurable process model whose syntax as well as variability constraints are represented by an ontology. We call this ontology CPM ontology and we published a first release of it in (El Faquih et al., 2014a). In the following subsections, we present the components of the framework and their usage for syntactic verification and semantic validation of CPM.

4.1 CPM Ontology for Syntactic Verification of CPM

As mentioned above, our approach is ontology based. In what follows we present the CPM ontology which is the core of the framework. The CPM ontology adds meaning to each element of the CPM in order to make it machine-readable. In addition, it will also allow reasoning on the process description. Although some BPMN ontology proposals are available, to the best of our knowledge, the CPM Ontology is the first attempt to provide an ontological formalization for VR BPMN (Schnieders and Puhlmann, 2007). Our choice is motivated by the fact that VR BPMN is the most popular solution for capturing variability in BPMN process models. Moreover, it is based on annotation mechanisms of BPMN elements (by using stereotypes) which allow adding semantics to the CPM. The CPM ontology encodes both the constraints of the VR BPMN notation as well as the variability constraints between the model elements.

The core business process diagram elements are represented in the CPM ontology using classes having appropriate attributes as defined in the BPMN Specification. Therefore, the semantic enrichment of a CPM (or the annotation of a CPM with CPM ontology) means creating instances of its concepts. Moreover, the variability constraints are expressed in the ontology using the object properties (relations between classes). A CPM contains configurable elements and non- configurable elements. In this paper, we focus on configurable elements which are of three types: Configurable Activity, Configurable data and Configurable Resource. We presented the rules related to configurable elements in (El Faquih et al., 2015). Figure 2 shows a graphical representation of the class' hierarchy of the CPM Ontology rooted at CPM. The CPM ontology classes are represented by circles, and the relations between them are illustrated using arrows. The relations names are indicated as arrows labels. The classes variant, variable and variation point which capture the variability concepts are linked to the ontology's root CPM.

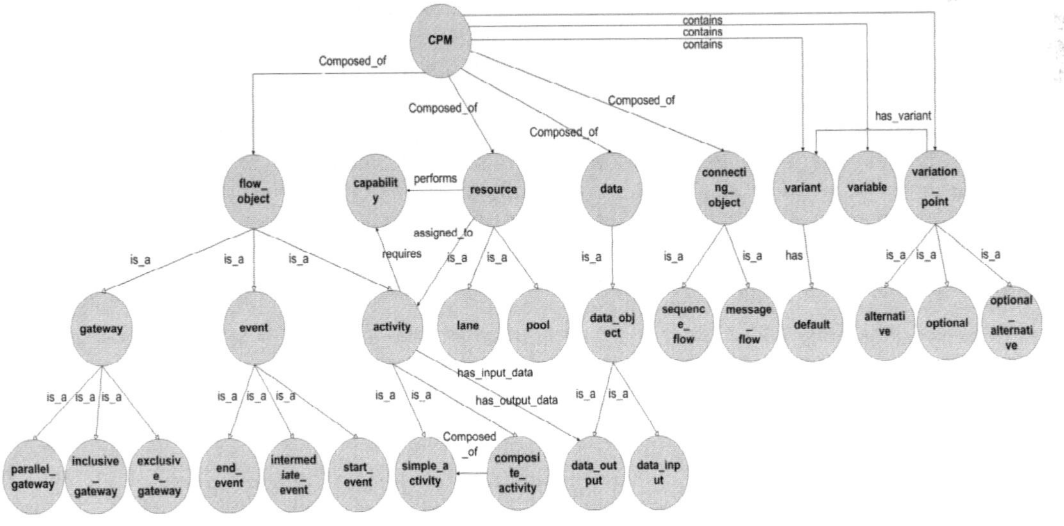

Figure 2. CPM ontology classes

To illustrate our approach, we consider an initial CPM model modelled in VR BPMN presented at Figure 3. This model is related to an e-healthcare business process and is taken from the case studies presented in (Ayora et al., 2013). More details about the e-health CPM are available in (El Faquih et al., 2015). The relation between the CPM and the CPM ontology instances is depicted in Figure 3. The CPM elements (activities, resources...) are represented as instances of the CPM ontology (cf. Figure 3). For example, the activity "Perform examination" is linked to the object "Perform examination" which is an instance of two concepts of the CPM ontology: "simple activity" and "variation point". The object properties represented in the CPM ontology are used to express validation rules since the OWL 2 language is not able to express all relations. The expressivity of OWL can be extended by adding SWRL (Semantic Web Rule Language) rules to the ontology.

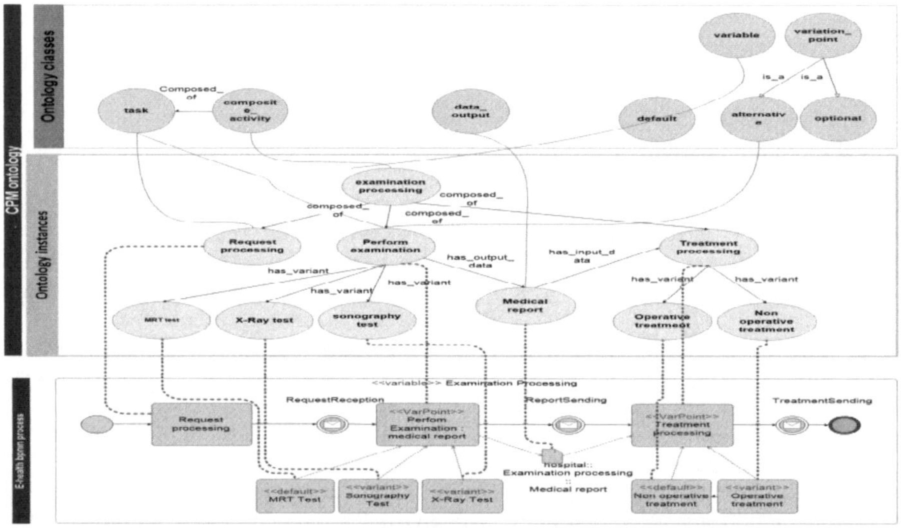

Figure 3. Relation between CPM ontology instances and the CPM

We expressed the syntactic rules cited in order to verify the syntactic quality of a given CPM (El Faquih et al., 2015). If the CPM respects all the rules, we can affirm that it is syntactically correct. Example of these rules:

Rule R1: A variation point must have at least one variant (default variant).

SWRL rule: variation_point (?x), hasVariant min 1 variant (?y) -> R1(?x, true)

4.2 Domain Ontology for Semantic Validation of CPM

The semantic validation of CPM must be established against a set of rules related to a specific domain. In our framework, the domain ontology describes a specific business domain. In this paper, we apply the framework in the context of e-healthcare. The domain ontology describes the E-hospital domain. Its definition is not in our scope. We use a customization of the ontology presented in (Aidarus et al., 2013). Concerning the configurable process models which are defined as a collection of variants, each variant must respect a fragment of the domain ontology. The domain ontology must include concepts for all the variants of the CPM. In the Figure 4, the domain ontology (the upper part of the figure) is composed of five classes related by object properties. Instances of these classes represent the objects needed for the mapping with the CPM ontology. For example, "Staff" which is an instance of the class "Person", could be a "doctor" or an "assistant". These two objects represent resources for a CPM activity.

Many constraints could by established to link the CPM (represented by CPM ontology instances) and the domain ontology. In order to verify these constraints, we define the semantic type relation (**SType**) between domain ontology instances and CPM ontology instances. The SType relation is represented in Figure 4 by the dashed blue line linking the CPM ontology instances and the domain ontology instances.

For the relation between activities, SType defines *the relation "a variant is a type of a variation point"*.

For the relation between resources and activities, SType represents *the relation between the capability required by the activity and the capability assured by the resource* (Sbai et al., 2014).

We present below some of these rules related to activities and resources:

- **Semantic rules for activities:** The semantic of a given variation point activity is derived from the semantic of a given concept in the domain ontology. For instance, if the designer wants to add a variant for a given variation point activity, a check must be performed in the domain ontology to verify whether the variant is a type of the variation point. Example: the variation point activity "perform examination" must have three variants which correspond to the three subclasses of the class medical test in the domain ontology. Moreover, each variant is defined by a set of features and the feature must have the same semantic type as the activity.

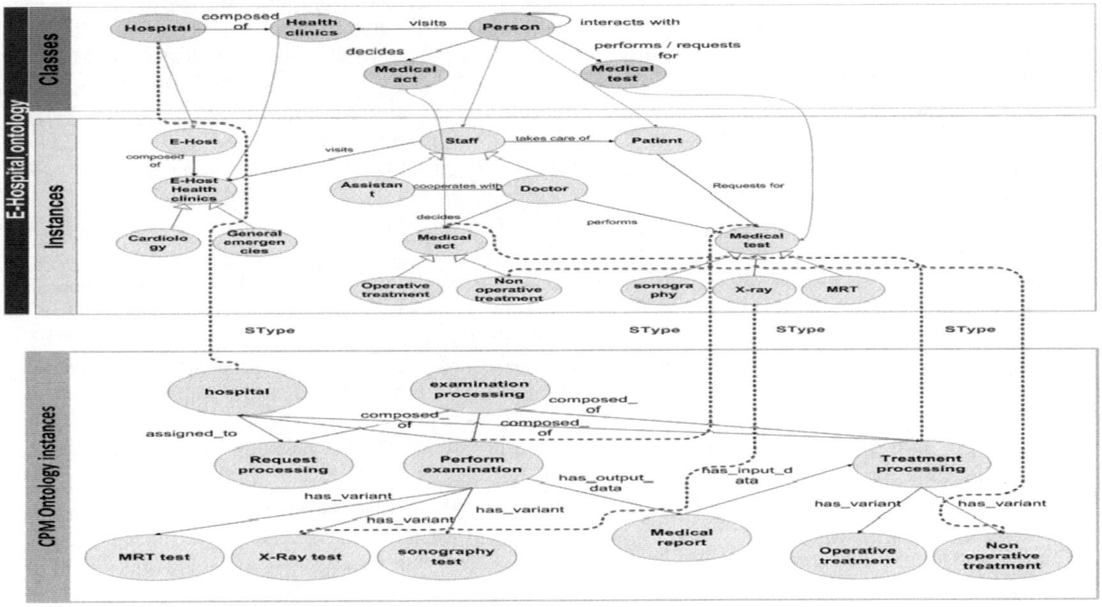

Figure 4. Relation between domain ontology instances and CPM ontology instances

- **Semantic rules for resources:** The semantics of a given variation point resource is derived from the semantics of a given concept in the domain ontology. For instance, if the designer wants to add a variant for a given variation point resource, a check must be performed in the domain ontology to verify whether the variant is a type of the variation.
- **Semantic rules for resources-activities assignment:** In the modeling phase, before assigning a resource to an activity, it is necessary to verify the semantic relation between the corresponding instances in the domain ontology. Example from Figure 4: the variation point activity "perform examination" could be performed by the resource "doctor" and not by the resource "assistant".

The above cited examples could be resolved by using the relations between the domain knowledge (represented by the domain ontology) and the CPM ontology. We propose to use SWRL to express these constraints. In order to have a complete semantic validation, other semantic relations have to be defined.

5. CONCLUSION

Insuring business process models quality has been recognized as a key success factor for modeling at an enterprise level. This is justified by the fact that a good process model can help avoiding errors at an early stage and decreases the cost of errors over the development lifecycle. Despite being an actively researched field in the business processes, the quality of CPM is still in its early stages. In this paper, we proposed a quality framework for CPM which employs semantic technologies (ontologies and rule language) to establish the syntactic verification and the semantic validation of CPM. In addition to the syntactic rules defined by the CPM ontology, the validation of CPM can also occur on a semantic level by the usage of a CPM ontology and domain ontology. As the notion of semantic validation is wide and complex, we adopt in this paper a definition that relies on the domain of interest. Our solution will also include a tool which implements the proposed framework. We are developing a prototype implementing the proposed approach for CPM quality. The prototype will be validated by conducting a large case study.

REFERENCES

Aalst, W. M. P., Dumas, M., Gottschalk, F., ter Hofstede A.H., La Rosa, M. and Mendling, J. (2010). Preserving correctness during business process model configuration. Formal Aspects of Computing 22.3-4 459-482.

Aidarus, I., Hussein, M., Hashi, A. and Mohamed, A.A. (2013). Ontology-driven information retrieval for healthcare information system: a case study. International Journal of Network Security & Its Applications 5, no. 1: 61-69.

Asadi, M. (2014). Developing and Validating Customizable Process Models. PhD diss., Communication, Art & Technology: School of Interactive Arts and Technology.

Ayad, S., Si-Said Cherfi, S., and Comyn-Wattiau, I. (2012). Towards a semantic quality based approach for business process models improvement. Australasian Conference on Information Systems.

Ayora, C., Torres, V., Weber, B., Reichert, M. and Pelechano, V. (2013). Enhancing Modeling and Change Patterns. BMMDS/EMMSAD, pp: 246-260.

De Oca, I.M, Snoeck, M, Reijers, H.A, and Rodríguez-Morffi, A. (2015). A systematic literature review of studies on business process modeling quality." Information and Software Technology 58 : 187-205.

El Faquih, L, Sbai, H and Fredj, M. (2014a). Towards a semantic enrichment of configurable process models. Information Science and Technology (CIST), Third IEEE International Colloquium on Information Science and Technology, pp. 1-6. IEEE, Tetouan, Morocco, October 20-22.

El Faquih, L, Sbai, H and Fredj, M. (2014b). Semantic variability modeling in business processes: A comparative study. Internet Technology and Secured Transactions (ICITST), 9th International Conference for Internet Technology and Secured Transactions, pp. 131-136. IEEE, London, UK, December 8-10.

El Faquih, L, Sbai, H and Fredj, M. (2015). Configurable process models: a semantic validation, 10th International Conference on Intelligent Systems (SITA), 20-21 Octobrer 20-21, Rabat, Morroco.

Gottschalk, F. (2009). Configurable process models. PhD diss., Technische Universiteit Eindhoven, 2009.

Gröner, G., BošKović, M., Parreiras, F.S. and GašEvić, D. (2013). Modeling and validation of business process families. Information Systems 38, no. 5: 709-726.

Hallerbach, A., Bauer, T. and Reichert, M (2009). Guaranteeing Soundness of Configurable Process Variants in Provop", IEEE Conference on Commerce and Enterprise Computing.

Hammer, M. (2014). What is business process management? Handbook on Business Process Management 1, pp. 3-16. Springer Berlin Heidelberg.

ISO, International Organization for Standardization: ISO 9000:2005: Quality management systems – Fundamentals and vocabulary (revised 2015).

Krogstie J., Lindland O. I., Sindre G. (1995). Defining quality aspects for conceptual models. In Proceedings of the IFIP international working conference on Information system concepts, pp 216-231.

La Rosa, M. (2009). Managing Variability in Process-Aware Information Systems, PhD Thesis, Queensland University of Technology, Brisbane, Austria.

Lautenbacher, F, Bauer, B. and Seitz, C. (2008). Semantic Business Process Modeling-Benefits and Capability. AAAI Spring Symposium: AI Meets Business Rules and Process Management, pp. 71-76.

Lohrmann, M. and Reichert, M. (2013). Understanding business process quality. Business Process Management, pp. 41-73. Springer Berlin Heidelberg.

Maßen, V.T. and Lichter, H. (2002). Modeling variability by UML use case diagrams. Proceedings of the International Workshop on Requirements Engineering for product lines.

Mendling, J., Leopold, H, and Pittke, F. (2014). 25 Challenges of Semantic Process Modeling. International Journal of Information Systems and Software Engineering for Big Companies: IJISEBC 1.1: 78-94.

Nelson, H. J., Poels, G., Genero, M. and Piattini, M. (2012). A conceptual modeling quality framework." Software Quality Journal 20, no. 1 (2012): 201-228.

Nguyen, T., Colman, A. and Han, J. (2014). Comprehensive Variability Modeling and Management for Customizable Process-Based Service Compositions. Web Services Foundations, Springer, pp.507–534.

Reijers, H.A, Mendling, J, and Recker, J. (2014). Business process quality management. Handbook on Business Process Management 1, pp. 167-185. Springer Berlin Heidelberg.

Schnieders, A. and Puhlmann, F. (2006). Variability Mechanisms in E-Business Process Families. BIS 85: 583-601.

Sbai, H, Fredj, M and Kjiri, L. (2014). Support for resources changes in configurable process models. The 4th International Conference on Multimedia Computing and Systems (ICMCS'14), pp. 1082-1087, April 14-16 2014, Marrakech, Morocco, 2014.

Wetzstein, B., Ma, Z., Filipowska; A., Kaczmarek, M., Bhiri, S., Losada, S., Lopez-Cob, J.M. and Cicurel, L. (2007). Semantic Business Process Management: A Lifecycle Based Requirements Analysis. In SBPM.

Short Papers

GEOREFERENCING HISTORICAL DOCUMENTS: THE CASE OF THE DUME BOUNDARY

Natália Botica, Francisco Andrade and Luís Fontes
Unidade de Arqueologia da Universidade do Minho
Edifício dos Congregados, Avenida Central, 100 - , 4710 228, Braga, Portugal

ABSTRACT

Much of the information of historical documents about the territory and property are defined on textual form. This information is mostly geographic and defines territorial areas, its limits and boundaries. For the treatment of this data, we have defined one information system where the treatment of the documental references for the study of the settlement and landscape implies a systematization of the information, normalization, integration and graphic and cartographic representation.

This methodology was applied to the case study of the boundary of the monastery-diocese of Dume, in Braga - Portugal, for which there are countless documents and references to this site, but where the urban pressure has mischaracterized very significantly the landscape, making the identification of territorial limits quite difficult. The work carried out to give spatial and cartographic expression to the data, by defining viewing criteria according to the recorded information, proved to be a central working tool in the boundary study and in understanding the dynamics of the sites in the various cultural periods.

KEYWORDS

Cultural heritage, Information technology, Information system, Historical documents, Landscape evolution.

1. INTRODUCTION

Knowing the genesis and evolution of a territory, characteristics and boundaries, involves collecting and processing data from documental, bibliographic, archaeological, toponymic and cartographic sources.

The case study of the genesis and evolution of the Dume monastic domain had as its main source the archaeological and documental data. The archaeological evidence from excavations and surveys made it possible to identify and characterize the sites and boundaries of the territory referred to in the documental sources. The data related to limits, organization, inventory, possession and transmission of the properties and to the description of land assets, were mainly drawn from documental sources, including the Liber Fidei (Costa, 1965; 1978; 1990), cartulary which compiles various documents relating to the heritage of Braga diocese. We've also consulted the censual from the late eleventh century 'dito do Bispo D Pedro' (Costa 1997), the 'Inquirições' of 1220 (PMH, Inq.) and 1288 (Pizarro, 2012) and the 'Memórias Paroquiais' of 1758 (Capela, 2003). The data of the micro toponimia of Dume that allowed the validation of some of the older data, have been collected in the indices of Casais do Cabido and Mitra Bracarense.

The documental sources have various textual references to sites, boundaries and confrontations in such a number and form that implies an organization and integration of the information, without which this study and treatment would be slow and difficult.

The Archaeology Unit of the University of Minho (UAUM) has developed one information system for the management of the information coming from the excavations, surveys and archaeological interpretation (2ArchIS) (Botica & Martins, 2008). From this system it is possible to view all the information, including to geo-reference the sites in a Geographic Information System. However, mapping historical documents involves creating references to sites whose meaning is wider than the archaeological site and also crossing all the references with the sites.

So, after we've identified the main sources of historical data, we established as a first priority to set a module for the Information System of historical documents, integrated with the already existing Information System of the Archaeological and Architectural Heritage (2ArchIS), allowing to organize, process and georeference all documents and references made to sites. This module, subsequently characterized, allowed the storage and the management of information coming from the archaeological and documental data, helping to identify the boundaries of the property of the former Dume monastery.

Connecting a Geographic Information System to the data of georeferenced sites, it is possible to represent the sites and documental references on current and ancient maps, whose reading and interpretation will support the study of human occupation and the evolution of the landscape, as demonstrated in this monastic set of Dume case study.

2. THE MONASTERY-DIOCESE OF DUME

The development of the Information System module for Historical Documents was applied to the study of the origin and chrono-cultural evolution of the human occupation in the monastic-diocese of Dume, its territorial expression and architectural evidence (Andrade, 2015).

The study of boundary of Dume was based on the existing archaeological data for the study area (Fontes, 1987; 1991-92) and the various documents that provide data on their domain, with special focus on confirmation of possession of the domain area, in 911 (Figure 1), the bishop of Sabarico Mondonhedo (Fontes, 2006).

The Dumiense monastic-diocesan domain was directly linked to the Roman domain. A considerable part of the known Roman villa structures were later reused, as well as bounding elements that are consistent with Roman times. Documentary data seem to indicate that the monastic limits have remained mostly stable until its extinction.

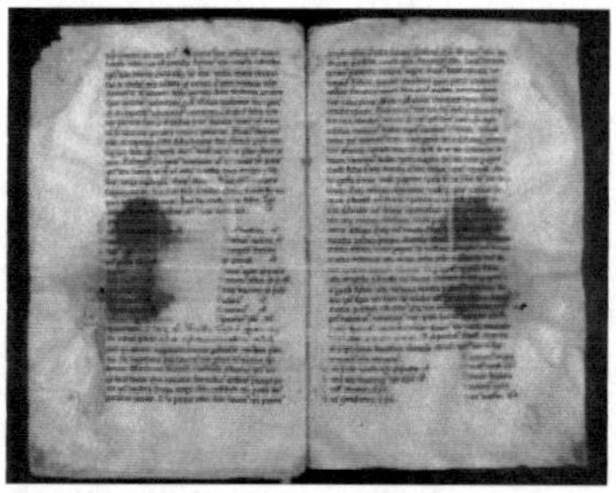

Figure 1. Image of Document 19 Liber Fidei, 911 Confirmation.

3. INFORMATION SYSTEM

The Information System of the Archaeological and Architectural Heritage (2ArchIS) developed by UAUM, was based on a relational database and implemented in MySQL. Integrates information from diverse sources as historical, archaeological, bibliographic and cartographic. The 2ArchIS was structured to store data characterization of archaeological sites, including its name, ownership and geographic location, by specifying the geographic coordinates. 2ArchIS still connects sites with archaeological data as stratigraphy, materials or epigraphy. Each of these elements may be associated with photos, drawings, topographic charts of the site as well as bibliographical and documentary sources.

However, the study of the evolution of the territorial contours takes one step further the association of sites with documentation, as it is already done in 2ArchIS. For this type of study, each document should be decomposed in References. Each reference is associated with two or more sites and should be recorded where and how in the Document these sites are related. Therefore, we developed a historical document management module, integrated with 2ArchIS system that link sites to References in a Document.

This module of historical documents management links the characterization and geo-referencing of the sites to the geographical, environmental and historical context. It also relates all references of a document. The type of reference, identification and other sites associated are interrelated between references.

3.1 Data Base

This historical document management module has as its central element the site and its characterization, including the name, type, description, toponyms and geographic location, specifying the geographic coordinates of the location. Associated with the site we also have the characterization of the environmental context, particularly with regard to the deployment site, water resources and use of soils. We link the site to graphics, photos, drawings and topographic map associated. (Figure 2).

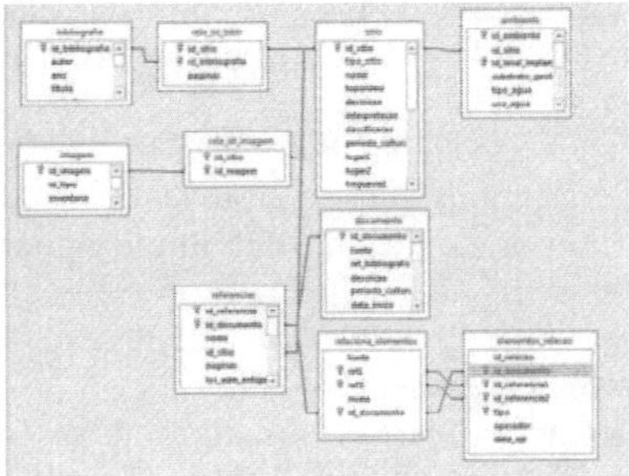

Figure 2. Simplified database diagram of the 2ArchIS historical documents management module

The documents were associated with general data such as font, description, bibliographic references, the document date, or date range, to link the document to a wider chronology, as the century or a cultural period. The type of act presented in the document, its object, value, issuer and addressee, can also be registered in database.

Each Each document can have one or more references to a site. Each reference is characterized by name and a link to the respective site. We can also add to references the old administrative location of the site, ancient toponyms, type of settlement, type or composition of the property and the delimitation.

All references of a document are associated with one or more sites and, as all sites are georeferenced, it is possible to map all references associated with sites, and define queries according to the type of reference which was made.

3.2 Back Office

For the storage and management of data from historical documents we developed a back office application, in PHP language, with the main menu shown in Figure 3.

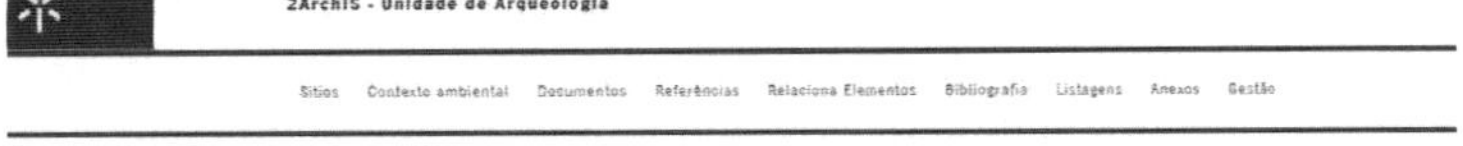

Figure 3. Back Office application main menu

It is through this application forms that can be done the register the documentary sources, bibliography, archaeological, toponyms and cartographic images. All these items are integrated and linked to each other.

Historical documents are characterized according to the source, description, chronology, type, object and value of the act, as well as the issuer and addressee of the act.

Each Document can contain one or more References. The references are associated with a site, keeping the page(s) where the association is made, toponyms of the site, the current and ancient locations, and the type of settlement, property and delimitations. A reference relates always two sites and defines the type of relationship between them. The systematic processing of this information and its organization and visualization enables a better understanding of the dynamics of the landscapes and sites.

In the menu Relaciona elementos , references are associated with sites as well as the type of relationship existing between them. This relationship can be "delimitação", "integra" or "integrado por", "confina" or "confinado" or yet "composto por", according to the descriptors used by André Marques (A. Marques & David, 2013 pp . 8-9).

The Menu also allows to attach, to a Site or Document registered in the Database, graphic documentation, 3D models, images or videos, plus a glossary of terms.

4. GEOREFERENCING HISTORICAL DOCUMENTS

The case study of the genesis and evolution of the Dume monastic domain, focuses on the territory situated in a part of the current municipality of Braga and along the middle reaches of the basin of the river Cávado. The study area has a very ancient settlement dating back to an occupation of the Chalcolithic / Bronze Age (Fontes 2006; Andrade, 2015).

For each site in the Back Office application, were recorded all references made to them in the historical documents. For this purpose, the concept of the site is wider than the archaeological site concept where you can identify remains or ruins. For historical documentation management, you can consider a site even when there are only documentary references, since they clearly have evidences that can be identified in the landscape. The distinction between these two types of sites is registered in the corresponding form, making clear if the site has known archaeological remains or not.

Crossing the documentary references to sites with data from archaeological prospection and cartographic databases allowed us to validate the location of the sites. We use a Geographic Information System, the ArcMap from ESRI, to project sites in the current and ancient maps, making a connection to the MySQL Database by ODBC Drivers and using the coordinate fields X and Y of the database table Sítio.

Through the correlation between documents and archaeological data, we drawn a map with the settlements for the study area (Figure 4).

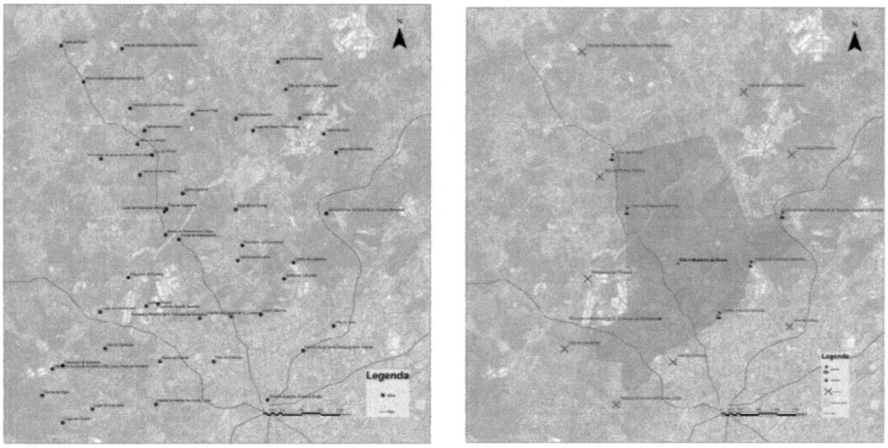

Figure 4. On the left the distribution of the sites in the study area and Dume monastery boundary on the right.

Some queries to references of each site allows us to select data according with filters like the date of documents or the type of relation established between the sites. So, to study the boundary of Dume Monastery we represent on the ArcMap all the sites that in "Doc. 19 Liber Fidei " document are direct or indirectly connected to" Boundary Dume Monastery ", namely:" Boundary Dume Monastery " " delimited " " Cipo of Felgueiras "or" Castro Maximum " " delimiting " " Monastery of the Boundary Dume".

The map uses different symbols that represent sites according to the kind of reference made to him. References a sites like "defines" or "is bordered by" are usually associated with sites like "Milestone", "Road" or "Bridge". These types of sites have an exact location and are usually delimiters or property markers. These sites are references for the study of territorial areas whose outlines are not always completely known, as is the case of the Dume boundary and sites with types like Town, Village, Habitat, Necropolis or Farm.

The information system designed supported the analysis of the historical documents and allowed the display of sites with different attributes and make their overlapping in different maps to validate some of the data evidences, like some landscape changes. Those actions would be very difficult to perform without this capability offered by the Information System to cross data in a very effective way.

5. CONCLUSION

Historical documents describes space in very different ways and deals with a large amount of textual information with spatial expression. In addition we have a strong urbanistic pressure in many study areas where the landscape changes and it is quite difficult to develop the fieldwork.

Using the Information System for historic documents management and making the association of textual references to a georeferenced sites, it is possible to transform textual data into cartographic representations, to improve the analyze and understanding of the data. The information system and the suggested workflow, allows us to manage the complex amount of data in a rational way and to increase the productivity of the territory studies. This work can be improved if combined with algorithms that automatically extracting facts from documents.

REFERENCES

Andrade, F., 2015. *Arquitetura e paisagem monásticas no território bracarense. O caso de Dume (S. Martinho),* Braga: Universidade do Minho (Dissertação de mestrado policopiada)

Botica, N. & Martins, M., 2008. *Gestão de sistemas de informação em arqueologia. A experiencia de Bracara Augusta.* Lugo, s.n.

Capela, J., 2003. As freguesias de Braga nas Memórias Paroquiais de 1758, A construção do imaginário minhoto setecentista. Braga.

Costa, A., 1965. Liber Fidei Sanctae Bracarensis Ecclesiae. Braga: Braga: Junta Distrital de Braga.

Costa, A., 1978. Liber Fidei Sanctae Bracarensis Ecclesiae. Braga: Braga: Junta Distrital de Braga.

Costa, A., 1990. Liber Fidei Sanctae Bracarensis Ecclesiae. Braga: Braga: Junta Distrital de Braga.

Costa, A., 1997. O Bispo D. Pedro e a organização da Arquidiocese de Braga, 2ª ed.. Braga: Irmandade de S. Bento da Porta Aberta.

Fontes, L., 1987. Salvamento arqueológico de Dume: Primeiros resultados, Cadernos de Arqueologia, Série II, nº4. Braga: UAUM/MDDS, pp.111-148.

Fontes, L. 1991-92. Salvamento arqueológico de Dume (Braga): Resultados das campanhas de 1989-90 e 1991-92, Cadernos de Arqueologia, Série II, nº 8-9, Braga: UAUM/MDDS, pp.199-230.

Fontes, L., 2006. A basílica sueva de Dume o túmulo dito de S. Martinho. Braga: NARQ/Junta de Freguesia de Dume.

Marques, A. & David, G., 2013. Base de dados e povoamento (diocese de Braga, séculos IX-XI). Porto: s.n.

Pizarro,J., 2012. *Portvgaliæ Monvmenta Historica. A Sæcvlo Octavo Post Christvm Vsqve Ad Qvintvmdecimvm Ivssv Academiæ Scientiarvm Olisiponensis Edita, Inqvisitiones — Inquirições Gerais de D. Dinis de 1288. Sentenças de 1290 e execuções de 1291*, Nova Série, Volume IV/1. Lisboa: Academia de Ciências de Lisboa.

PMH.INQ., 1888. *Portugaliae Monumenta Historica A Sæcvlo Octavo Post Christvm Vsqve Ad Qvintvmdecimvm Ivssv Academiæ Scientiarvm Olisiponensis Edita, Inquisitiones,* Fasciculi I&II, volume I. Lisboa: Academia de Ciências de Lisboa.

INFLUENCING FACTORS OF IN-MEMORY DATABASES FOR BUSINESS INFORMATION SYSTEMS

Hans-Peter Steinbacher and Hendrik Teerling
University of Applied Science Kufstein
Andreas Hofer Str. 7, 6336 Kufstein, Austria

ABSTRACT

Nowadays companies have to face the exponential increasing amount of data and therefore to manage the complexity of storing, analyzing and organizing it. The challenge is the economical usage of this information and known database management system might have reached their limitations. New concepts and database types have to be used for managing this big data. In the following, the driving and restraining factors of the use of In-memory databases for business information systems are analyzed. To identify critical factors of the use, a structural equation model based on the information-system success model of DeLone and McLean was used. A literature research and quantitative survey have been used for verify or falsify the hypothesis.

KEYWORDS

Bigdata, Inmemory-Database, Issm, Structural Equation Model

1. INTRODUCTION

Today, enterprises are facing the challenge of managing efficiently the exponentially growing amounts of data generated in their information systems in order to gain competitive advantage. In academic literature, the In-Memory databases are described as a potential solution to overcome these challenges (Weber 2014). In-Memory databases are databases, which store their data in the main physical memory. Compared to the conventional databases, which store their data mainly on a disk, the In-Memory databases are designed to provide high-speed access to the data (Krueger et al. 2010). Although the academic literature attests this technology a high potential, the current use in enterprises is not very widespread (Halper 2014). In this respect, this paper identifies the reasons for using In-Memory databases and the reasons refraining from this technology. The research mainly focus on the interest of medium sized and large enterprises.

In order to identify the factors that influence the use of this technology, a structural equation model was deduced from academic literature. The structural equation model was designed to identify the main factors for using In-Memory databases in business information systems. With the help of an online survey, which collected the data set, the structural equation model was evaluated. Furthermore, the research hypotheses were verified and falsified with using that model and the critical factors were related.

2. THEORETICAL FOUNDATIONS

The idea of storing an entire database in the main memory isn´t new. In the 80's Eich (1989) researched that topic. However, due to high cost of main memory modules and the unreliability of storing data in main memory, the research of Eich had not a big impact to the practical implementation in enterprises (Eich 1989). Some years later the situation changed. Declining prices of the main memory and the 64-bit technology overcame the early problems. The price of main memory dropped from \$1.000 in 1999 to \$8 in 2012. As result of the decreasing prices, the technology came to the fore of the academic literature and information systems provider (Wessel et al 2013).

The In-memory databases improve the performance of the information systems. The Enterprise Resource Planning vendor SAP promises that their In-Memory database SAP HANA is 3600x faster than a traditional disk based solution (SAP AG 2012). A special feature of In-Memory databases is the way they organize the data. Compared to traditional databases, where the data sets are organized row oriented, In Memory databases organized their data sets column-oriented. This improves the performance of analytical operations and read only requests (Krueger et al 2010).

In case of the rising data depending in decision processes, Plattner claims a technological revision of database management systems. The In-Memory technology is a potential technical solution that could handle the new demands (Plattner 2013).

In order to evaluate the success of information systems DeLone and McLean developed a model with scores the success of information systems from the user's perspective. DeLone und McLean deduce three quality dimensions – information quality, system quality and service quality. Each of them has an influence on two further dimensions - the intention to use/use and the user satisfaction. These two dimensions affect the net benefits, which interact again with these dimensions. The following analysis modifies the success model of DeLone and McLean to identify both driving and re-straining factors for the use of In-Memory databases in information systems (DeLone, McLean 2003).

The dimensions information quality and the system quality have been adopted for the research. Furthermore, a new dimension was introduced in order to measure the possibility to change the business processes when using In-memory databases. These three dimensions have a theoretical influence to the modified dimension net benefit. Furthermore, the restraints for the implementation of In-Memory databases in information systems should also be detected. Therefore, a new dimension, the use obstacle, was created. Based on the academic literature, the dimensions innovation cost (Gemlik et al 2010, Kosch et al 2013, Leppler 2014), investment uncertainly (Benlian et al 2009, Pillai et al 2009) and the enterprise integration (Klesse et al 2005, Markl et al 2013) were created for this research,

The analysis should measure the relationship and the impact of these three dimensions to the dimension using obstacles. Finally the two dimensions- use and use obstacle-were to be analyzed with respect to their impact to another dimension, which is adopted from the IS model, intention to use/use. The figure 1 sums up the modified model for measuring the influence factors of using an in memory database for information systems.

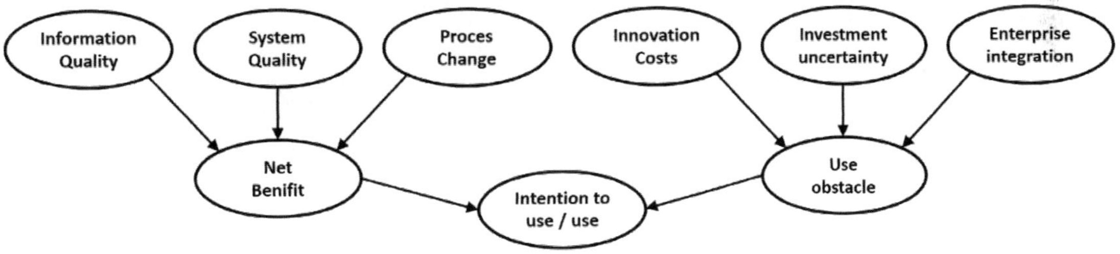

Figure 1. Modified structure model based on DeLone and McLean (2003)

3. METHODS

Because the hypotheses and dimensions are in a comprehensive hypothesis braid, a structural equation model is used. The target group of this research are medium sized and large businesses of different affiliates. They got the online survey with the 41 items. 1800 IT managers, responsible for the database management in their company in Austria, Germany, Italy and Swiss, have been invited to take part in the survey. The return rate of the survey was 110 questionnaires where 47 were not filled in completely. Therefore, the final sample of the research comprised 59 medium sized and large companies with the return rate of 3.3% (Table 1). The Partial-Least-Squares method was used as the evaluating strategy because this method allows good results with a comparatively small sample (Ruge 2010).

Table 1. Overview sample size

Criterion	Parameter	Frequency	Percentage
Questionnaire	Complete filled in	59	53.64 %
	Partly filled in	51	46.36 %
Affiliates	Industry	29	49.15 %
	Bank and Insurance	3	5.08 %
	Information Technology	5	8.47 %
	Trade	7	11.86 %
	Service	3	5.08 %
	Other	12	20.34 %
	Total final sample	59	100 %

The evaluation method was built as follows. First, the outer models was measured. The outer model specifies the relationship between the dimensions, also called latent variables and the empirically measurable indicators. It is used to obtain values for the dimensions, which could not directly measured. Second, the inner model is analyzed. That model gauges the relationship between the latent variables, using the estimate values of the latent variables of the outer model. With the help of the path coefficients, the critical influence factors were identified. By means of the t-statistics, the hypothesis of the research could verify or falsify (Weiber, Mühlhaus 2010).

4. RESULTS

For evaluation and analysis of the structural equation, model statistical evaluation criteria are used. In summary, the values for the outer model are passable. In case of the number of modifications of the IS model and the explorative character of the research the values are acceptable and good. Based on the values of the outer model, the inner model with the relationships from the dimensions were evaluated. The following table 2 sums of the results of the research.

Table 2. Results of the structural equation model

Hypothesis	**quality criterion**		
	path coefficients	t-statistics	conclusion
H1: Information Quality ▶ Net Benefit	0,182	1.783	temporarily confirm
H2: System Quality ▶ Net Benefit	0,223	2.110	temporarily confirm
H3: Process Change. ▶ Net Benefit	0,479	4.295	temporarily confirm
H4: Innovation cost. ▶ Use obstacle	0,242	1.991	temporarily confirm
H5: Investment uncertainly ▶ Use obstacle	0,464	5.411	temporarily confirm
H6: Enterprise integration▶ Use obstacle	**0,073**	**0.700**	temporarily rejected
H7: Net Benefit ▶ Intention to use /use	0,312	1.991	temporarily confirm
H8: Use obstacle. ▶ Intention to use /use	-0,429	3.332	temporarily confirm

All hypothesis were confirmed except the hypothesis 6. In case of the low value of the t-statistic the hypothesis gets rejected temporality.

5. CONCLUSION

The statistical research has confirmed five influence factors of using in memory databases for business information systems. The information quality, system quality and the process change could attest as drivers for the technology. In case of the high path coefficient the dimension process change, could identify as the critical factor in relation to the Net Benefit. Interpreting this effect, the conclusion is that the benefit of this technology only can be increased if its implementation is stimulated by anticipated enhancements of business processes. Increasing their technological support can improve Business processes qualities. Beginning by a clear documentation of the business processes until semi-automation of such processes, can increase the acceptance by the process users. This enables easier and accepted process change activities.

Based on the statistical values the dimensions innovation cost and investment uncertainty are identified as obstacles to the technology. The enterprise integration does not have an influence on the use obstacle. The critical factor, which affects to the use obstacle, is the investment uncertainty.

The net benefit has a smaller affect to the intention to use/use then the use obstacle. That means that actually the enterprise judge the obstacle of the use of In-Memory databases is bigger than the benefit. Reduced to a simple meaning of In-Memory databases the main benefit is speed. To foresee the benefit of speed is a complex calculation and has to face the easy calculation of investment costs of In-Memory databases.

To eliminate the situational dependences, the results of the short term have to be examined be a long-term study. Especially the rejection of hypothesis 6 needs a more detailed investigation. To get a representative results the sample size have to be increased even when the needed sample size for a PLS analysis have been reached.

REFERENCES

Benlian, Alexander; Hess, Thomas; Buxmann, Peter (2009): Treiber der Adoption SaaS-basierter Anwendungen. In: Wirtsch. Inform. 51 (5), S. 414–428.

DeLone, William H.; McLean, Ephraim R. (2003): The DeLone and McLean Model of Information System Success: A Ten-Year Upgrade. In: Journal of Management Information Systems 18 (4), S. 9–30.

Eich, Margaret H. (1989): Main memory database research directions. In: G. Goos, J. Hartmanis, D. Barstow, W. Brauer, P. Brinch Hansen, D. Gries et al. (Hg.): Database Machines, Bd. 368. Berlin, Heidelberg: Springer Berlin Heidelberg (Lecture Notes in Computer Science), S. 251–268.

Gemlik, Arkadius; Neumann, Markus; Sprenger, Jon; Breitner, Michael H. (2010): Praxisrelevanz des Modells von DeLone und McLean zur Erfolgsmessung von Informationssystemen. In: Informatik 2010. Bonn: Ges. für Informatik (GI-Edition : Proceedings, 176), S. 615–620.

Halper, Fern (2014): Next-Generation Analytics and Platforms. For Business Success. Hg. v. The Data Warehouse Institute. Renton. http://tdwi.org/research/2014/12/best-practices-report-next-generation-analytics-and-platforms/asset.aspx? tc=assetpg, 24.09.2015.

Klesse, Mario; Wortmann, Felix; Schelp, Joachim (2005): Erfolgsfaktoren der Applikationsintegration. In: Wirtschaftsinformatik 47 (4), S. 259–267.

Kosch, Lubov; Zakhariya, Halyna; Breitner, Michael H. (2013): Beeinflus-sen Auswahlkriterien den Erfolg eines CRM-Systems? eine Strukturgleichungsmodellierung basierend auf dem DeLone und McLean IS-Erfolgsmodel. In: Proceedings of the 11th International Conference on Wirtschaftsinformatik. Leipzig: Univ., S. 229–243.

Krueger, Jens; Grund, Martin; Tinnefeld, Christian; Eckart, Benjamin; Zeier, Alexander; Plattner, Hasso (2010): Hauptspeicherdatenbanken für Unternehmensanwendungen. Universität Potsdam. Potsdam (3).

Leppler, Stephan (2014): TCO Vergleich von neuzugelassenen konventionellen und (teil-)elektrischen Fahrzeugen aus Nutzersicht. Entwicklung eines VBA-Excel-basierten TCO-Modells zur Untersuchung der wirtschaftlichen Konkurrenzfähigkeit neuzugelassener (teil-)elektrischer Pkw. 1. Aufl. s.l.: diplom.de.

Markl, Volker; Löser, Alexander; Hoeren, Thomas; Krcmar, Helmut; Hemsen, Holger; Schermann, Michael et al. (2013): Innovationspotenzial-analyse für die neuen Technologien für das Verwalten und Analysieren von großen Datenmengen (Big Data Management). Hg. v. Volker Markl, Thomas Hoeren und Helmut Krcmar. Berlin, München, Münster.

Pillai, Rajani Ganesh; He, Xin; Echambadi, Raj (2009): 660 Advances in Consumer Research Volume 36, © 2009 Inclusion versus Exclusion: The Effect of Perceived Uncertainty on Screening Strategies. In: Advances in Consumer Research 36, S. 660–661.

Plattner, Hasso (2013): A Course in In-Memory Data Management. Berlin, Heidelberg: Springer Berlin Heidelberg.

Ruge, Marcus (2010): Prognosen mit dynamischen Strukturgleichungsmodellen – ein Ausblick. Hg. v. Universität Potsdam. Wirtschafts- und Sozial-wissenschaftliche Fakultät. Potsdam

SAP AG (2012): Top 10. Zehn Gründe, warum Unternehmen ihre Zukunft mit SAP HANA gestalten. Hg. v. SAP AG. http://www.ifi-lios.de/pdf/sap_hana/SAP_HANA_Top_10.pdf, 25.03.2015.

Weber, Mathias (2014): Big-Data-Technologien. Wissen für Entscheider. Leitfaden. Hg. v. Bundesverband Informationswirtschaft, Telekommunikation und neue Medien e. V. Berlin.

Weiber, Rolf; Mühlhaus, Daniel (2010): Strukturgleichungsmodellierung. Eine anwendungsorientierte Einführung in die Kausalanalyse mit Hilfe von AMOS, SmartPLS und SPSS. Berlin, Heidelberg: Springer (Springer).

Wessel, Patrick.; Köffer, Sebastian.; Becker, Jörg. (2013): Auswirkungen von In-Memory-Datenmanagement auf Geschäftsprozesse im Business Intelligence. In: Proceedings of the 11th International Conference on Wirtschaftsinformatik. Leipzig: Univ., S. 1781–1795.

PROJECT SATCO - SMART AIRPORT TRAFFIC CONTROL

Deborah Mendes Ferreira and Flávio de Barros Vidal
Department of Computer Science, University of Brasilia, C.P. 4466
Brasilia - DF 70910-900, Brazil

ABSTRACT

Brazil has the largest air transportation network in South America, it works as a hub to connect other. Although Brazil has a robust air traffic framework, there is still room for improvements, the entire region would be benefited from such improvements. We still don't have an optimal and automated air traffic management system. Most of the control is carried out empirically by Air Traffic Controller with the aid of some automatic equipment. A less efficient management can frequently lead to departure and landing delays and even serious incidents. We propose Project SATCo, Smart Airport Traffic Control, which is a middleware that automates the process of airport ground control, making the link between flights and airport data with possible optimizations for sequences of departures or arrivals. The process of arriving and departing of aircraft is broken into several stages in order to find local points of optimizations and thus reach a global optimization. The advantage of using this middleware is its simplicity and easy implementation, which will not require major changes in the current Brazilian air traffic management structure. Moreover, with this middleware we could test many different optimizations and find the best suitable solution to each scenario.

KEYWORDS

Air traffic control, Middleware, Flight optimization, Air traffic management.

1. INTRODUCTION

The present bottleneck of aviation is in the airports, the airspace is huge compared to the number of airports that exists in a region. What determines the number of aircraft that can travel is the airport capacity to carry out these aircraft arrivals and departures. Because of this bottleneck, many airports have saturated capacities and as a result, many flights arrive and depart outside the schedule. According to the Federal Aviation Administration (FAA), flight delays in the United States generate an approximate loss of 22 billion dollars annually to the airlines (FAA, 2015).

The runway is the main bottleneck inside the airport since only one aircraft can use the runway at a time. The cost of building new runways is quite high and sometimes there is no physical space for it. The cheapest and simplest option is to optimize the current structure of the airport without making physical changes. In order for the airport to have an efficient utilization of its structure, it is necessary to use optimization methodologies and techniques for aircraft arrivals and departures.

Researches financed by the National Aeronautics and Space Administration (NASA) about the cause of delays concluded that automated tools to aid the optimization of flight scheduling are beneficial for flight controllers, and for aircraft operators.

Brazil has the responsibility to manage the territorial airspace (8,511,965 km^2) and the airspace of the overlying ocean area, which extends to the meridian 10° W, making a total of 22 million km^2. Brazil has the busiest airspace in South America, more than 190 million people pass through Brazilian airports every year (INFREAERO, 2013).

Brazilian airports act as a router for other South American countries, allowing them to have access to other continents. They have a robust framework, but there are still many improvements that could be made and which would benefit the entire region of South America. The activity of airport control in Brazil is carried out empirically by flight controllers, who must negotiate the positioning of aircraft with airlines companies and with the pilots without clear criteria, which may result in more problems for the flight controller, who already has to deal with other complex situations in their profession. Due to the increased number of aircraft on the ground, the time required for the controller to make decisions has increased considerably, they often find saturated runways, crowded gates and various aircraft simultaneously in transit.

In this paper we present a middleware called Project SATCo that is currently being developed. SATCo is designed as a mediator between airport information and possible optimizations for each part of the airport. We divide the flight process in several steps so each step can be optimized locally to create a global optimization. We can optimize the gate allocation, taxi and runway sequencing with different optimization algorithms, choosing the one that is more adequate for each structure. The middleware makes it easier to apply such optimization by hiding the complex details of airport structure.

2. SATCO

This section presents the structure of the middleware and its behavior. Figure 1 presents an overview of the middleware and how it connects with other parts of the system.

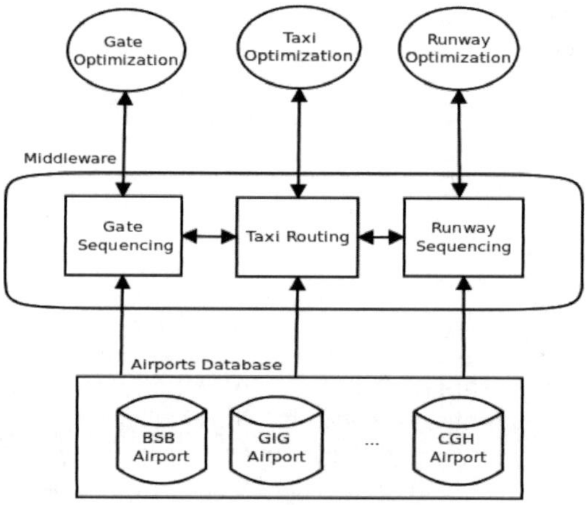

Figure 1. SATCo overview.

SATCo is a middleware created with the goal of providing an interface between the data from airports and the possible optimizations for each part of the airport ground control. The airports database contains the airport structure and all the arriving and departing flights. With this information we can control all landings and take-offs.

Data from all airports in a region are also connected, so we have access to all flights that are on their way to a specific airport. If any airport cancel its landings, we can redirect flights to nearby airports using the information obtained from different airports. SATCo divides the complete process of arrivals and departures into smaller parts to find local optimizations and optimizations that reach a global level.

First we have an optimization at level of structure, this optimization will ensure that the each of the airport structure is used with efficiency. Then, we have an optimization at airport level, by using each structure with efficiency, we should reach a global optimization at airport level. Finally, with the optimization of several airports, we will reach also an optimization at air space level. In Figure 2, we present an example on how this optimization would work on Brazilian air space.

Since the Middleware connects each part of the flight to differente optimizations, we can, for example, use Genetic Algorithms to optimize the taxiing (Pessoa et al., 2013), Game Theory to optimize departures (Ferreira et al., 2014) and several other possibilities in just one platform, connecting all these optimizations.

The first necessary configuration for this middleware is determining the airport that will be optimized, with this information the middleware will have access to the entire structure of the airport: taxi routes, lanes, location of gates, runways, etc. The following information about the airport is available:

n_g = number of gates;

G_i = gate *i*, where $i = 1, \ldots., n_g$;

n_r = number of runways;

R_i = runway *i*, where $i = 1, \ldots, n_r$;

$T = (V, E)$ = taxiway directed graph, with set *V* of vertices together with a set *E* of edges;

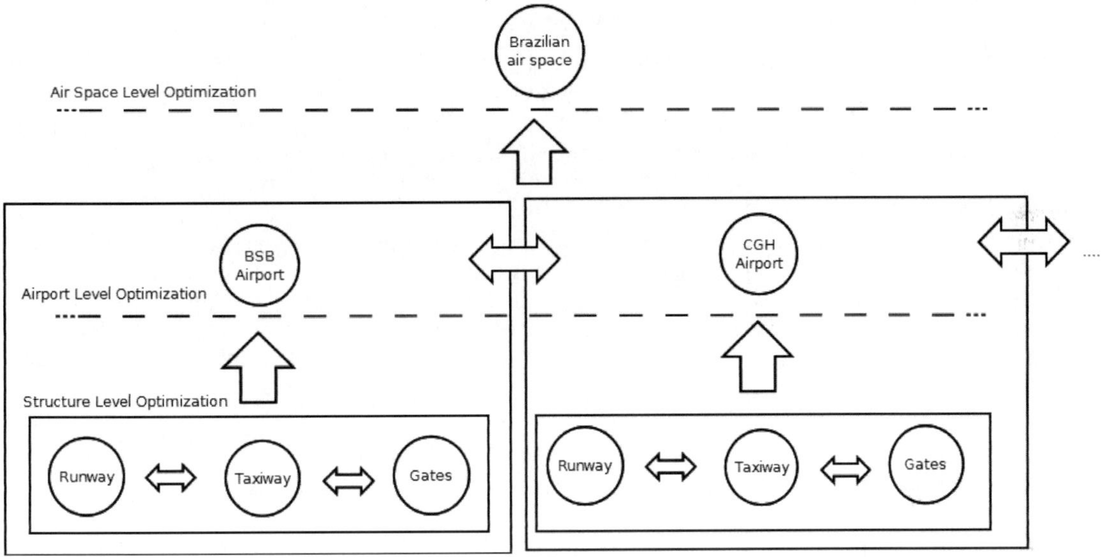

Figure 2. Optimization levels of SATCo.

n_v = number of vertices in T;

V_i = taxiway vertex *i*, where where $i = 1, \ldots, n_v$;

n_e = number of edges in T;

V_i = taxiway edge *i*, where where $i = 1, \ldots, n_e$;

$Dt(X, Y)$ = distance between point *X* and point *Y* at the airport, where *X* and *Y* could be a gate, a runway or a taxiway vertex/edge.

The following aircraft information is known by the middleware, it can obtain information about the aircraft that are near the airport since it has a connection with other airports:

A_{id} = aircraft with its respective flight id;

$S_{A_{id}}$ = aircraft status (on route= 3, landing = 2, departing = 1, done = 0);

$P_{A_{id}}$ = position of aircraft A_{id};

$V_{A_{id}}$ = velocity of aircraft A_{id};

$DT_{A_{id}}$ = destination of aircraft A_{id};

$ST_{A_{id}}$ = scheduled take off of aircraft A_{id};

$SL_{A_{id}}$ = scheduled landing of aircraft A_{id};

$S_{A_{id1},A_{id2}}$ = necessary separation between A_{id1} and A_{id2}.

The following variables will define the state of the airport at a given time:

CT = current time;

$LT_{A_{id}}$ = real landing time of aircraft A_{id}, defined if $S_{A_{id}} = 2$;

$TT_{A_{id}}$ = real take off time of aircraft A_{id}, defined if $S_{A_{id}} = 1$;

SR_i = status of runway R_i (busy =1, not busy =0);

SG_i = status of gate G_i (busy =1, not busy =0);

SV_i = status of V_i (busy =1, not busy =0);

PA_{G_i} = current aircraft at gate V_i, defined if $SG_i = 1$;

PA_{R_i} = current aircraft at runway R_i, defined if $SR_i = 1$;

PA_{V_i} = current aircraft at vertex V_i, defined if $SV_i = 1$;

The middleware connects this information with the optimization algorithms, so it is possible to apply such algorithms without worrying about the complete structure of the airport. Also, we can compare different algorithms using the same scenario. The middleware stores everything that is happening at the airport, such as aircraft that is on the ground and the position of each one, so we can arrange landing and take-off in parallel. SATCo works as a state machine by storing the state of the gates, the taxiway and runway and modifying these states as the aircraft move.

3. CONCLUSION

This paper presented the Project SATCo, a middleware to connect airport structure to its possible optimizations. Project SATCo presents a significant improvement at the airport ground control and is especially useful for countries that have saturated airports, such as Brazil, and is still on its way to implement new technologies to improve airport control. This middleware is capable of adapting itself to the dynamic scenario of air traffic control.

The advantage of SATCo is the fact that the optimizations happen at a local and at a global level, allowing us to find a better result. Also, the optimization module is separated from the airport structure, hiding the complex details of the airport to the optimization, making it easier to test several possible optimizations.

Brazil is going to pass through some intense periods in the aviation, during the 2016 Olympics, and SATCo represents an inexpensive and simple solution to aid the Brazilians airports at this period.

SATCo is being implemented and tested with data from the 2014 World Cup, using different optimizations.

REFERENCES

Anagnostakis, I., Clarke, J. P., B-ograve, D., hme, V-ograve, U., & lcker. (2001) Runway operations planning and control: Sequencing and scheduling. *Journal of Aircraft* v. 38, n. 6, p. 988-996.

FAA. Federal aviation administration. Available Online, July 2015. http://www.faa.gov/.

Ferreira, D. M., Rosa, L. P., Ribeiro, V. F., de Barros Vidal, F., & Weigang, L. (2014). Genetic Algorithms and Game Theory for Airport Departure Decision Making: GeDMAN and CoDMAN. *In Knowledge Management in Organizations* p. 3-14 .

Gotteland, J. B., & Durand, N. (2003). Genetic algorithms applied to airport ground traffic optimization. *In Evolutionary Computation*, 2003. CEC'03 v 1., p. 544-551.

Gotteland, J. B., Durand, N., Alliot, J. M., & Page, E. (2001). Aircraft ground traffic optimization. *In ATM* 2001, 4th USA/Europe Air Traffic Management Research and Development Seminar.

Infraero. Empresa brasileira de infraestrutura aeroportuária. Available Online, July 2015. http://www.infraero.gov.br/.

Kontoyiannakis, K., Serrano, E., Tse, K., Lapp, M., & Cohn, A. (2009). A simulation framework to evaluate airport gate allocation policies under extreme delay conditions. *In Winter Simulation Conference* p. 2332-2342.

Nikoleris, T., Gupta, G., & Kistler, M. (2011). Detailed estimation of fuel consumption and emissions during aircraft taxi operations at Dallas/Fort Worth International Airport. *Transportation Research Part D: Transport and Environment* v.16, n. 4, p. 302-308.

Rosa, L. P., Ferreira, D. M., Cruciol, L. L., Weigang, L., & Deng, X. J. (2013). Genetic algorithms for management of taxi scheduling. *In The 2013 International Conference on Artificial Intelligence*.

Stroiney, S., Levy, B., & Knickerbocker, C. J. (2010). Departure management: Savings in taxi time, fuel burn, and emissions. *In Integrated Communications Navigation and Surveillance Conference* (ICNS), 2010 p. J2-1.

INNOVATION-DRIVEN MODEL DESIGN AND KEY FACTORS ANALYSIS

Jinluan Ren, Jing Wang, Rui Huang, Xinzhu Huang and Shu Zhang
School of Economics and Management, Communication University of China, Beijing, China

ABSTRACT

When economic development reaches a higher level, innovation become the main driven force for economic increasing. Innovation-driven development is a dynamic and open cyclic process. Based on analyzing the relationships among the innovation elements, the innovation data from 2005 to 2013 of Beijing as an example, 25 key factors of innovation-driven development are filtered from 47 factors by neural network model. The innovation-driven system dynamics model is constructed based on these selected key factors. Then the innovation-driven development model is designed, in which innovation input, science & technology output, innovation performance and innovation environment are key apartments. Finally the paper proposes some advice on how to advance the innovation-driven development, and points out the future research direction.

KEYWORDS

Innovation-Driven; Key factors; Driving Relationship

1. INTRODUCTION

With the development of economic globalization and the arrival of the knowledge economy, innovation has penetrated into all aspects of economic development and social life. Innovation capability is one of important factors to evaluate the comprehensive competitiveness of countries or regions. Innovation-driven economic pattern is gradually replacing the traditional investment driven economic pattern, and becoming the main form of economic development. Innovation-driven development process involves many links and elements. Whether the important degree of different factors is same or not, and what kind of driving relationship exists between the elements are the basis for making innovation policies. This study uses the neural network model to determine the key elements in the innovation-driven development process.

2. LITERATURE REVIEW

Michael Porter (1990) proposed the concept of "innovation-driven". He suggested four distinct stages of national competitive development: factor-driven, investment-driven, innovation-driven and wealth-driven. In innovation-driven stage, the high technology and knowledge are the most important resource to advance economy development.

Some scholars pointed out that the economic growth relies on science & technology innovation more and more, especially independent design, R&D, inventions as well as the production and creation of knowledge (Liu, 2011 and Hong, 2013). In the background of knowledge economy, innovation-driven has transformed from the closed, single, technology and artificial environment innovation to the global configuration of innovation resources, regional cooperation and innovation, non-technical innovation, ecological self-organizing system and other innovation models (Gan, 2013). As many factors involved in the process of innovation-driven and the complex relationship between these factors, related empirical studies had been done about the relationship among innovation factors. An analysis framework of national innovation capacity had been put forward, which was determined by the interplay between the innovation system infrastructure and innovation environment (Furman et al, 2002). This analysis framework used international patent data to measure the innovation ability of national innovation system and calculate the influence of innovation inputs, innovation environment and other related factors. The study found that the performance of innovation system was affected not only by innovation input but also innovation system environment factors. Foreign direct investment (FDI), institutions and governance and economic freedom affected innovation output (Ghazal et al. 2015). There is a relationship between national R&D expenditure and GDP. Development of innovation economy was not solely decided by R&D expenditure, and the efficient investment and strict implementation of innovative strategy are more important (Gackstatter et al, 2014).

In summary, most of the research focus on the relationships between two factors. There are a few study focusing on relationships among all innovation elements. This study analyses the influence of different factors on innovation-driven development based on neural network model and the relationships among them.

3. CONNOTATION AND KEY FACTORS OF INNOVATION-DRIVEN DEVELOPMENT SYSTEM

3.1 Connotation of Innovation-Driven Development

Innovation-driven the economic and social development is a dynamic, open and cyclical process. Innovation inputs, science & technology innovation, and innovation performance and innovation environment are the crucial components. There are driven effects among them.

The level of economic development, education and scientific research environment, social and culture environment and opening environment are the basic driving force of innovation. Innovation input generally includes capital input and talent input. Knowledge output is reflected in science and technology papers and patents. Knowledge flowing in the market or their own development promotes the development of new products and economic efficiency of enterprises. With the support of technological innovation, the economic benefits of enterprises can be improved significantly, so as to promote the adjustment of the whole social economic structure, and improve the ability of sustainable development. Ultimately it improves the economic efficiency and innovation environment.

3.2 Analyzing the Primary Index of Innovation-Driven

Innovation and innovation-driven research have different indicators in different systems. Representative index systems are below. The Innovation Union Scoreboard (2015) distinguishes between 3 main types of indicators – Enablers, Firm activities and Outputs. There are 8 innovation dimensions capturing in total 25 different indicators. "The Enablers capture the main drivers of innovation performance external to the firm and cover 3 innovation dimensions: Human resources, Open, excellent and attractive research systems as well as Finance and support." The Global Innovation Index (GII) (2015) includes two sub-indexes—the Innovation Input and the Innovation Output Sub-Index. Innovation Input includes five dimensions - institutions, human capital and research, infrastructure, market sophistication and business sophistication. Innovation input defines aspects of the environment conductive to innovation within an economy. Indicators of innovation input can be said to be the indicators of driving innovation. The Global Competitiveness Report (GCR) (2014-2015) is made up of 114 variables and provides an overview of the competitiveness performance of 144 economies. The report suggests that the key pillars are business sophistication and innovation in innovation-driven economy.

This paper designs innovation-driven development index system based on the connotation of innovation-driven development and the related index framework. This index system includes 4 types indicators: innovation input, science & technology output, innovation performance and innovation environment, 13 secondary indicators and 47 third level indexes.

3.3 Innovation-Driven Development Index System

Because of existing redundancy among indicators, neural network model is used to select the key indicators of innovation-driven development. Based on this index system, the data of Beijing from 2005 to 2013 were collected as the research foundation.

In order to analyze the driving relationship between innovation input and science& technology output, 9 indicators of innovation input of neural network model were used as input variables, and 7 indicators of science & technology output were used as target variables neural network model, then the importance of input variables could be got. Then those indicators whose importance is bigger than 1 are selected as preliminary alternative indicators. And so forth, preliminary alternative indicators of science & technology output, innovation performance and innovation environment were selected by the same method.

Based on the frequency of indicators, key indicators were select by whose appear frequency is bigger than or equal to 2. The optimized index system contains 25 indicators, as shown in table 1.

Table 1. Innovation-driven Development Index System

Primary level indexes	Second level indexes	Indicator
Innovation input	R&D expenditure	R&D Expenditure percentage of GDP (%)
		R&D Expenditure of Large and medium-sized enterprises (10000 Yuan RMB)
		R&D Expenditure on per capita (10000 Yuan RMB)
	Innovative talent	Full-time equivalent of R&D personnel per 10000 population (Person)
	Innovation platform	Number of industrial technology innovation strategy alliance
	Innovation service	The number of enterprises in incubating in national tech-enterprise incubators
Science & technology output	Knowledge output	The number of science & technology paper indexed by SCI
	Technology diffusion	Total technical contract turnover (hundred million Yuan RMB)
		Amount of technology import contracts (hundred million US$)
		International income of technology per 10000 RMB of GDP (US$/10,000 RMB)
Innovation performance	Innovation product	New product sales revenue
	Economic output	GDP (Hundred Million Yuan RMB)
	Industrial structure adjustment	Capital productivity
		Overall society labor productivity (RMB Yuan/Person)
	Sustainable development	Water consumption per GDP
		Energy consumption per GDP
		Environmental quality index
Innovation environment	Political environment	Government expenditure on purchasing new technologies and products as percentage of public finance budget
		Corporate tax deduction (hundred million Yuan RMB)
	Culture environment	Public finance expenditure on education as percentage of GDP (%)
		The number of public library collections per capita (Copies/Person)
		Green coverage (%)
	Communication environment	Total amount of import and export as percentage of GDP
		Amount of utilized foreign investment

4. ANALYSIS OF INNOVATION-DRIVEN DEVELOPMENT

4.1 Building the Innovation-Driven Model

Based on the analysis of the connotation of innovation-driven, this study proposes an innovation-driven development model, as shown in figure 1.

R&D expenditure, innovation talent, innovation platform and innovation service are used to measure innovation input. Science & technology output is mainly includes knowledge output and technology diffusion. Innovation performance is mainly measured by innovation products, economic output, industrial structure adjustment and sustainable development. The innovation environment mainly includes Political environment, culture environment and communication environment. Each parts of innovation-driven development process drives each other.

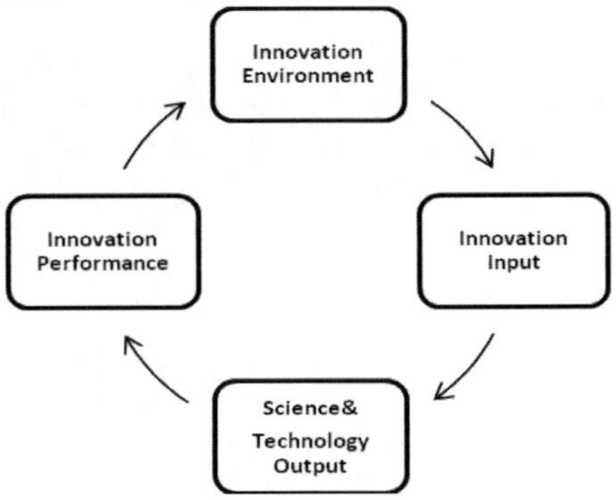

Figure 1. Innovation-driven development model

4.2 Analyzing the Driving Relationship in the Innovation Development System

Innovation-driven development system contains a lot of factors. Multiple feedback relationships exist between the various factors. There are time lags between the factors interaction. It is not easy to analyzing these relationship and interaction effect by intuitive understanding or experience. This study analyzes the driving relationship in the innovation development system using the system dynamics method. Some results are obtained.

Innovation input had positive driven effect on scientific & technological output. R&D expenditure percentage of GDP and the number of industrial technology innovation strategy alliance simultaneously affect three indicators of science & technology output positively. This note the funds support and the cooperation alliance are key factors in affecting knowledge output and technology diffusion.

Science& technology output has positive driven effect on innovation performance. International income of technology per 10000 RMB of GDP and Total technical contract turnover simultaneously affect capital productivity, new product sales revenue and water consumption per GDP positively. This notes technology diffusion plays a key role in the process of creating innovation performance.

Innovation performance has positive driven effect on innovation environment. Overall society labor productivity, GDP, environmental quality index are the most important indexes in innovation performance, they affect political environment and culture environment positively. Reduction of energy consumption per GDP will increase total amount of import and export as percentage of GDP. The reduction of water consumption per GDP will increase the amount of utilized foreign investment.

Innovation environment has positive driven effect on innovation input. Government expenditure on purchasing new technologies and products as percentage of public finance budget, international income of technology per 10000 RMB of GDP, total technical contract turnover and new product sales revenue affect many other factors, and at the same time are affected by other factors.

5. POLICY RECOMMENDATIONS AND FUTURE RESEARCH

5.1 Policy Recommendations

The imperfect system of innovation-driven system is one of the key factors that restrict of innovation development. The government should support the cultivation of innovation talent and increase investment to promote innovation-driven development, guide and support enterprises, universities and research institutions to increase R & D investment through preferential policy.

Improving innovation platform, industrial technology alliance and technology market can facilitate technology exchange and increase the rate of transformation of achievements in science and technology. Accelerating the formation of integrated, open, competitive and orderly modern market and technological innovation service system will help the market to play important role in optimizing allocation of resources for science and technology.

Government should pay more attention on constructing culture environment, creating positive social atmosphere, and increase input in infrastructure. Improve the living environment is help for attracting more innovation talent to Beijing. In this way, Beijing's innovation-driven economy society can be continuously promoted.

5.2 Future Research

In the future we can consider the following works: It is suggested analyzing and judging innovation-driven status in different area based on this model. The innovative status is very different in different regions in China and other countries, so it is necessary to study innovation-driven development in different level not only in the country level. It is also necessary to study not only the driving process in the internal innovation system, but also the process of innovation driving economic development systematically from both the macro and micro level promoting innovation. The clear index and data are important parts of the further research.

ACKNOWLEDGEMENT

This research is financially supported by the National Science Foundation of China, Grant No. 71172040 and the Beijing Science Research Center, Project No. HG1508.

REFERENCES

Cornell University, INSEAD, and WIPO, 2015. The Global Innovation Index 2015: Effective Innovation Policies for Development, Fontainebleau, Ithaca, and Geneva.

European Commission, 2015. Innovation Union Scoreboard 2015, Brussels.

Furman, J.L. et al, 2002. The determinants of national innovative capacity, *Research Policy.* Vol. 31, pp. 899-933.

Gan, W. H., 2013. Four dimension of innovation-driven analysis based on the methodology, *Journal for Party and Administrative Cadres(In Chinese).* No. 1, pp. 49-52.

Gackstatter, S. et al, 2014. Building an innovation-driven economy – the case of BRIC and GCC countries, *Foresight.* Vol.16, pp. 293-308.

Ghazal, R. et al, 2015. Determinants of innovation outputs in developing countries: Evidence from panel data negative binomial approach, *Journal of Economic Studies*. Vol. 42, pp. 237-260.

Hong, Y. X., 2013. Some conceptions on innovation-driven growth and collaborative innovation, *Economic Theory and Business Management(In Chinese).* No. 5, pp. 5-12.

Liu, Zhibiao, 2011. From late-development advantage to first-mover advantage: theoretic thoughts on implementing the innovation-driven strategy, *Industrial Economics Research (In Chinese).* No. 4, pp. 1-7.

Porter, Michael E., 1990. *The Competitive Advantage of Nations*. The Free Press.

World Economic Forum, 2015. The Global Competitiveness Report 2014-2015, Switzerland.

DIGITALIZATION: THE DILEMMA IN HIGHLY STANDARDIZED COMPANIES AND ORGANIZATIONAL DEVELOPMENT

Paavo Heikkinen[1] and Bernd Hilgarth[2]
[1]*MCI Management Center Innsbruck, Universitätsstraße 15, 6020 Innsbruck / Austria*
[2]*Ostbayerische Technische Hochschule Amberg-Weiden, Hetzenrichter Weg 15, 92637 Weiden / Germany*

ABSTRACT

Many so called disruptive trends like the Five SMART Technologies (Gartner, 2014) affect more and more existing business models with high dynamics and complexities. At the same time the affected organizations do show more or less settled business models with partly long traditions of process improvement work. During researching the Business Process Management (BPM) last-mile phenomenon in the past five years (Kurz et al, 2012), some general reasons arise for failures of process improvements and implementations in highly standardized organizations. At the same time for the authors of this paper it became clear that this research might be expanded to aspects coming from other disciplines like project management, strategy management, quality management or change management are nearby the BPM approaches. In the era of the widely discussed trend of digitalization, the number and intensity of process improvements an organization has to react on with the adaptation of their business processes and organizational structures increases from the authors experience and point of view in an enormous way. Mature organization show often that the problem to react on necessary changes are initiated by the use of new technologies. This article serves as (1) a first summary of the observations were made during the past three years in context of adaptations of disruptive technologies and business models like 3D printing in standardized process organizations and (2) it will draft from the authors point of view the need and way for researching on this complex.

KEYWORDS

Digitalization, BPM, Organizational Development, Disruptive Technologies, Last-Mile Problem, Dynaxity

1. INTRODUCTION

New manufacturing technologies are changing the industries as standardized production processes are facing a need for change. These new alternative production technologies do not fit into the scope of the existing processes, and therefore a necessity for adapting the current procedures has risen. This leads to create obstacles in the implementation of the new technologies. The need for adapting existing processes and creating new ones has its challenges in multinational enterprises (MNEs). These challenges are often called the last mile problem (Kurz et. al., pp. 166, 2012). This paper discusses the restrictions faced while implementing new technologies in practical environment of a standardized MNE.

The paper contributes as a first observation report to the disciplines of information science, organizational development, business process management, quality management, change management and operational excellence. It shall act as a *teaser* to reflect the need for further researching and developing a comprehensive systemic framework will improve the efficient management of these highly impacting changes do come from this digitalization stream.

For this in the paper the Action Design Research (ADR) (Sein et. al., 2011) is referenced as the basic research method for this work; secondly the authors describe their insights gained from the observation and research in context of adaptations or implementation of disruptive technologies and business models in highly standardized MNEs. Beforehand the conclusions, the authors derive the identified need for doing further activities by drafting the research hypothesis and the intended line of research. This report is in context of empirical work of the authors in the automotive industry, especially in the after sales business.

2. RESEARCH METHODOLOGY

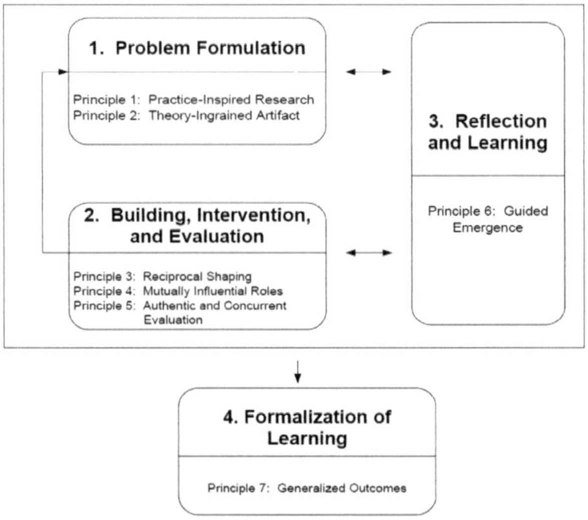

Figure 1. Action Design Research cycle (Sein et al., 2011)

ADR is a rather young research method derived from a combination of design research and action design. It was originally proposed by Sein et. al. (2011) to include organizational relevance to the creation of new artifacts. Their method brings the academic research and the operations and insights of an organization together by introducing a continuous cycle of evaluation between the parties. In other words, they show a need for tight collaboration between the researchers and end-users. The ADR consists of four stages (see Figure 1). This paper only enters the stage one.

The initial trigger for the first stage of the ADR research cycle is either the observation of problems in the operations of organizations, or an anticipation of such obstacles by the researchers. These triggers provide the impetus to formulate research efforts that shall tackle the initial problem by combining practice and theory. The ADR has a wide variety of possible shareholders, who give valuable inputs to the problem formulation. This mix includes practitioners, end-users, researchers, existing technologies, and/ or prior researches. These inputs are often combined with first empirical enquiries of the problem. High value is given to the *practice inspired insights* which are formulated from the collaboration between the organization (practitioners and end users) and the researchers. Moreover, the first stage supports in defining the scope of research, the roles and influence of the participation of practitioners, and finally in the formulation of the research questions.

Morandi et al. (2013) state that there should be a clearly defined action between the organization studied and researches in order to be classified as an action research. The researches have taken critical part as an embedded observer. That is, the researchers are officially a part of the system as practitioners with the possibility to step outside the system to see the organism. Where the role of a practitioners is shared with the studied organization, which is also seen as the end-user.

3. DIGITALIZATION AND ITS HAZARDS FOR ORGANIZATIONS

While piloting alternative production technologies, additive manufacturing (AM) and additive tooling (AT) in the after sales department of a prominent automotive enterprise, various obstacles were identified. These obstacles may prevent the successful application of new technologies, and processes linked to them, in typical standardized MNEs. Moreover, the new production technologies may require unordinary activities from all the involved process partners. Companies facing struggles in adapting processes to changes from digitalization often show highly complex structures and turbulent process dynamics. This situation has been explained as the area between the second and third zone of *dynaxity* introduced by Henning and later adapted by Titlman et. al. (2006). Henning's explained how organizations acting in such environments behave in *techno bureaucratic management* style. It is questionable if the linear progression in the model of Henning's applies as such to MNEs. That is, it is uncertain if more chaotic dynamics directly increase the complexity of a firm. Furthermore, *process innovation,* defined by Davenport (1993) as a continuum to process improvement, explains the need for a deeper dive to organizational functions to achieve process time and quality improvements, and process cost reductions. Nevertheless, these approaches are means-to-an-end solutions, and thus are not directly applicable to highly standardized organizations with thought-to-be mature process structures. Our observations show that techno bureaucratic management and process innovation alone are not capable of addressing these obstacles, and there is a clear need for further research. Next the paper will show some arguments to express this demand.

3.1 Lack of Process Orientation

The current field of research does not pioneer solutions for adapting current process landscapes to emerging and disruptive technologies, such as AM and AT. The implementation of new IT solutions and processes has been widely researched (Davenport, 1990 & 1993; Hammer & Champy, 1993; Boehm & Turner, 2005). Nevertheless, the researches can be considered the following steps and answers for supporting the new production ways – not implementing them. From the authors point of view, the infrastructural artefacts do not solve the organizational problems. This leads to further increasing complexity when amending concepts such as AM. Moreover, the existing processes are not capable of addressing the required process and product qualities of alternatively produced products. Especially with the current product liability scandals in the automotive industry, there is no room for uncertainty.

While analyzing the as-is situation in the field of observation, it was found out that the existing process orientation is not as expected. In other words, there is no common understanding of process architecture, and no clear responsibilities and roles. This creates problems in accessing the current business process models. Also the understanding of such models varies between departments and roles. Therefore, the dynaxity comes from the digitalization, and cannot be handled by the organization in an efficient way. This leads to more chaotic process dynamics. The assumed effects coming from new technologies are not achievable, and the high level of standardization increases the blockades to adapt. The need for alignment throughout the organization limits the flexibility of adapting to fast moving technological changes. This is a deadlock-dilemma such highly standardized MNEs will more often be faced with in the future.

3.2 The Dilemma and the Role of Existing Operational Management Approaches

In the field of observations, the authors have seen that these approaches are not comprehensive enough to handle this dilemma. Normally MNEs have, in the focus of the authors, already implemented approaches like organizational development, business process management, operational excellence, change management, project management, or quality management. Nevertheless, the question here is why these approaches fail to tackle the described dilemma?

In addition to the researches by Henning, Tiltman, Davenport and other experts of the field, during researching the Business Process Management (BPM) last-mile problem phenomenon in the past five years (Kurz et. al., 2012), it was found out that some general reasons may lay in the wrong understanding and use BPM methods. The ineffective management of the cultural change, and the insufficient use of Information Technology were identified as potential failing points in process improvements during its adaptation phase. With the identified dilemma, that organizations needs to adapt trends coming from digitalization and its technologies, from the authors point of view the probability of insufficient implementation of failure increases without an integrative approach of process-oriented operational management.

4. RESEARCH IMPLICATIONS

To reflect the identified hazard in the implementation of the disruptive technology 3D printing in the highly standardized MNE, from the authors point of view following questions for the future research activities can be formulated:

1. How is the adaptation of digitalization trends handled in the different scientific disciplines?
2. What are the in literature suggested methods to avoid the observed dilemma and efficiencies which can be applied in a general manner?
3. Do these identified theories direct the comprehensiveness the organizations needs?
4. If needed what can be an improved approach (framework or artifact) and does it really help these MNEs (in sense of testing)?

Addressing these questions, the authors will follow the ADR cycle for the ongoing research activities. In a next step additional cases will be reflected to get more insights, from the empirical point of view, for the identified dilemma (ADR principle 1). Parallel to this a broad and multi-disciplinary literature review shall help to identify methods and approaches that do exist in different scientific disciplines to handle these phenomena (ADR principle 2). This will lead directly to the second step in the overall research progress – deriving an artifact that might be used for intervention and evaluation in similar situations.

5. CONCLUSION

From a scientific point of view this work might be seen as the beginning for a set of research activities. Therefore, it is addressed to the authors to check their research hypothesis by running through the ADR research process. This paper shows of course limitations in validity of the observed and described situation (dilemma) for the adaptation of digitalization trends in MNEs, but it should be the beginning of rigorous research.

REFERENCES

Boehm, B. & Turner, R. (2005). Management challenges to implementing agile processes in traditional development organizations. in Software, IEEE , vol.22, no.5, pp.30-39. doi: 10.1109/MS.2005.129

Davenport, T.H. and Short, J.E. (1990), "The new industrial engineering: information technology and business process redesign", Sloan Management Review, Summer, pp. 11- 27.

Davenport, T. (1993). Process Innovation: Reengineering Work Through Information Technology.

Gartner (2014). The Five SMART Technologies to Watch. Retrieved on 10.01.2016 from: https://www.gartner.com/doc/2669320?refval=&pcp=mpe

Hammer, M. and Champy, J. (1993), Reengineering the Corporation: A Manifesto for Business Revolution, McGraw-Hill, New York, NY

Kurz, M., Huber, S. & Hilgarth, B. (2012). ProcessWiki: A Contribution for Bridging the Last Mile Problem in Automotive Retail. S-BPM ONE - Education and Industrial Developments Volume 284 of the series Communications in Computer and Information Science pp 151-167

Mendis D., Secchi, D. & Reeves, P. (2015). A Legal and Empirical Study into the Intellectual Property Implications of 3D Printing. Centre for Intellectual Property Policy & Management.

Sein, Henfridsson, Purao, Rossi, & Lindgren (2011). Action Design Research. MIS Quaterly, Vol. 35, 1, 37-56 (2011)

Tiltmann T., Rick, U. & Henning, K. (2006). Concurrent Engineering and the Dynaxity Approach. How to Benefit from Multidisciplinarity. *Leading the web in concurrent engineering: next generation concurrent engineering: 13th ISPE International Conference on Concurrent Engineering Location: Antibes, France, Sep 18-21, 2006*. pp.: 488-49

Morandi, M. I. W. M. et al. (2013). Foreseeing ironore prices using system thinking and scenario planning. Systemic Practice and Action Research, n. Janeiro, 1-20.

STRATEGIC ALIGNMENT WITH A BALANCED SCORECARD APPROACH

Jorge Gomes and Mário Romão
ISEG, Rua Miguel Lupi, 20, 1200-781 Lisboa, Portugal

ABSTRACT

Strategic alignment is a topic which has received considerable attention over the last decades. There are many reasons why organisations have performed strategic alignment, but perhaps the most critical one is that it can help them improve performance and competitive advantage in the organisations when properly applied. Managers should be capable of interpreting the external business environment in order to capitalise the opportunities, and deal with threats. The Balanced Scorecard approach (BSC) recognises the rise of intangible assets in value creation strategies and the limitations of traditional financial measurements for this type of assets. Balanced Scorecard translates an organisation's mission and strategy into a comprehensive set of performance measures by providing a framework for the strategic alignment between an organisation's strategy and its business units. BSC uses a balanced mix of financial and non-financial measures to evaluate performance through four perspectives, based on a cause-and-effect logic. This paper highlights the importance of adopting this type of frameworks in line with the organisation's strategic alignment and its focus on implementing its mission and strategic objectives at all organisation levels.

KEYWORDS

Balanced Scorecard, IS/IT Strategic Alignment, Performance Measurements, IS/IT Investments, Project Management

1. INTRODUCTION

Recently, the focus of the IS/IT literature has shifted from the importance of IS/IT and its potential to change a whole range of strategic and industry structure variables (Clemons, 1986) to the relationship between IS/IT and specific components of firm strategy, such as, business environment (Maier, Rainer and Snyder, 1997), competitive advantage (Mata, Fuerst and Barney, 1995), organizational performance (Bharadwaj, 2000), and knowledge accumulation (Grant, 1996). Systems and Information Technology (IS/IT) has become an extremely important tool for the sustainability and business growth of organisations. According to Henderson and Venkatraman (1993), the inability to realise value from IS/IT investments is due to the lack of alignment between the business and the IS/IT strategies of the organisation. For more than two decades, the need for alignment of IS/IT with business strategy has called the attention of researchers and practitioners alike. It seems clear that, even though IS/IT has evolved from its traditional role of administrative support toward a more strategic role, there is still a lack of a proper framework for exploring and understanding its potential for organisations (Henderson and Venkatraman, 1993) and for shaping new business strategies (Konsynski and McFarlan, 1990). From the IS/IT perspective, the lack of alignment with business strategy typically leads to a reactive stance regarding IS/IT, where IS/IT is seen as a cost, rather than a strategic business partner. From a business perspective, the lack of alignment with business strategy results in a decrease in return from investments in IS/IT, and consequently in reduced competitive capabilities (Tallon, Kraemer and Gurbaxani, 2000). A direct advantage of strategic alignment is a perception of higher business value of IS/IT (Tallon et al., 2000). Many studies highlight the difficulty of identifying business-value related to IS/IT investments. Methods and frameworks were tested to try and collect benefits that cannot be exclusively justified by financial measures, neither in the form of intangible benefits, such as customer satisfaction, or employee training. The Balanced Scorecard (Kaplan and Norton, 1992), is one of the most widely-used management tools today, aiming to overcome the inadequacy of traditional management systems and their dependency on financial measures which reports lag indicators that reflect actions from the past. Balanced Scorecard is a powerful tool, which combines financial and non-financial measures in a single report that aims to provide managers with the relevant information needed to manage their activities (Olve et al., 1999). Addressing some of the weaknesses and vagueness of previous management approaches, and attempting to provide a clear prescription as to what organisations should measure, the main objective of BSC is to provide management with precise information about critical success factors that will provide a better understanding of the business, and a more efficient and faster decision-making process (Mooraj, Oyon and Hostettler, 1999). BSC is a strategic planning and management system that is used extensively in business and industry, government, and non-profit organizations worldwide to align business activities to the vision and strategy of the organizations (Gomes and Romão, 2015).

2. IS/IT STRATEGIC ALIGNMENT

The sole purpose of undertaking any business activity is to create value. Should an activity destroy value, then this activity should not be started. There is no commonly agreed definition concerning IS/IT business value (Grembergen, 2001). Cronk and Fitzgerald (1999) define IS/IT business value as being the sustainable value added to a business by IS/IT investments, and Banker and Kauffman (1991) state that it is the IS/IT contribution towards the management goal of profit maximisation that is paramount. With the rapid progress of development and the presence of new advanced technologies, the application of IS/IT in today's business environment has opened opportunities by strategically using technology for the benefit of organisations and businesses (Galliers and Leidner, 2003). The effective and efficient use of IS/IT requires the alignment of IS/IT strategies with business strategies in order to enhance overall competitiveness and productivity by improving the core business processes, and by exploiting the opportunities provided by technology to redesign business processes (Luftman, 2000). What is an IS/IT strategy? An IS/IT strategy is the one that contributes to the creation of business value. IS/IT managers need to understand the external environment, and the affect that this has on the organisation. Business strategy should be shaped and aligned with external information, whilst being driven by information from IS/IT (Ward and Peppard, 2000). Over the last two decades, several authors have carried out an extensive research on strategic alignment, and they highlight some of the important aspects of this concept (e. g. Henderson and Venkatraman, 1993; Lederer and Salmela, 1996; Reich and Benbasat, 2000). Applying IS/IT in an appropriate and timely way, in harmony with business strategies, goals and needs, not only helps firms realise the potential benefits from investments in IS/IT (Tallon et al, 2000), but also enhances business performance by aligning both organisational and technological infrastructures (Croteau et al 2001). For organisations to stay competitive in a dynamic business environment, they have to understand how to manage IS/IT strategically. The strategic use of IS/IT for effective organisational performance provides an important contribution to the creation of business value (Henderson and Venkatraman, 1993). A high priority business issue concerns the alignment between business strategy and strategic choices of IS/IT deployment (Silvius, 2007; Ward and Peppard, 2002). Over the last years, IS/IT alignment has consistently appeared as a top concern for researchers, practitioners and company executives alike (Luftman et al., 2005). The business and IS/IT performance implications of alignment have been demonstrated empirically and through several studies (Chan et al., 1997; Irani, 2002; Kearns and Lederer, 2003). Alignment leads to a more focussed and strategic use of IS/IT, which, in turn, leads to improved performance (Chan et al., 2006). Henderson and Venkatraman (1993) claimed that the inability to realise value from IS /IT investment is in part due to a lack of alignment between the business and IS/IT strategies of organisations. Lederer and Salmela (1996) note that alignment between IS/IT strategies and business occurs when implemented projects fulfil business needs. The strategic alignment of a business with IS/IT is considered to be a very important issue, mainly when IS/IT becomes an essential part of the business and is used as a leverage for special business trends (Silvius, 2007; Peppard and Ward, 2004). Alignment of organizational and technological infrastructures has also been found to enhance business performance (Croteau, Solomon, Raymond, & Bergeron, 2001). According to Ward and Peppard (2002), the consequences of not having a IS/IT strategy that is aligned with business include the following issues: 1) IS/IT investments that do not support business objectives; 2) no integration, resulting in a duplication of effort; 3) poor information management; 4) a misunderstanding of the purpose of investments; 5) the redesign and redevelopment of systems, and; 6) potential business advantages from IS/IT are not realised. Kaplan and Norton (2001) note that BSC facilitates the communication of strategy throughout the organisation, enabling the alignment of personal and departmental goals. As part of this strategic process, long term strategic initiatives will be identified, which are aligned through a reduced emphasis on short term financial measures, and a greater focus on drivers of long term success (Kaplan and Norton, 2001). Aligning the organisation to the strategy involves evaluating current organisational structures, as well as reporting lines and policies and procedures, in order to ensure that they are consistent with the strategy. This can include the re-alignment of business units, or the re-definition of the roles of different support units, in order to ensure that each part of the organisation is positioned to best support the strategy (Kaplan and Norton, 2001). The authors explain that organisational alignment is an explicit part of the management process. They write that the execution of strategy requires the highest level of integration and teamwork among organisational units and processes. The authors also emphasized that management systems must have a clearly defined strategy as their core, and that all parts of the management process can be designed to create alignment. Strategic alignment has the following crucial components (Kaplan and Norton, 2001): 1) Strategic fit - the internal consistency of the activities that implement the unique parts of the strategy; 2) Organisation alignment - how the various parts of a company synchronise their activities to create vital integration and synergy; 3) Human capital alignment - which is achieved when employees' goals and incentives are aligned with the strategy; 4) Alignment of planning and control systems - which happens when management systems for planning, operations and control are linked to the strategy. All of these components show how success depends on the successful alignment of the strategy, the organisation, the employees and their management systems.

3. THE BALANCED SCORECARD

Research studies found that 98% of private sector clients were unable to implement their own strategic objectives in daily operations (Niven, 2003). Accordingly, there is a need to find a tool that has the ability to measure the impacts, influence and the leverage of organisational activities and other long-term goals in general. Luftamn and Brier (1999) note that companies that have achieved strategic alignment with ISI/IT was able to build a strategic competitive advantage that will provide them with greater visibility, efficiency and profitability in the changing markets. BSC is a framework that combines financial and non-financial measures of performance with the objective of aligning strategy with business, motivating better communication and consequently leading to improved performance (Rompho, 2011). The BSC approach balances measures of the customer, internal process and learning and growth against traditional financial measures. BSC translates vision and strategy, and defines the linkages to integrating performance across an organisation, communicates objectives and measures to the business units, provides feedback to management about the strategy implantation and finally, and aligns all the strategic initiatives with business challenges (Kaplan and Norton, 1992). Mapping a strategy is an important way of evaluating and making an organisation's perspectives, objectives and measures visually explicit, and also the causal linkages between them. Process mapping represented by strategy maps (Kaplan and Norton, 2000) makes this alignment more explicit, as well as the relationship between a performance scorecard and the organisation's strategy. Strategy maps facilitate the communication of strategy throughout the organisation, enabling the alignment the goals of people and business units. In order to develop a strategy map, managers need to select a few strategic objectives within each of the perspectives, and then have to define the cause-effect chain among these objectives, by drawing links between them. A BSC of strategic performance measures is then derived directly from the strategic objectives. As an important part of this strategic process, long-term strategic initiatives are then identified and aligned, which reduces the attention on short-term financial measures, and increases the focus on drivers of long term success (Kaplan and Norton, 2001). To create an organisational alignment, a BSC needs to be designed for all levels of the organisation, as a means of ensuring that all the employees are pursuing goals that are consistent with, and lead to, the achievement of the organisation's strategy (Kaplan and Norton, 2006). Despite the advantages and disadvantages of BSC, it is important to recognise that this tool is truly beneficial for the alignment of organisational strategy with business, and it represents a powerful strategic tool for internal communication when it is fully integrated and adopted by an organisation. Although the considerable impact on worldwide organizations, has also attracted some sort of criticism (Frigo, 2002). This criticism mostly comes from the academic community, who dislike the empirical nature of the framework. The technical flaws in the methods and the BSC original seems to be the main sources of disagreement (e.g. Atkinson et al., 1997; Maltz et al., 2003; Reilly and Reilly, 2000; Kennerley and Neely, 2003; Norreklit, 2000, 2003).

4. CONCLUSIONS

We can say that there is alignment between IS/IT and business when: 1) IS/IT capabilities support the business capabilities and have the flexibility to accommodate business strategy changes; 2) IS/IT investments are justified by business, on the basis of the benefits from the transformations that they bring about; 3) Topics such as principles, policies, standards or architectures of IS/IT are driven by business strategies.

A tomorrow firm's success depends on its current ability to deal with intangible assets, such as customer relationships, internal business processes and employee learning. Measuring organisational success and implementing effective strategies for sustainable performance and future success, represent a continuous challenges for managers, researchers and practitioners.

Although a growing number of firms have been using non-financial performance measures in areas such as customer loyalty and employee satisfaction, few of them have realised the potential benefits of these relatively new measurement systems. Although it is subject to some criticism, mainly from academic sectors, BSC nevertheless emerges as a worldwide referential for measuring organisational performance, for helping organisations implement their vision and mission and communicate the strategic objectives to all organisational levels focussed on the alignment of all investment initiatives with the organisation's strategy, particularly in IS/IT investments.

REFERENCES

Atkinson, A. A., Waterhouse, J. H. and Wells, R. B., 1997. A Stakeholder Approach to Strategic Performance Measurement. *Sloan Management Review*, Vol. 38, pp. 25-37.

Bharadwaj, A. S., 2000. A Resource-Based Perspective on Information Technology Capability and Firm Performance: Am Empirical Investigation. *MIS Quarterly,* Vol. 24, No. 1, pp. 169-196.

Banker , R. and Kauffman, R., 1991. *Quantifying the Business Value of IT: An illustration of the Business Value Linkage Framework.* Sterm School of Business, NewYork, Working paper nº IS-91-21.

Chan, Y. E., Huff, S. L., Barclay, D.W. and Copeland, D.G., 1997. Business Strategic Orientation, Information Systems Strategic Orientation, and Strategic Alignment. *Information Systems Research,* Vol. 8, Nº. 2, pp. 125-150.

Clemons, E. K., 1986. Information systems for sustainable competitive advantage. *Information & Management.* Vol. 11, No. 3, pp. 131-136.

Cronk, M. C. and Fitzgerald, E. P., 1999. Understanding "IS business value": derivation of dimension. *Logistics Information Management,* Vol. 12, No. 1-2, pp. 40-49.

Croteau, A. M., Bergeron, F. and Raymond, L., 2001. Business Strategy and Technological Deployment: Fit and Performance. *Information System and Management,* Vol. 6, No. 4.

Croteau, A. M., Solomon, S., Raymond, L. and Bergeron, F. 2001. *Organizational and technological infrastructures alignment.* In Proceedings of the 34th Hawaii International Conference on System Sciences, Maui, HI, USA.

Frigo, M., 2002. Strategy and the Balance Scorecard. *Strategic Finance,* Vol. 84, No. 5, pp. 6-9.

Galliers, B. and Leidner, D., 2003. *Strategic Information Management*, 3ª edition. Oxford: Butterworth Heisemann.

Gomes, J. and Romão, M., 2015. Achieving project success through alignment with organizational strategy: Balanced Scorecard approach. *In Proceedings of 8th IADIS International Conference - Information's Systems 2015*, Funchal, Portugal.

Grant, R. M., 1996. Toward a knowledge-based theory of the firm. *Strategic Management Journal*, Summer Special Issue Vol. 17, pp. 109–122.

Grembergen, W. V., 2001. *Information Technology Evaluation Methods & Management*. London: Idea Group Publishing.

Henderson, J. C. and Venkatraman, N., 1993. Strategic Alignment: Leveraging Information Technology for Transforming Organisations. *IBM Systems Journal*, Vol. 32, No. 1, pp. 4-16.

Irani, Z., 2002. Information Systems Evaluation: Navigating through the problem domain. *Information Management,* Vol. 40, No. 1, pp. 11-24.

Kaplan, R. S. and Norton, D. P., 1992. Using the Balanced Scorecard as a Strategic Management System. *Harvard Buisness Review,* Vol. 74, No. 1, pp. 75-85.

Kaplan, R. S. and Norton, D. P., 1993. Putting the Balanced Scorecard to Work. *Harvard Business Review*, September-October.

Kaplan, R. S. and Norton, D. P., 2000. *The Strategy-Focused Organisation.* Cambridge, MA: Harvard Business School Press.

Kaplan, R. S. and Norton, D. P., 2001. *The Strategy Focused Organisations: How Balanced Scorecard Companies Thrive in the New Business Environment.* Boston: Harvard University Press.

Kearns, G. S. and Lederer, A. L., 2003. A Resource-Based View of Strategic IT Alignment: How knowledge sharing creates competitive advantage. *Decision Sciences,* Vol. 34, No. 1, pp. 1-29.

Konsynski, B. R. and McFarlan, W. F., 1990. Information Partnerships: Shared Data, Shared Scale. *Harvard Business Review,* Vol. 68, No. 5, pp. 114-120.

Lederer, A. and Salmela, H., 1996. Towrds a theory of strategic information systems planning. *Journal of Strategic Information Systems,* Vol. 4, No. 14, pp. 1-50.

Luftman, J. N., 2000. Assessing business IT-alignment maturity. *Communications for the Association for Information Systems,* Vol. 4, No. 14.

Luftman, J. and Brier, T., 1999. Achieving and Sustaining Business–IT Alignment, California Management Review, Vol. 42, No. 1, pp. 109-122.

Luftman, J., Kempaiah, R. and Nash, E., 2005. Key Issues for IT Executives 2005. *MIS Quarterly Executive*, Vol. 5, No. 2, pp. 81-101.

Maier, J. L., Rainer, R. K., and Snyder, C. A., 1997. Environmental scanning for information technology: an empirical investigation. *Journal of Management Information Systems*, Vol. 14, No. 2, pp. 177-201.

Maltz, A. C., Shenhar, A. J. and Reilley, R. R., 2003. Beyond the balanced Scorecard: Refining the search for organisational success measures. *Long Range Planning*, Vol. 36, pp. 187-204.

Mata, F. J., Fuerst, W, L., Barney, J. B., 1985. Information technology and sustained competitive advantage: a resource-based-analysis. *MIS Quartely,* December, pp, 487-504.

Mooraj, S., Oyon, D. and Hostettler, D., 1999. The Balanced Scorecard: a necessary good or an unnecessary evil. *European Management Journal*, Vol. 17, No. 5, pp. 481-491.

Neely, A. and Kennerley, M., 2003. Measuring Performance in a Changing Business Environment. *International Journal of Operations & Production Management*, Vol. 23, No. 2, pp. 213-229.

Niven, P., 2003. *Balanced Scorecard: Step-by-Step for Government and Nonprofit Agencies*. Hoboken, New Jersey: John Wiley & Sons, Inc.

Norreklit, H., 2003. The Balanced Scorecard: What is the score? A rhetorical analysis. *Accounting, Organisations and Society*, Vol. 28, pp.591-619.

Norreklit, H., 2000. The Balanced Scorecard: a critical analysis of some assumptions. *Management Accounting Research*, Vol. 11, pp. 65-88.

Olve, N. G., Roy, J. and Wetter, M., 1999. *Performance Drivers.* Chichester: John Wiley & Sons.

Peppard, J. and Ward, J., 2004. Beyond strategic information systems: Towards an IS capability. *Journal of Strategic Information Systems,* pp. 167-194.

Reich, B. H. and Benbasat, I., 2000. Factors that Influence the Social Dimensions of Alignment between Business and Information Technology Objectives. *Management Information Systems Quarterly*, Vol. 24, No. 1, pp. 81-113.

Reilley, G. and Reilley, R., 2000. Using a measure network to understand and delivery value. *Journal of Cost Management,* pp. 5-14.

Rompho, N., 2011. Why the Balanced Scorecard Fails in SMEs: A Case Study. *International Journal of Business and Management*, Vol. 6, No. 11, pp. 39-46.

Silvius, G. A. J., 2007. Business and IT alignment in theory and practice. *In Proceedings of the HICSS '07, 40th Annual Hawaii International Conference on System Sciences.*

Tallon, P. P., Kraemer, K.L. and Gurbaxani, V., 2000. Executives perceptions of the Business Value of Information Technology: A process-Oriented Approach. *Journal of Management Information Systems*, Vol. 16, No. 4, pp. 145-173.

Ward, J. and Peppard, J. (2002). *Strategic Planning for Information Systems 3th edition*, New York: John Wiley & Sons.

CURRENT STATUS AND PROSPECTS FOR E-LEARNING MANAGEMENT IN THE PROMOTION OF DISTANCE EDUCATION IN SAUDI ARABIA

Norah Sultan Aifa Alshahrani and Abdul Khader Jilani Saudagar
Information Systems Department, College of Computer and Information Sciences
Al Imam Mohammad Ibn Saud Islamic University (IMSIU)
Riyadh, Saudi Arabia

ABSTRACT

The rapid growing trends in web-based education motivate e-learning development methods to a huge extent. Thus, it can be sense that the dynamic nature of online systems, the development of technologies, and networks channels make the e-learning process more sophisticated and complex. E-learning developers face many challenges and obstacles to deliver these services efficiently. This research work seeks to shed light on e-learning management systems and some of its challenges by concentrating on the success factors found specifically in the context of improving e-learning management systems. This research work also presents the key findings, success factors in the field of e-learning management from literature and the e-learning management systems of some reputed neighboring Arab Universities. The future work of this research proposes factors that can be used to overcome problems and deficiencies that arise in the e-learning management environment of Saudi Arabia universities.

KEYWORDS

E-learning, challenges, services, management.

1. INTRODUCTION

In recent years, the e-learning environment has rapidly developed and it has become a very important educational alternative to traditional teaching methods. Therefore, this research will focus on studying the current status of e-learning management in distance education of Saudi Arabia. There are some problems existing in the e-learning management systems of Saudi Arabia and other countries which are not technologically equipped. Also there are many significant factors influencing e-learning management system of distance education that must need to be identified. These factors will help to propose e-learning management model with solutions to overcome the weaknesses of e-learning management system and improve the level of students' satisfaction with the current e-learning management systems of universities offering distance education in Saudi Arabia.

Currently there are three electronic education modes for teaching viz e-learning, online learning and distance learning. To start with the distance education, this is known as an "umbrella" mode for all these types of education (Keegan, 1996). The main difference between distance learning and campus-based is about delivering the learning material using computer base to different geographical place and with different time zone (Moore, et al., 2011). Many of top universities over the world offer full or partial online programs including Bachler Master's and Ph.D. such as Harvard University by uses edX learning platform. In addition University of Leicester one of the most suppliers for distance learning in UK and University of Nebraska at Kearney at US that offering a lot of distance learning programs like Bachelors, master, some programs for blended student. Central Queensland University in Australia uses CQUniversity's Distance Education Study Centres to facilitate the learning process. Albidewi and Tulb (2014) in California State University used Moodle learning management system and Blackboard learning management system. They conclude that the Moodle system is the more efficacious and effective than the Blackboard system. Also it implements virtual courses and find improvement on their students' scores and there is more interaction between students. In the Middle East there are some fully electronic universities like Egyptian E-Learning University that combines between the advantages of both the traditional education and the e-learning education in a distinguished blended model. Also Hamdan bin Mohammed smart university that have virtual learning environment that use Horizon Wimba as virtual class room.

There are some institutional factors that affect the student's success in distance learning which are categorized into two types academic and social interaction factors (Ibrahim et al. 2007). Also Aljabre (2012) mentioned the cultural background and faculty members training has a major effect on the student's acceptance and ability to participate in Saudi Arabia distance learning. In other study (Aydogdu and Tanrikulu 2013) classify the success factors of the e-learning system into five dimensions based on instructors teaching methods and guidance, students IT skills and demographics, courses and its content, technology design and quality. Asiri, et al., (2012) research using Learning Management Systems (LMS) on Saudi universities results in two types of factors, internal factors and external factors. The internal factors are the faculty member's attitude about suggested LMS must be positive and comfortable with it. The external factors are external barriers like organizational acceptance of suggested LMS and the demographic factors like gender, computer experience and training. Al-Busaidi and Al-Shihi (2010) concentrated in their study on the instructors' factors such as user self-efficacy which is about the instructor's capabilities to use the LMS to get required performance followed by instructor's attitude toward e-learning, instructor's experience, skills and abilities to use technologies. Apart from these instructor's teaching style and personal innovativeness like the instructor's acceptance of any adoption of new technologies. Claar, et al., (2014) in his work expresses students concern towards systems, flexibility and responsiveness. Huandong, et al., (2009) have suggested some principles to design the e-learning system which are systematises, openness level, practicability, efficiency, safety and expansion. Finally, Miller and Schiffman (2006) said the e-learning systems enhanced usually for two main reasons the student access and the learning quality. The work presented by Tu and Yuan (2014) was theoretical study by applying critical success factors approach. They grouped these factors into six key factors which are business alignment, organizational support, organizational awareness, IT competence, security control development, and performance evaluation.

The current status of the e-learning in Saudi Arabia is still in its infancy as suggested by Al-Harbi (2011). From Saudi student acceptance perceptive Al-Harbi concluded that the students like to know about the e-learning before, who have self-efficacy, confidence of using the internet and university support to the e-learning are more embraced to be an e-learning student. Ali, et al., (2003) survey result with almost 35% of the Saudi students prefer taking the course in a class and around 29% of them prefer taking the course at home and the rest 36% are uncertain.

The advantages of e-learning are numerous, but the ability to share learning material anytime and anywhere is perhaps the most obvious one. E-learning allows anyone to be a learner anywhere, thus reducing the costs associated with education. Therefore, e-learning is increasingly seen as an approach to facilitate and enhance learning by the use of computerized devices and communication technologies (Baby and Kannammal, 2014).

Despite of many positive functions and advantages of using e-learning when compared to more traditional modes of learning, e-learning also raises significant challenges in many areas. One major obstacle that is often discussed is the technological challenges associated with e-learning. To be in a successful e-learning environment, rapid technology developments must be kept on track (Defta, et al., 2013). There are different ways to cope with these changes, including introducing new techniques to understand and support learning communities, and developing e-learning systems to support mobile communities of learners. Also, introducing different forms of e-learning to enhance the interaction between students and teachers is also another method to support information sharing across different learning channels to facilitate the e-learning process (Rana and Lal, 2014). The challenges of applying the distance education in Saudi Arabia by Abdel and Al-Masaud (2014) are poor culture of using PCs, the computer networks are not well structured, no sufficient preparation for universities' labs, poor English and not enough training on the e-learning program. Furthermore, information security threats are some of the more unpleasant consequences of using the internet in an e-learning environment. E-learning developers must maintain a secure e-learning environment by applying the following information security measures: identification and authentication, confidentiality, authorization, non-repudiation, availability, and integrity (Mihai, 2012).

The main purpose of this study is to collect factors that effect on the e-learning organizations success. After that it explore and discover the current status of an e-learning in reputed neighboring Arab Universities. It aims to find the proper e-learning management system that contains solutions to overcome the current problems and deficiencies.

The results of this research are useful for the universities offering distance education to enhance their e-learning management system. Its helps to get an appropriate LMS with success factors like flexibility, integration, ease of use, accessibility, interactivity, high availability, usability, scalability, interoperability, stability and security.

2. RESEARCH DESIGN

After studying the current status of LMS in Saudi Arabia and neighboring universities, the research work continue through two phases sequentially that are Quantitative and Qualitative as described below:

2.1 Phase One: Quantitative

Online questionnaire is distributed to the e-learning participants viz students, instructors. The results are treated and interpreted using statistical application like SPSS, by using the frequency (counts) determine the number of 'yes' answers for each factor to be selected by respondents and percentage from the whole sample. It helps to determine the critical success factors that actually affect the level of students' satisfaction about current LMS based on information systems success model of Delone and McLean (2003).

2.2 Phase Two: Qualitative

Upon completion of phase one, interviews are conducted with students, instructors, e-learning experts and developers by visiting the universities offering the distance education to know their problems about current LMS. The interviews are aimed to explore the needs of the stakeholders, enhancements, improvements to the existing LMS. The interviews are analyzed and synthesized using popular qualitative techniques, along with content analysis these steps help to know the deficiencies and find the best solutions to overcome these deficiencies in the e-learning management system.

2.3 Proposed Framework

This research works to enhance available LMS by designing a framework as shown in Figure 1 that evaluate the current LMS based on success factors system quality, service quality, information quality and user (student and instructors). The proposed factor dimensions obtained from the quantitative and qualitative research are as shown in Table 1.

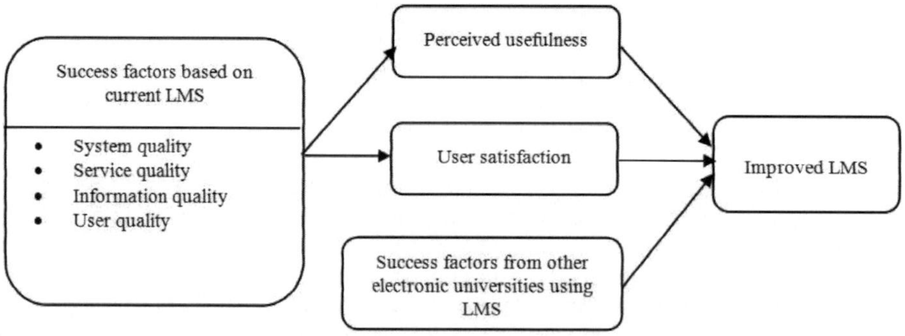

Figure 1. Proposed framework of improved LMS

Table 1. Proposed factor dimensions to evaluate the LMS

Quality dimensions	Factor dimensions
System quality	1. Comfortability 2. Ease of use 3. Availability 4. Responsiveness 5. Well designed 6. Adaptable 7. Reliable
Service quality	1. Well supported 2. Responsiveness 3. Effectiveness 4. Availability
Information quality	1. Easy to understand 2. Time less 3. Well formatted 4. Secure communication 5. Availability
User Quality (Student and Instructors)	1. Interaction 2. Learning style 3. Assessment ability 4. Control level
Perceived usefulness	1. Improves students learning performance 2. Improves instructors job performance
User satisfaction	1. Satisfaction level 2. Effectiveness 3. Adequacy 4. Usefulness

3. CONCLUSION

The dynamic nature of online systems, the development of technologies, and networks channels make the e-learning process more sophisticated and complex. This encourages the researcher to conduct this study about the e-learning environment to improve the LMS for distance education. Additionally, the e-learning management processes faces lot of challenges to be effective and efficient learning environment. This research collects information from the literature review to help on finding the e-learning management success factors, problems and deficiencies and its solution. It explores how these factors successfully managed and implemented as an improved e-learning management system. Additionally, how this management system will overcome the founded problems and deficiencies. Finally, it results in a new proposed framework for the e-learning management system in Saudi Arabia universities.

REFERENCES

Abdel, G. A. and Al-Masaud, K., 2014. Impediments of Activating E-Learning in Higher Education Institutions in Saudi Arabia. *International Journal of Advanced Computer Science and Applications*, Vol. 5, No. 4, pp 12-18.

Albidewi, I. and Tulb, R., 2014. Promise and Challenge of E-Learning Literature Review. *European Scientific Journal*, Vol. 10, No. 1, pp 210-217.

Ali, S. H. et al, 2003. Perceptions about e-Learning in Saudi Arabia. *Proceedings of World Conference on Science & Technology Education*, Penang, Malaysia, pp. 393-399.

Aljabre, A., 2012. An Exploration of Distance Learning in Saudi Arabian Universities: Current Practices and Future Possibilities. *International Journal of Business, Humanities and Technology*, Vol. 2, No. 2, pp 132-137.

Al-Busaidi, K. and Al-Shihi, H., 2010. Instructors' Acceptance of Learning Management Systems: A Theoretical Framework. *Communications of the IBIMA*, Vol. 2010, pp 1-10.

Al-Harbi, K. A. S., 2011. E-Learning in the Saudi Tertiary Education: Potential and Challenges. *Applied Computing and Informatics,* Vol. 9, No. 1, pp 31-46.

Asiri, M. J. S. et al, 2012. Factors influencing the use of Learning Management System in Saudi Arabian Higher Education: A Theoretical Framework. *Higher Education Studies*, Vol. 2, No. 2, pp 125-137.

Aydogdu, Y. and Tanrikulu, Z., 2013. E-learning Success Model Development. *Education and Science*, Vol. 38, No. 170.

Baby, A. and Kannammal, A., 2014. Information Security Modelling in an E-learning Environment. *International Journal of Computer Science Issues,* Vol. 11, No. 1, pp. 195-200.

Claar, C. et al, 2014. Student Acceptence of Learning Management Systems: A Study on Demographics. *Issues in Information Systems*, Vol. 15, No. 1, pp 409-417.

Defta, C. et al, 2014. Threats Analysis for E-learning Platforms. *Knowledge Horizons Economics,* Vol. 6, No. 1, pp. 132-135.

Delone, W. and Mclean, E., 2003. The Delone and Mclean Model of Information Systems Success: A Ten-year Update. *Journal of Management Information Systems*, Vol. 19, No. 4, pp. 9-30.

Huandong, C. et al, 2009. E-Learning System Model Construction Based Constructivism. *Proceedings of Fifth International Joint Conference on INC, IMS and IDC*, Seoul, South Korea, pp. 1165-1169.

Ibrahim, M. et al, 2007. Institutional Factors Affecting Students Intentions to Withdraw from Distance Learning Programs in the Kingdom of Saudi Arabia: The Case of the Arab Open University. *Online Journal of Distance Learning Administration*, Vol. 10, No. 1.

Keegan, D., 1996. *Foundations of distance education*. Routledge, London.

Mihai, I., 2012. E-learning Security Management. *Journal of Criminal Investigations,* Vol. 5, No. 2, pp 116-121.

Miller, G.E. and Schiffman, S., 2006. ALN Business Models and the Transformation of Higher Education. *Journal of Asynchronous Learning Networks*. Vol. 10, No. 2, pp 15-21.

Moore, J.L. et al, 2011. E-Learning, Online Learning, and Distance Learning Environments: Are they the same? *The Internet and Higher Education*, Vol. 14, No. 2, pp 129-135.

Rana, H. and Lal, M., 2014. E-learning: Issues and Challenges. *International Journal of Computer Applications,* Vol. 97, No. 5, pp 20-24.

Tu, Z. and Yuan, Y., 2014. Critical Success Factors Analysis on Effective Information Security Management: A Literature Review. *Proceedings of Twentieth Americas Conference on Information Systems*, Savannah, United States of America, pp. 1-13.

AUTOMATIZING SUBJECT SYLLABUS UPDATING

Elsa Mª Macías-López[1], Álvaro Suárez[1], José Aurelio Santana[2], Domingo Marrero[1] and Vicente Mena[2]
[1]*Departamento de Ingeniería Telemática*
[2]*Departamento de Señales y Comunicaciones*
Grupo de Docencia de Arquitectura y Concurrencia (GDAC) - Grupo de Arquitectura y Concurrencia (GAC)
Universidad de Las Palmas de Gran Canaria, Campus Universitario de Tafira s/n, 35017 Las Palmas de Gran Canaria (Spain)

ABSTRACT

Subject syllabus is a contract between the University and Society. Every year syllabus must be updated to contain last advances, the subject staff... The syllabus updating is a process that can be automated in order to reduce bureaucracy and eliminate errors generated by inclusion or elimination of some contents unintentionally. Usually this process is centralized in the subject staff but authorities (e.g. Government, Rector's office, teaching advice commissions) previously approve many of the information contained in syllabus file. Connoisseur of the problematic behind of this syllabus updating process, our University funds our work in progress to do a study of how to automatize as much as possible this process and propose some ideas for the design of a Web tool to do it.

KEYWORDS

Syllabus, University coordination, Web 2.0, Cloud, Free software.

1. INTRODUCTION

Before starting the next academic course, every university subject syllabus must be updated until it will be finally approved and published by the authorities (e.g. Government, Rector's office, teaching advice commissions) (Zabalza, 2012). This is a process in which different persons participate (professors, reviewers, University staff) due to the significance of these guides that are not only an agreement between the future student and the University, but also a contract between University and Society. The process the University of Las Palmas de Gran Canaria implements is resumed in (Macías, 2014).

The syllabus updating for every subject implies a hard bureaucratic process. The first time the subject will be taught its syllabus is initialized. Previous the beginning of the academic course, the subject syllabus must be updated. This hard process lasts four months, occupies several University staff (professors, reviewers, management staff...) and is error prone.

As far as we know, previous works have focused on providing to the students the access automatized of the university syllabus's content previously edited by professors and university staff (Callejo, 2009). At present, this information is available via Web on most Universities. In this paper we propose a study of how automatize as much as possible syllabus creation or updating process to save time in bureaucracy to professors and reduce errors with help of information technology support involving as many agents as possible (professors, reviewers, students, staff). The motivation behind is that we, as reviewers of academic commissions from the Department and School of Engineering, detect these facts with more frequency than the desired one. As a result, we have recently received a funding from our Institution to make a research that proposes the design of a tool to automatize the edition in order to reduce time and errors.

The structure of the paper is as follows. Section 2 is devoted to present the current process to update subject syllabus and the proposal we have in mind to automate it. Finally some conclusions are derived.

2. AUTOMATING THE SYLLABUS EDITION

With the aim of reducing the updating time and errors and to easy, the coordination among the different agents involved in this syllabus updating, a proposal that can be implemented with Web 2.0 tools and free software is considered. In our university context, automating this process will imply a process innovation since at present the subject syllabus updating is done with a proprietary software. It is used via the Web interface accessible in the Intranet of the University and it only makes easier the introduction of some fields of the syllabus.

2.1 The Syllabus Content Structure

Each university defines a structure for the subject syllabus that is stored in an electronic file. Table 1 presents some fields that are included in this file, stressing which of them are or not introduced by the tool automatically (column *Filled* set to *Yes* or to *No* respectively). The fields we mention are the ones we consider are present in many syllabuses beyond our University. Analyzing the nature of these fields, we conclude that:

1. There are fields that not filled by the tool (they are most of them) despite the fact they are available in external documents approved by proper University Authority. Moreover, this information remains invariable between courses until the University and Spanish Government undertake a global updating of the university degree. This is the case for fields like *requirements*, *professional profile contribution*, *abilities*, *objectives*, and *learning results*. As a result, every year is introduced or copied from the previous edition the same content when it is not necessary in the sense this information should be shown to the professors when they start the updating process.
2. There is information that can be introduced by other university staff rather professors but the fact is that currently it is made by professors. This information is approved every year for the proper authority and therefore is variable course after course. Examples of these fields are *tutorial schedule* (on-line, individual, group, by telephone…), and *additional material* (bibliography, Hardware and Software resources).
3. There are filled fields like the one related to *information about the subject* (ID subject, Degree, Faculty or School, credits, level, …) and *professors* (name, location, e-mail, …) and we agree the way the tool does.
4. There are also fields such as the *description of the learning and teaching methodologies and assessment* that are a combination of information available in external documents and can be applied to different subjects but they must be personalized for the subject's context.
5. Finally, the subject staff (professors) must update the *program* (theoretical and/or practical) and the *scheduling of tasks and activities per week.* Students of previous years and professors belonging to teaching advice commission can assist them.

Table 1. Fields included in most university syllabus

Field	Filled
General information about subject	Yes
Requeriments	No
Professional profile contribution	No
Abilities	No
Objectives	No
Program (contents)	No
Learning and teaching methodologies	No
Assessment	No
Schedule with tasks and activities per week	No
Learning results	No
Tutorial Schedule	No
General information about professors	Yes
Bibliography	No
Hardware and Software resources	No

2.2 The Use Cases Presentation

As we said previously, we propose that in the process can collaborate as many people as possible: professors, reviewers attached to Departments and Schools or Faculties, students, and administrative staff (Figure 1). We envision these guides can be elaborated almost automatically accessing to databases updated for the corresponding person and in the proper time, that is to say, whenever there are changes in the related fields. For example, Figure 2 shows one use case diagram in which the Department approves the tutorial schedule for each professor and the management staff from that Department udpates authomatically all syllabus with this information. Figure 3 shows the case diagram in which fields with contents available in external documents invariable during years can be automatized as it was described in the bullet 1 for Table 1 above. These figures are only some examples of the process edition automation.

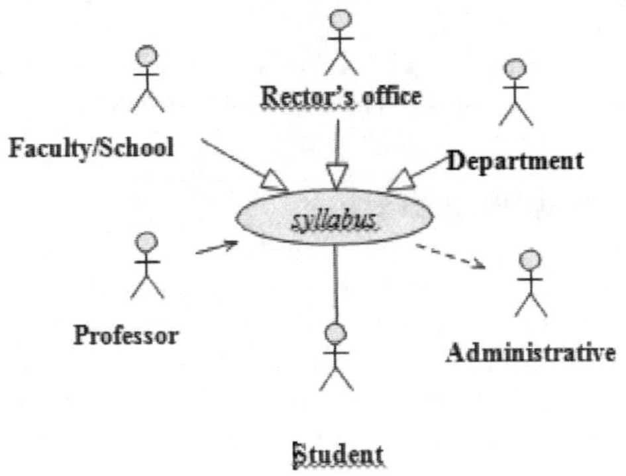

Figure 1. People involved in the syllabus edition

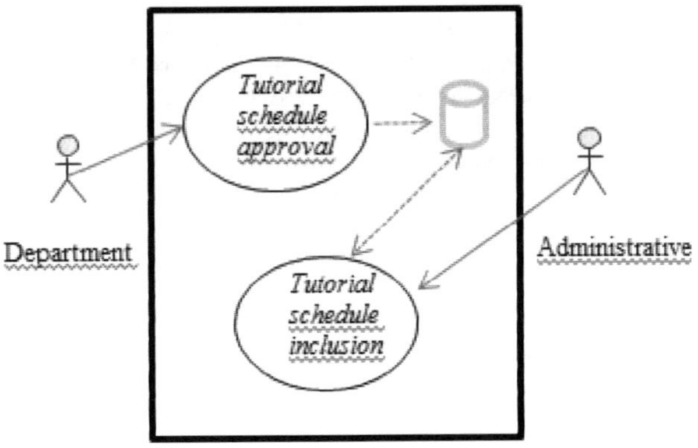

Figure 2. Use case diagram for the updating of tutorial schedule field

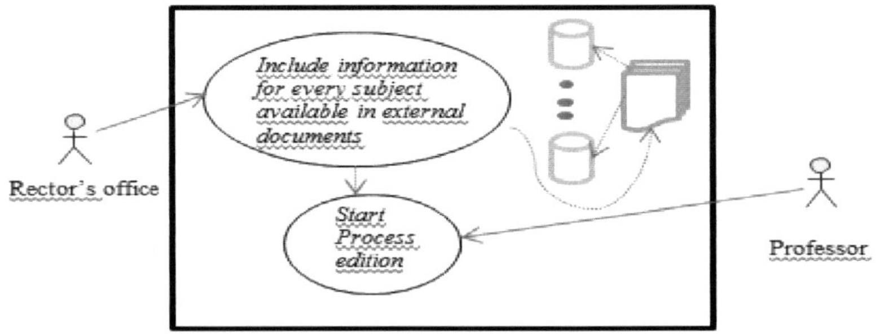

Figure 3. Use case diagram for the updating of the fields requirements, professional profile contribution, abilities, objectives, and learning results

2.3 Initial Ideas about Implementation

We propose that the different databases contained in the private Cloud in the Intranet of the University must be connected. We can define new databases that are synchronized with the existing databases. For example, we propose to create a database containing the information related to learning methodologies, abilities, learning results… for each degree. The subject staff in charge of filling e.g. the particular abilities and learning results for their subject only will have to choose (using a rich Web 2.0 interface) the ones they consider are adequately. The reviewing process will consist in observing if they were appropriately chosen instead of doing a syntactic revision to the text.

3. CONCLUSION

In this work in progress, we have presented the subject syllabus content file for our University. Currently, this file is filled most by hand in a large process that does not guarantee the resultant file does not contain serious errors. This is undesirable because the subject syllabus is the contract between the University and Society (students in particular). We also propose some initial ideas about how to fully automatize this process minimizing the work to be done by subject staff and other management staff in the University. We think the tool we will implement will reduce errors and updating time considerable.

ACKNOWLEDGEMENT

Researched supported by Las Palmas de Gran Canaria University under contract CPIE2015-43 (published at: https://www2.ulpgc.es/hege/almacen/download/7118/7118256/boulpgc_febrero_2016_5_febrero.pdf, page 7).

REFERENCES

Zabalza, M. A. and Zabalza Cerdeiriña, Mª. A., 2012. *Planificación de la docencia en la universidad: Elaboración de las Guías Docentes de las materias*. Narcea Ediciones, Madrid.

Macías, E. et al, 2014, Propuesta de mejora de la coordinación temprana vertical y horizontal de asignaturas. *I Jornadas Iberoamericanas de Innovación Educativa en el ámbito de las TIC*. Las Palmas de Gran Canaria, España, pp.289-298.

Callejo, A. et al, 2009, Elaboración de guías docentes atractivas: Formato Web. *I Congreso de Docencia Universitaria*. Vigo, España.

Doctoral Consortium

AN EXPLORATORY MODEL OF KNOWLEDGE TRANSFER PROCESS THROUGH INFORMATION SYSTEM IMPLEMENTATION: CASE STUDY (NHS IN THE UK)

Firas Masri[1], Prof. Peter Kawalek[2] and Prof. A. Trevor Wood-Harper[3]
[1]*Ph.D. candidate (Knowledge Management In Health Sector), Alliance Manchester Business School. IMP and Health Division Manchester M15 6PB*
[2]*Professor, University of Manchester., Alliance Manchester Business School, Booth Street East Manchester M15 6PB*
[3]*Chair in Information Systems & Systemic Change, Alliance Manchester Business School Manchester M15 6PB*

ABSTRACT

Grant (1996) cited that *"Knowledge is viewed as residing within the individual and the primary role of the organisation is the knowledge application rather than knowledge creation"* (p. 109). Kogut and Zander (1992) wrote: *"what firms do better than markets is the sharing and transfer of the knowledge of individuals and groups within an organisation"* (p.383). From above citations, we can *adopt* that the interaction and sharing of knowledge on an individual level will generate new organisational knowledge *through* knowledge transfer (KT) which achieves high organisational performance (Maurer, 1998 and Holsapple *et al.*, 2000; Argote, 2013). Despite the importance of transferring and sharing knowledge as the basic and crucial function in organisations, employees frequently resist sharing their knowledge (Ciborra, and Patriotta, 1998; Bock, and Kim, 2001; Tsai *et al.,* 2013). To this end, "Knowledge Transfer" (KT) emerged in the 1990s as a process by which research messages were "pushed" by the source to the users (Lavis *et al.* 2003; Pentland et al., 2011; Argote, 2013). Thus, this paper adopts that knowledge embedded in the interactions of people, tools, and tasks provides a basis for competitive advantage in firms.

Healthcare is mainly knowledge-based, where the transfer of knowledge is imperative for suitable health outcome (Willem et al., 2007). In the health industry, knowledge is still widely scattered; it is collected at different times and by different people or information systems which make it difficult to understand, to compare and to exchange (Bate & Robert 2002). Moreover, in most studies, effective transfer of knowledge increases productivity, creates competitive advantage and enhances the organisational performance. Thus, the ability of health organisations to capture, disseminate, and organize knowledge (what we can call knowledge transfer functions) allows them to improve the quality of the outcome, process efficiency, patient satisfaction, reducing errors, and cost control (El Morr, and Subercaze, 2010).

However, knowledge is complex, dynamic and embedded in people, and transferring it between agents (i.e. Sender and receiver) is problematic (Grol *et al.*, 2013). This issue becomes more evident in the systems which are mainly dependent on people (e.g. Healthcare systems). In the healthcare systems Levin and Cross, (2004), Lin *et al.,* (2008) and Nicolini *et al.,* (2008) found that professionals (i.e. physicians and nurses etc.) are not aware of the various enablers and barriers that effectively influence Knowledge Transfer (KT). Thus, it is strongly recommended to explore these factors from different perspectives and how they could enhance the KT systems that would influence the system performance, which has aspects such as; outcomes, quality and appropriateness of services, and productivity.

My main aim to join this conference is to enhance and develop my thesis in a way to create a model for knowledge transfer in the healthcare situation which can be linked to theories; Knowledge Based View, organisational learning and Socio-technical aspects.

KEYWORDS

Knowledge transfer processes, Socio-technical thinking, and Healthcare.

1. RESEARCH OBJECTIVES AND QUESTIONS

It has been argued that knowledge management (KM) and KT system studies are especially limited in the healthcare (Lin *et al.*, 2008, Nicolini *et al.*, 2008, Pentland et al., 2011, Lin *et al.*, 2012). In particularly the focus on a Middle East and Arabic context is limited (Wilkesmann, et al., 2009). Thus, from socio-technical perspective, this research **aims** to understand the mechanism and elements of the KT system within the UK context which is relatively under-researched. This study attempts to develop a holistic approach to deal with issues such as the enablers and barriers of KT system. Moreover, it will try to discover their complex interactions and relations with regard to the characteristics of; knowledge, sender, receiver, relationship between them, and the context and tools in Healthcare situation taking the particular case of the UK healthcare.

In summary, the technical challenges (e.g. Software and hardware of KT systems) as well as human challenges (e.g. Healthcare professionals and their beliefs, the nature of work and time constraints) are considered as major barriers in the way of successful KT mechanism in the UK healthcare context. These challenges, which have been analysed theoretically, should be managed carefully in the NHS and generally to achieve successful KT mechanism.

Therefore, the main research question that will be answered upon the completion of this PhD research is:

- Research Question- How are the enablers and barriers of successful KT systems perceived in the UK healthcare sector?

The main research question will be supported by the followibgb sub-questions:

1. *Who are the key stakeholders involved in the KT system in the UK healthcare sector?*
2. *What are the enablers and barriers associated with the KT system in the UK healthcare sector?*
3. *What are the best practices of the successful KT system in the UK healthcare system?*

2. RESEARCH METHOD

In this research, "multi-case studies" approach is adopted as a research strategy. Also data will be generated as a result of observations and interviews with key stakeholders (system developers and system users) in the the UK hospitals. The semi-structured interview protocol will be designed to conduct semi-structured interviews to collect data, as this will allow participants to discuss and help the researcher to acquire information about KT factors from socio-technical perspective. The factors (enablers and barriers) of KT were collected from earlier studies in different fields, including healthcare and then categorized into the following five characteristics using the socio-technical theory to analyse characteristics of; knowledge, sender, receiver, context, and tools. Moreover, the in-depth semi-structured interviews with the above mentioned stakeholders will be conducted to get a deep and a holistic view of factors affecting the KT mechanisms in the UK healthcare context.

In this study, three phases of distinct methodologies will be conducted in order to get a Holistic picture and deep understanding about KT's factors. These phases are:

- Phase 1 (Pilot study): In this phase 3-4 KT system developers and 2-3 KT system users from a hospital in UK will be interviewed. These participants will be called the first group.
- Phase 2: These interviews will be analysed and developed throughout continuous interactions between the interviewer and the 1st group participants. This analysis will help the researcher to better understand the particular situation of the healthcare in UK and to enhance the interview protocol.
- Phase 3: as the objective of this research is to get a deep understanding about the KT of the healthcare situation in UK, the expected number of interviews is between (35-40) interviews participants from different backgrounds or until *saturation* is reached.

In the following pages I draw figures which are; the first is a theoretical research framework which illustrates the relationship between the theoretical framework, methodology and the area of concern or what it is called (FMA) (Checkland, & Holwell, 1998) (See Figure1). The second one is the Structure of the Thesis which illustrates the processes and steps of the thesis and the methods of each one (see Figure2).

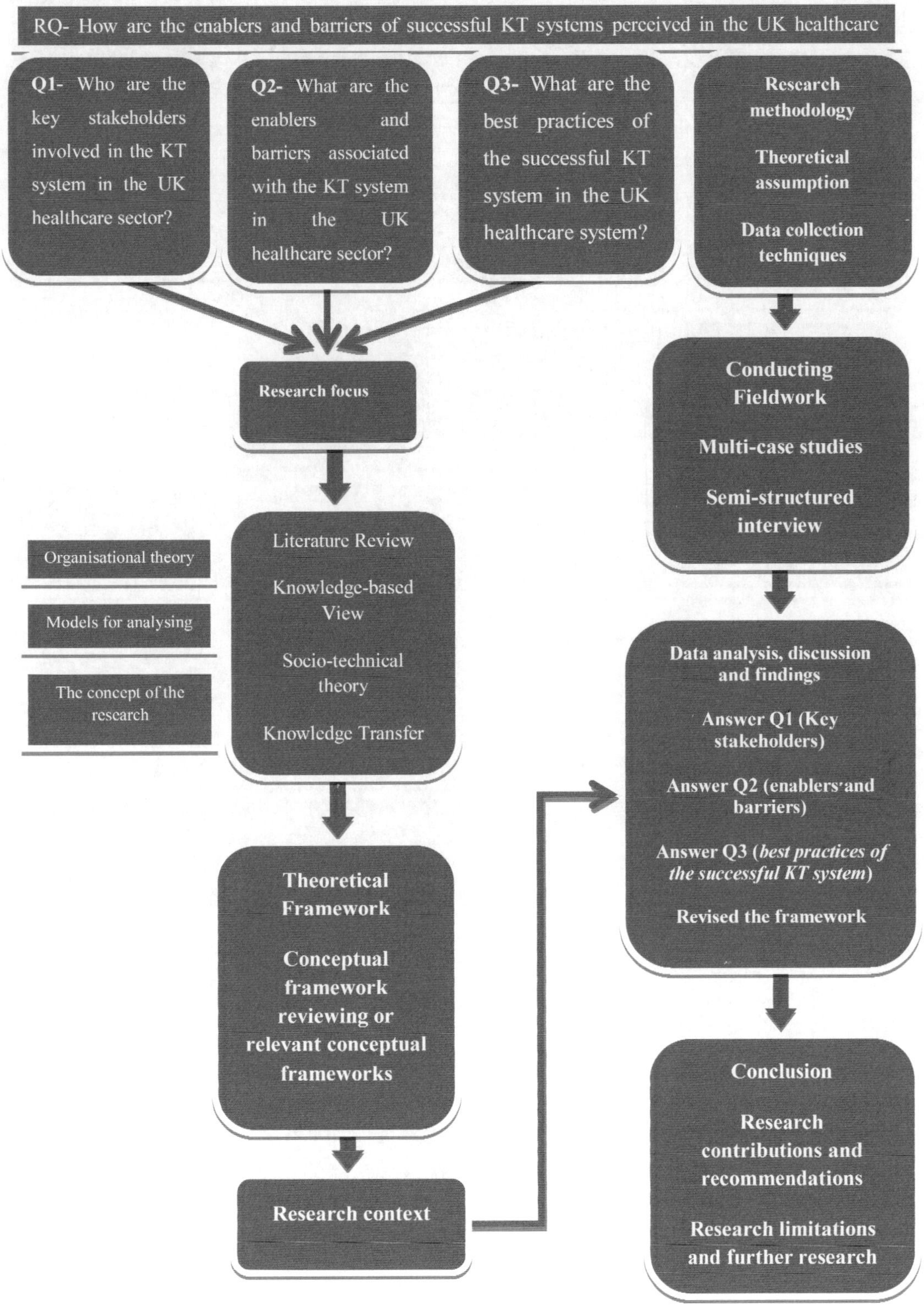

Figure 1. Research Framework

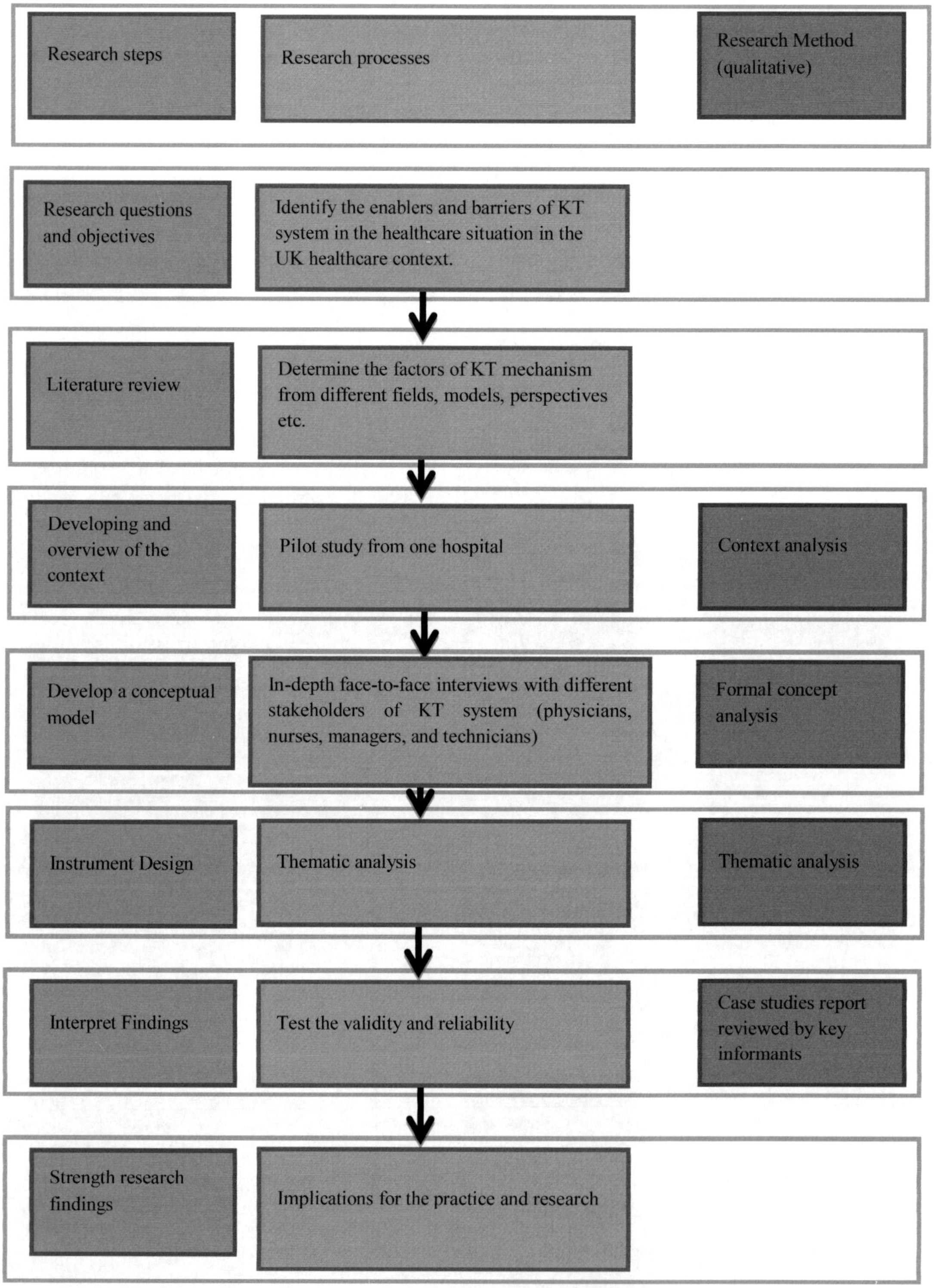

Figure 2. Conceptual Structure of the work

REFERENCES

Argote, L., 2013. Organization Learning: A Theoretical Framework. In *Organizational Learning* (pp. 31-56). Springer US.

Bate, S.P. and Robert, G., 2002. Knowledge management and communities of practice in the private sector: lessons for modernizing the National Health Service in England and Wales. *Public Administration*, *80*(4), pp.643-663.

Bock, G.W. and Kim, Y.G., 2001. Breaking the myths of rewards: An exploratory study of attitudes about knowledge sharing. *Pacis 2001 proceedings*, p.78.

Ciborra, C.U. and Patriotta, G., 1998. Groupware and teamwork in R&D: limits to learning and innovation. *R&D Management*, *28*(1), pp.43-52.

El Morr, C. and Subercaze, J., 2010. Knowledge management in healthcare.*Handbook of research on developments in e-health and telemedicine: Technological and social perspetives*, pp.490-510.

Grant, R.M., 1996. Toward a knowledge-based theory of the firm. *Strategic management journal*, *17*(S2), pp.109-122.

Grol, R., Wensing, M., Bosch, M., Hulscher, M. and Eccles, M., 2013. Theories on implementation of change in healthcare. *Improving Patient Care: The Implementation of Change in Health Care, Second Edition*, pp.18-39.

Holsapple, C.W. and Joshi, K.D., 2000. An investigation of factors that influence the management of knowledge in organizations. *The Journal of Strategic Information Systems*, *9*(2), pp.235-261.

Kogut, B., & Zander, U. 1992. Knowledge of the firm, combinative capabilities, and the replication of technology. *Organization science*, *3*(3), 383-397.

Lavis, J.N., Robertson, D., Woodside, J.M., McLeod, C.B. and Abelson, J., 2003. How can research organizations more effectively transfer research knowledge to decision makers?. *Milbank quarterly*, *81*(2), pp.221-248.

Lawler, E.K., Hedge, A. and Pavlovic-Veselinovic, S., 2011. Cognitive ergonomics, socio-technical systems, and the impact of healthcare information technologies. *International Journal of Industrial Ergonomics*,*41*(4), pp.336-344.

Levin, D.Z. and Cross, R., 2004. The strength of weak ties you can trust: The mediating role of trust in effective knowledge transfer. *Management science*, *50*(11), pp.1477-1490.

Lin, C., Tan, B., & Chang, S. (2008). An exploratory model of knowledge flow barriers within healthcare organizations. *Information & Management*, *45*(5), 331-339.

Lin, C., Wu, J. C., & Yen, D. C. (2012). Exploring barriers to knowledge flow at different knowledge management maturity stages. *Information & Management*, 49(1), 10-23.

Maurer, H., 1998. Web-based knowledge management. *Computer*, *31*(3), pp.122-123.

Nicolini, D., Powell, J., Conville, P. and Martinez-Solano, L., 2008. Managing knowledge in the healthcare sector. A review. *International Journal of Management Reviews*, *10*(3), pp.245-263.

Checkland, P., & Holwell, S. (1998). Action research: its nature and validity. *Systemic Practice and Action Research*, 11(1), 9-21.

Pentland, D., Forsyth, K., Maciver, D., Walsh, M., Murray, R., Irvine, L. and Sikora, S., 2011. Key characteristics of knowledge transfer and exchange in healthcare: integrative literature review. *Journal of advanced nursing*, *67*(7), pp.1408-1425.

Tsai, M.T., Chang, H.C., Cheng, N.C. and Lien, C.C., 2013. Understanding IT professionals' knowledge sharing intention through KMS: a social exchange perspective. *Quality & Quantity*, *47*(5), pp.2739-2753.

Wilkesmann, U., Fischer, H. and Wilkesmann, M., 2009. Cultural characteristics of knowledge transfer. *Journal of Knowledge Management*, *13*(6), pp.464-477.

Willem, A. and Buelens, M., 2007. Knowledge sharing in public sector organizations: The effect of organizational characteristics on interdepartmental knowledge sharing. *Journal of public administration research and theory*, *17*(4), pp.581-606.

AUTHOR INDEX